MICHAEL
OWEN
THE BIOGRAPHY

MICHAEL
OWEN
THE BIOGRAPHY

OLIVER DERBYSHIRE

JB

JOHN BLAKE

Published by John Blake Publishing Ltd,
3 Bramber Court, 2 Bramber Road,
London W14 9PB, England

www.johnblakepublishing.co.uk

First published in hardback in 2007
This edition published in paperback in 2010

ISBN: 978-1-84454-643-5

British Library Cataloguing-in-Publication Data:

A catalogue record for this book is available from the British Library.

Design by www.envydesign.co.uk

Printed in Great Britain by CPI Bookmarque, Croydon CR0 4TD

1 3 5 7 9 10 8 6 4 2

Photogr   s,

Papers u   icts
made from   ocesses
confor   Askews   n.

Every att   ders,
but som   iate

Photogr

CONTENTS

PROLOGUE

'I want to live the life that enables me to be a top-class footballer,' he said simply.

Michael Owen had always had the attitude to go to the very top of whatever he turned his mind to and, fortunately for England, that was football. Rather than embrace the celebrity lifestyle that seems to be the motivation for far too many of his contemporaries, Owen has shied away from the cameras off the pitch lest it affect his performance on it.

It is this dedication that enabled Owen to become the Premiership top scorer at the age of eighteen, to win the European Footballer of the Year award by twenty-two, win fifty caps before his twenty-fourth birthday. After his climb to the top so early in his career, it can be easy to forget quite how unplayable Owen is when on form, especially after suffering two long-term injuries in recent years.

He worked hard to get to the top of the England pecking order, and, although he will always be considered as one of the youngsters after making the breakthrough aged seventeen and being the youngest player to pull on the famous Three Lions shirt in the twentieth century, Owen is now one of the most experienced strikers in world football. Each goal for his country takes him one step closer to Sir Bobby Charlton's record of forty-nine and, if he can remain relatively injury-free for the remainder of his career, Owen could well become the first Englishman to score a half-century of goals.

1

BOY WONDER

'He played for Deeside Primary School in Wales, he broke my scoring record and he played in the Ian Rush tournament in Wales as well, so we do go back many years,' Rush told Wales's daily, the *Western Mail*. 'From our point of view we would have loved him to have been Welsh or played for Wales, but he's chosen England and for him it's the right choice.'

Long before that night in St Etienne and the global acclaim that came with it, Michael James Owen achieved notoriety as North Wales's most prolific schoolboy goalscorer. But there was never any choice for him regarding his nationality – he is definitely not Welsh.

Born in England, at 10.20 pm in the Countess of Cheshire Hospital on 14 December 1979, weighing 7 pounds 15½ ounces (3.6 kilograms), to English parents, Terry and Janette Owen, Michael was the fourth of five children: he has two elder brothers, Terry and Andy, an elder sister, Karen, and a younger sister, Lesley.

He went to school in Wales and played football for Deeside Schools and Flintshire Schoolboys, both representational teams in northeastern Wales. He once had a trial for Wales Schoolboys but never played for them and would never have qualified to play a full international for Wales. Michael Owen is English, although he could have qualified to play for Scotland through his grandmother on his father's side.

As Owen told the *Western Mail*, 'I've spent virtually my entire life in Wales so there's something Welsh inside me, although it's not blood. The only countries I could play for were England or Scotland. My only connection with Wales is that I grew up there and that I have a house there.'

Owen's dad played professional football for nearly fifteen years from 1966 to 1981. A striker, like his son but far less prolific, Terry scored seventy goals in 299 league games during a career that took him all across England. He started as a trainee at Everton but left Merseyside for Yorkshire in 1970, when he joined Bradford City. In 1972 he moved on again, this time to Chester, where he made more than half his total league appearances, playing 161 times for the then Sealand Road club.

Owen Sr left Chester in 1976 and had spells at Cambridge United and Rochdale before he ended his career at Port Vale, when they failed to offer him a new contract in 1981. But Terry Owen was never one to brag about his time as a footballer, and didn't advertise the fact by adorning the family home with shirts or team photos from his playing days. When Michael was growing up he didn't even realise his father had played professionally until his big brothers told him.

Quite a shy and reserved man, the elder Mr Owen was as unassuming as his journeyman career through the lower leagues of English football. As far as young Michael was concerned, the most significant clubs his dad played for were Chester and

Everton – Chester because this was where Owen Sr had been happiest as a footballer and thus where he decided to settle with his young family when his playing days were over; and Everton because they were the team Owen Jr supported as a kid, since they still gave his dad match tickets.

When Terry's footballing career ended, he went straight to work in a 'real' job. Back in the days of modest wages for players, a man with five kids to support was a long way from retirement. Michael's parents ran a clothes shop, which his mum's side of the family owned, and, when that was forced to close, Janette moved to an office job and Terry became an insurance salesman.

Despite the financial pressures of raising five children and paying for a mortgage on a big family home, Terry was his son's most loyal supporter and made sure he got to every single one of his games. The strength of the family bond was evident as Janette and Lesley also came to many of his matches, and it was this level of support that helped Michael to achieve his dream of becoming a professional footballer.

Terry was very committed to his family and it wasn't just his footballing protégé of a son he watched: he also travelled far and wide to watch Karen running or playing hockey, or Lesley's netball competitions.

With such a tight-knit family, Michael has always shown great loyalty to his relatives. When the money started rolling in, the first thing the young Owen did was to pay off the mortgage on his parents' house, and, the richer he has become, the more he has done for his family, going so far as to buy each of his siblings a house in the same close.

It started when Owen bought his first house at eighteen, and, when more money became available to him, he bought two more – one for his parents and one for Andy. But he didn't think this was fair to the others, so soon Karen and Terry Jr had their own houses, and when Lesley was old enough Michael got her in on the act. When the last house on the close came up for sale they had run out of family, though, so there was one house on the road without an Owen. The family's footballing millionaire eventually moved out of the close, but it was nice while it lasted.

'When I was little, I never said, "I want to be a footballer because I want to become rich",' Owen once told the *News of the World*. 'But it has enabled me to look after my family. I've been able to buy a house for my mum and dad and my older brother, Andy, and I hope to do the same for my other brother and sisters.'

Michael was never pressured into anything by his father. Terry would just do everything to make sure his son had the best shot at being a footballer. And, although Owen Sr never said anything to his son, he did tell some friends that Michael would play for England one day, and the sensible ones among them made some money out of the bookies from it.

Although he never verbalised his pride in his son's footballing prowess, Terry Owen would clean Michael's boots, and make sure that they were the best-polished pair on the park every week. His young lad was the best player in Terry's eyes, so he wanted him to look the part.

Because of this care and attention from his father, it was natural that Michael would try his hardest to please his old man, whether that was with his performances on the pitch or how he behaved off the park. From those early days until today there is very little that the lad has ever done to let Terry down.

As his dad would watch him play on a Saturday, the schoolboy Owen would caddy for his dad on a Sunday, and there began young Michael's first love away from football – golf. He is still a big fan of the game and plays off a handicap of eight, but he was almost addicted to the sport as a schoolboy. As Owen revealed recently, 'I was completely hooked on the game. When I was thirteen, I would fit in fifty-four holes.'

A natural sportsman, Owen was good at whatever he turned his hand to: athletics, with a personal best of 11.4 seconds over 100 metres as a young sprinter; rugby, using his pace to score many tries from centre; cricket, where he was captain of Hawarden Under-16s, opening the bowling and batting with a top score of ninety-two; snooker, with a top break of sixty-four; and even boxing.

He spent three years training at Deeside Boxing Club from the age of ten, and had two organised fights. Owen won the first bout on a split decision, and took the rematch on another split decision on 14 March 1990. He had a third bout scheduled but his opponent failed to turn up, and, as his footballing career began to grow, so the bell sounded on his time in the ring.

'I boxed for a few years. I wasn't bad – but I certainly prefer goal-scoring to boxing,' Owen recalled in the *News of the World*. 'It was really scary. I always played football and was used to having ten team-mates around me to help. But now suddenly I was in there on my own, facing someone who wanted to give me a real pasting. I won both of my bouts, but ended up each time with a bloody nose.

'I decided that was enough for me. Trials for Liverpool and the Lilleshall School of Excellence in Shropshire were just around the corner, so football was about to take over my life.'

It didn't matter what sport he was playing, Owen just loved playing, and with his fierce competitive streak he always wanted to win. He told the press, 'Talk to my family and they will tell you the one thing I am very bad at – losing. If they ever beat me at anything I'm not very good company. Then again, that could be a quality. I certainly believe it is, though I don't think any of the family or any defenders I play against would agree. It's just that I hate to lose so much it drives me on. In fact, if I get beat I like to hurt – just like Alan Shearer.'

He thinks he probably developed this trait with all the games he played against his dad while growing up. As Owen Jr said, 'I'm sure he instilled it into me. He has a golf handicap of eleven and plays a great game but, if I ever beat him, I can see the hurt. I know how that feels.'

Wherever he got it from, it was certainly evident from an early age, as Bryn Jones, one of Owen's first managers, told the *Independent on Sunday*: 'Don't ever play Michael at snooker or golf; I wouldn't even bet with him on which raindrop would get to the bottom of the window first.'

Owen's will to win at least had a healthy outlet as he was growing up. With just fourteen years separating the five kids, they were always up to something, and Michael would often play two-on-two with his dad and his brothers even with the massive age gap of nine years between him and Andy. Michael would usually be on his dad's team, and playing against his brothers was good practice for him as he spent his early years playing against much older boys and young men, and has spent his entire career up against considerably bigger defenders.

Terry Jr and Andy were both talented footballers and were paid to play on occasion in their prime, but neither of his elder brothers had the same focus or dedication as Michael and the closest they came to the big time was the park kickabouts with the future star. But they've never been jealous of their little brother, and the whole family have been happy to share in Michael's success.

The training against his elder brothers was put to good use when Michael began playing competitive football with Mold Alexander Under-10s when he was still only seven. And with competitive football came his first pair of boots, as he recalled to the press: 'They were "Keegan Kids" boots and cost about a tenner. I was thrilled and couldn't wait to put them on. After that first game in the park I was completely hooked and didn't want to do or think about anything except football.'

At first Owen was just a substitute for Mold, appearing late in the second half, often to grab a goal or two and turn the game on its head, but he soon forced his way into the starting line-up. While at Mold he had his first taste of regional football as he was selected to play for Hawarden Pathfinders every couple of months. His performances at club and regional level made quite an impression on his dad. 'He'd play with boys who were a lot older than him,' Terry Owen said. 'He'd put the ball in the corner of the net, side-footing it in, and I thought, "Blooming 'eck, what have we got here?" He wasn't chasing the ball all over the place. He'd choose a spot. He'd pass the ball into the net from an early age. He wouldn't just take a swing and hope for the best.'

Owen's first footballing controversy came when he moved on from Mold Alexander to a new club side. He made a seamless transition to Hawarden Rangers with 116 goals in one forty-game season, but in the end-of-season awards he missed out on Player of the Year, with the goalkeeper getting the nod instead. Feeling unappreciated after the snub, Owen soon ended his relationship with the club.

The following season Owen intended to restrict himself to Liverpool youth and county games, but he came out of schoolboy club retirement to play a handful of games for St David's Park. It was no small coincidence that his first game for St David's was against Hawarden Rangers, and Owen was delighted with the result as he scored four goals in a 4–3 win.

As well as making the move into club football, Owen had

taken his first steps on a representative ladder, which stopped just short of Wales Schoolboys. He was first chosen to represent Deeside Schools, an under-11s county side, at the age of eight. In doing so he became the youngest boy ever to be picked for his county, beating a record previously held by Wales midfielder Gary Speed.

In his first year for Deeside, Owen didn't play many games, as managers Bryn Jones and Dave Nicholas protected their young star – and the feelings of the other boys who stood to lose their place to a boy three years younger. Jones fondly remembers his schoolboy superstar, and is glad he has developed so fully. 'He's an all-round player but it's his pace which makes him so incredible.' Owen's first manager told the press, 'There wasn't a lot I had to teach Michael – he was a natural. He'll take everything in his stride, as he has all along. I still see him every now and then, but he's so busy I don't get the chance very often.'

Owen still impressed enough in his few appearances that first year to be made captain in his second season. As skipper he played every match and bagged fifty-odd goals from just thirty-something games. But Owen still saved the best for last as, aged eleven, in his third and final season for Deeside Schools, he beat Ian Rush's record for goals in a season with ninety-two.

Rush's total had stood at seventy-two, and, although the boys played a lot more games in Owen's day, the English lad scored two more in the equivalent number of games, and by the end of the season he had smashed the Welsh legend's record by twenty goals.

Rush was a hero on Merseyside and throughout Wales, but, as Owen was growing up, it was another striker he looked to emulate. Gary Lineker was Everton's leading striker in 1985/6 and he was one of England's many heroes at the 1990 World Cup. 'My first hero was Gary Lineker,' Owen told *Kodansha*

BOY WONDER

Official World Cup 2002 Preview Guide. 'My first real memories of the World Cup are from 1990. I was only nine or ten at the time, and I remember running home from school every day to watch the games from Italy. Lineker, of course, scored some great goals for England in the World Cup, and it was always my ambition to follow him into the team one day. But it wasn't just the England games that fascinated me – it was everything about the atmosphere of the World Cup that totally enthralled me.'

Owen was soon on the road to the England team himself, as he attended a trial for the Football Association's School of Excellence at Lilleshall. His chance to impress came at Chester City's Deva Stadium on a cold and blustery evening, where the youngsters played in four twenty-minute matches. The conditions were so poor it would have been difficult to tell the difference between a Ronaldinho and a Martin Keown, but either Owen did enough or his reputation preceded him, and he was selected for the FA's Academy.

The biggest downside to life at Lilleshall for Owen was the move away from home. Coming from such a close family, he found it difficult to up sticks and leave everyone behind, but the boarders soon became like brothers, and he quickly felt at home down in the Midlands. The obvious positive to life at the FA School was that it marked Owen out as one of the finest footballers of his age group in England, and the dream of playing professionally was growing ever more tangible: recent graduates in the years before Owen arrived included Ian Walker, Sol Campbell, Andy Cole and Nick Barmby.

With only sixteen pupils on each year, the boys soon got to know each other on and off the pitch, and Owen still considers classmate Michael Jones to be his best friend. Jones didn't make it as a professional footballer but there were other success stories from their year group: Wes Brown, the injury-plagued Manchester United defender; Michael Ball, who impressed enough at Everton to win an England cap before moving to Glasgow Rangers and eventually PSV Eindhoven; and Steve Haslam, who played in the Premiership with Sheffield Wednesday before taking a step down to the conference with Halifax Town.

'At fifteen everybody dreams of playing Champions League football and of being a star, but you don't really appreciate the high percentage of players who don't make it,' Haslam recently revealed, in the *Daily Mirror*. 'At fifteen you have still got a long way to go to make it as a footballer and those years up to twenty-one are the easily the most difficult. You don't really understand that at that age. But in saying that, as well as Michael, Wes and Bally a few of us played league football so it wasn't a bad group at all.'

But Owen was already distancing himself from his contemporaries with his goal scoring displays, and John Owens, his manager for the England Under-15s team, was quick to notice his burgeoning talent.

'Listen,' Owens told the *Sunday Times* at the time. 'I don't want you to go too over the top because a lot can happen to kids between fourteen and eighteen, but there's this boy called Michael Owen who looks as if he's going to have it all – he's sensational. He's got a prodigious appetite for goals, excellent technique, very close control and skills and is very fast. Without having to rely on a large physique, he's very astute, very clever at losing defenders, using his brain rather than muscle, and he loves to run at defences.'

Looking back on his prediction and assessment, Owens added, in the same paper ten years later, 'I'd like to take credit for some blinding flash of insight but he was so good I'd have had to be blind not to identify him as something special. I worked with Ryan Giggs when he was a kid, too, but Michael remains the best young player I've ever seen.'

And Owen was composed in front of the press from an early age to boot. 'I remember him doing an interview with *Blue Peter* at fifteen.' Owens added. 'Some hardened pros freeze on microphone; Michael stood there confidently, unflustered and talking sense.'

The fourteen-year-old Owen remained focused when speaking to the *Sunday Times* as well. 'I just love scoring and I think I'm good at it,' he revealed. 'My dad knows all about the pitfalls – he is good at helping me keep my feet on the ground. If I carry on the way I have, I don't see why I couldn't make it.'

The talent kept coming for the coach, and in the subsequent seasons Owens had Francis Jeffers and Joe Cole in his England Under-15s teams. 'It was just a privilege to work with young players of that calibre,' the manager said in the *Independent on Sunday*. 'A player like Michael would have come through anyway, whatever I did or didn't do. The potential was there for all to see. But it is still a thrill to sit back and watch it come to fruition.

'There were none of the ricochets or messy little goals you'd expect from schoolboys,' Owens said, revealing Owen's on-pitch maturity from a young age. 'Michael only ever scored adult goals. He was very mature in all aspects of his life, not just on the pitch. He had such a strong mental attitude and such a willingness to learn and develop. There was never any doubt in his mind where he was heading.'

Owen impressed everybody with his performances on the pitch and he scored on his England Under-15s debut, a trick he would later repeat for the Under-16s and Liverpool. When Brazil came to Wembley later in the season to play against

Owen and his young compatriots, it caught the attention of the national press. The South Americans' full international side were World Cup holders and everyone was intrigued to see the talents of their next generation.

The young *Canarinho* weren't in great form and had lost 1–0 in Scotland the previous week. Struggling to acclimatise themselves to winter on the Clyde, the youngsters had failed to make an impact on the British public in Glasgow, but they had another chance to wow the fans in London.

The English lads towered over their rivals, in almost every position, and they put their added bulk to good use all over the park while the Brazilian boys, including the future World Player of the Year, Ronaldinho, in their ranks, played the only way they know how. A shimmy here, a dummy there, the ball fizzing around on the ground until the aerial route was occasionally called upon to beat the bigger guys. But even at such an early age Owen had enough skill to gain the respect of his opponents.

As Jonathan Rendall noted in the *Sunday Times*,

Sometimes innocence shone through from beneath the layers of coaching. Michael Owen, the England left winger, actually smiled. He had gone past his defender, raced to the by-line and then instead of doing the sensible thing and crossing he back-heeled the ball, beat the Brazilian again and nonchalantly laid it off with his right foot.

The Brazilians may have admired his trickery but everyone was impressed with the way he scored the only goal of the game after seventy minutes. Writing in the *Independent*, Julie Welch reported,

Jamie Burt darted up the right and sent over the cross which led to England's winner. Cesar and Owen both went

*for it and when Owen went stumbling, he could well have
held out for the penalty award. Instead he got up to thump
a classic shot home. It was a courageous and talented piece
of work and you only hope that Owen will be one of the
boys who make it to the top.*

The then England manager Terry Venables, who was guest of
honour at the schoolboy international, also thought highly of
the goalscorer, as he told the *Daily Mail*. 'He's well on the right
road and looks outstanding, reminds me a little of Nicky
Barmby at his age.

'It's not just about strength at this level these days. In recent
years our schoolboy sides have competed on skill as well as
determination. Last year's team was outstanding. Let's hope
they follow through. I've always been concerned that when
these boys get to eighteen or twenty they get disenchanted if
they don't make it straight away into their club's first or reserve
team. You can lose good players, like English football nearly did
with David Platt at Manchester United.'

Owen was destined to follow the former Aston Villa,
Juventus and Arsenal midfielder as a captain of his country, and
one former England coach had spotted his ability early on.
'Even back then, you could tell that Michael, Brownie and Bally
were going to be great players,' Don Howe said of Owen and
his more talented teammates in the *Daily Mirror*.

'Michael would always score – you could rely on him to score
you three in a match,' Howe continued. 'He had bags of natural
talent and he was so quick that defenders couldn't live with him.
He showed his predatory skills when he scored against Brazil
and that was a great day for all those lads. For many of them,
it was probably the highlight of their careers to play Brazil at
Wembley and some of them ended up in the non-leagues, but

that happens with any group of players. Although you have to say that three full England Internationals from one schoolboy team is not a bad return.'

That year's Lilleshall class was indeed blessed with talent, but even the guys who didn't make it to the very top could see that Owen was heading for great things. Jamie Day played against Brazil at Wembley, and, although the central midfielder shined against the South Americans, he failed to win a professional contract at Arsenal. 'The problem with footballers is that they all develop at different rates,' Day told the *Daily Mirror.* 'When I look back at myself as a schoolboy, I probably peaked at fifteen to sixteen. The lads who were younger than me were then able to overtake me, while someone exceptional like Michael just carried on improving to become the world-class player he is now. If I'm being critical of myself, I probably could have worked harder, but I was never the quickest player and I think in today's game you must have pace.'

Owen has always had speed to spare and the schoolboy striker's predatory instincts against Brazil took him to six goals in three games for his country. The prolific youngster had already bagged a hat-trick as England thrashed Belgium 7–0, and scored both goals in a 2–2 draw with Wales.

The goals were coming in copious quantities and most of them were of high quality, but one stood head and shoulders above the rest of his schoolboy strikes. Playing against Scotland in Newcastle on 28 April 1995, Owen scored the goal he still regards as his finest ever. England opened the scoring but the visitors hit back, and from the restart Owen accelerated past a couple of opposition players before cutting inside a third. Approaching the penalty area, he beat one centre-back with a drop of the shoulder and sidestepped the challenge of the other centre-half before smashing the ball into the far top corner from the edge of the six-yard box. A truly memorable goal to grace the magnificent St James' Park.

Owen remembers it well. 'It was an England schoolboy game against Scotland and we needed to win it to win the Victory Shield,' he later told the press. 'They'd just equalised and, from the kick-off, Kenny Lunt pushed the ball to me. I was just about to tap it back to him when he suddenly shouted at me to run. I looked up and half of the Scottish lads were still celebrating on the right-hand side of the pitch, so there were only about five to beat. I started running, went past the lot and whacked the ball into the top corner.

'Obviously it's not the most important goal I've ever scored, but certainly the best – better than the Argentina goal. I've got a video of it, and I watched it all the time for about three years until I broke into the Liverpool team.'

The goals continued to flow and the next month Owen scored a first-half hat-trick as England beat Austria 5–0 in Salzburg. That comprehensive victory extended England Under-15s' unbeaten season into May, but that came to an abrupt end when they lost 1–0 to the Republic of Ireland in Dublin and followed that up with a home defeat as Germany ran out 4–2 winners at Wembley.

Owen scored against the Central European side, putting a fine finish to some good work by Jamie Burt to make it 1–1 after half an hour, taking his total for the season to twelve and giving him yet another striking record. His dozen goals for England Under-15s made Owen the leading goalscorer at that level, breaking the record of nine, which had previously been held by Kevin Gallen of Queens Park Rangers, and Nick Barmby, who went on to play for England, Tottenham Hotspur, Everton and Liverpool, among other teams.

As well as games for his country, Owen also played the occasional game for the youth team at Liverpool, where he was on Centre of Excellence forms. And, during the 1995–6 season, Owen played for the Reds in their successful FA Youth Cup campaign. Although it was an Under-18s competition, the England Under-16s goalscorer's burgeoning talent had caught the attention of the Liverpool coaches and they got him released from Lilleshall for their tilt at glory.

In a team that included David Thompson and Jamie Carragher, Owen's first game was in the fourth round against Sheffield United and he scored two goals in a 3–2 win. After such a promising display it was of little surprise when the England lad was requested for the fifth-round tie with Manchester United at Anfield. It was another 3–2 victory but this time the young striker went one better and bagged a hat-trick.

Just as Robbie Fowler had been dubbed the new Ian Rush when he made the breakthrough at Anfield, Owen, because of his goals for the youth team, was likened to Fowler, the man the Kop referred to as 'God'. Ignoring the new attention, the youngster maintained his prolific form to ensure it wasn't too harsh a comparison.

After five goals in his first two Youth Cup games, Owen's place in the starting line-up was assured and he further justified his selection in the semifinal with three goals over two legs against Crystal Palace. Owen missed the first leg of the final against West Ham because he was on international duty, but his teammates managed without him and won 2–0 at Upton Park. The gifted youngster returned for the game at Anfield, but Liverpool got off to the worst possible start as Frank Lampard halved the aggregate deficit in the first minute, blasting home from outside the area as he so often does now. Owen was not to be denied his first piece of silverware, though, and equalised five minutes before the break. He was first to react when Hammers' keeper Neil Finn beat out a shot from Stuart Quinn and the England youngster nodded the ball home, in front of twenty thousand people.

Facing Rio Ferdinand for the first time in his career, Owen found time to return the favour to his strike partner and, in the fifty-fourth minute, his shot came off the post and Quinn was perfectly positioned to score. The match ended 2–1 on the night and 4–1 on aggregate to give Liverpool the FA Youth Cup for the first time in their history.

'I was proud to be part of the first Liverpool team to win the Youth Cup,' Owen later said in *The Times*. 'It is the biggest tournament for young players and you certainly got a great feeling before the games and in the games. It's a great competition, a learning curve to play at the big stadiums, play against the best players around the country, and you can only improve. The whole thing is about experience and learning. We were playing most of our games at Anfield in front of big crowds who were watching to see who was the next young lad to burst through.'

The youth team manager was delighted with his young striker, who seemed to be the leading contender in the breakthrough stakes, as the former Liverpool player and Irish international Steve Heighway said to the press, 'Owen has scored fantastic goals because his finishing is so clinical. He's single-minded and a bit of a free spirit. How far he goes is up to him.'

As his domestic season drew to a close Owen went to France for the European Under-18s Championship. England got their tournament off to a slow start with two draws, first 0–0 against Spain and then 1–1 with Italy as Owen revealed the bristling character beneath his innocent exterior.

Gennaro Gattuso, who would become of the world's finest midfielders at AC Milan, opened the scoring for the Italians after fifty-five minutes, but the lead lasted just five minutes as Coventry's Andrew Ducros levelled the scores. The match ended in controversy, though, as Owen was lucky to stay on the pitch after appearing to strike Claudio Mastrapasqua, who had been holding him back. This was just seconds after sweeper Marco Pecorari had been sent off for a trip on Owen and the Liverpool striker was thankful the referee didn't see him lash out.

A 1–0 win over Ireland saw England qualify second in Group B, and that put them into the third-place play-off, where they faced Belgium. Owen scored the winning goal in extra time as England won 3–2, and their victory in Besancon was followed by the final, where hosts France beat Spain 1–0 thanks to a strike by Thierry Henry.

Like most kids his age, Owen received his GCSE results that summer and although he hadn't applied himself to his schoolwork with the same dedication and devotion as he showed on the football pitch, the talented sportsman still managed to pass all ten of his GCSEs with C and D grades. 'You hear a lot of people saying how important school qualifications are, but I didn't seem to see the sense in that,' Owen told *The Times*. 'If I didn't make it as a professional footballer then I would want to do something in football.'

Owen has always had the right attitude to go far, and that especially applied to going out with his mates. 'I have never been out on the razzle before,' he went on. 'I don't think too much about the fact that I could be out with my mates going for a drink. I have always wanted to be a footballer and the things that go with it are just there and you cannot change them. It is good to be instilled with discipline right from the start and that is what my Dad gave me.' During his two years at Lilleshall Owen had attended Idsdall High School, but with his time up at the FA's School of Excellence it was time for the young striker to return home to Hawarden, and decide where to pursue his professional career.

Where he would go was still up for discussion, as Owen had yet to sign forms with Liverpool. Many other clubs were interested in signing this precocious talent. Owen met with Alex Ferguson at Manchester United, George Graham at Arsenal and Glenn Hoddle at Chelsea, and had trials at plenty of other clubs: Everton, Wrexham, Chester, Oldham, Norwich and Manchester City. But Liverpool made him feel most at home and Steve Heighway in particular made an excellent impression on the Owens with his honest straight-talking approach, so Owen rewarded the Reds' hospitality by deciding against the other suitors and joining the Anfield playing staff.

Owen signed YTS (Youth Training Scheme) forms with Liverpool on a weekly wage of £42.50, and his return to North Wales helped to kick-start a romance with the 'girl next door', Louise Bonsall. The fleet-footed footballer has been with her ever since. The Bonsalls lived a stone's throw from the Owens, and Louise and Michael had been at school together and had known each other for a long time, but it was only when the sixteen-year-old Owen returned from Lilleshall that things progressed.

Louise had got one of her friends to ask Owen to 'go out' with her, before his Lilleshall days, but little happened and he soon moved away for two years at the FA school. When Michael's football fame brought his relationship with Louise to the attention of the nation's media, his dad Terry remembered their school days together. He told the *Daily Post*, 'She is a lovely girl. They would walk home from school together and I suppose if you did that at their age it was classed as being boyfriend and girlfriend, but he would never tell his mum and dad – you don't at that age, do you?'

Schoolteacher Hugh Dodd, who taught both Michael and Louise, also remembers the close friendship between the two from an early age. He said in the *Daily Post*, 'It is one of those things which you think about when you remember children from school. I thought he may have been going out with Louise. They just seem right for each other.'

But during his two years spent playing for England and living in the Midlands, the young lovebirds saw very little of each other, so, when Owen returned from Lilleshall permanently and noticed Louise in a local pub, he sent a friend over to find out if she was still interested – and the rest is history.

The quiet and reserved striker is well matched by a woman who doesn't court the press in the way that so many other 'footballers' wives' do, and they are not a couple to be spotted parading up and down the red carpets at every premiere or opening. Since they are both from very similar backgrounds, Owen knows Louise is with him for the right reasons, and not just the fame and fortune that comes with being one of England's finest footballers. Long may it last.

2

PRINCE OF THE KOP

'You have got to aim for the top in your sport,' he said to *The Times*. 'If you believe yourself that you are better than whoever you are up against, you are halfway there. That is a major factor in it. I go out and play my own game and if I do well I would expect to play in the next game. The manager does not have any favourites, and if you are playing well, he will play you regardless of who else is around.'

It didn't take long for Michael Owen to force himself into the Liverpool team, and from there he was fast-tracked into the England team as his pace and prolific goalscoring drew him many admirers. And even before he had made his Liverpool debut, Owen was the subject of a transfer bid. When the Reds signed Patrik Berger from Borussia Dortmund after Euro '96, the German giants made enquiries as to Owen's availability but were swiftly rebuffed. 'I was amazed they'd heard of him but they said they'd been told all about him,' Anfield chief executive Peter Robinson recalled.

Still only sixteen years old, Owen spent much of the early part of the 1996/7 season splitting his time between Liverpool's youth team and the England Under-18s. In the white shirt of his country, Owen was as deadly as ever and scored all the goals in England's 4–0 win over Northern Ireland in a European Championship qualifier. With his development continuing unabated, the Reds were very keen to have their prodigy signed to professional forms as soon as possible, so, on 18 December 1996, Michael Owen put pen to paper on a three-year deal.

After just five months on his paltry YTS pay packet, Owen turned seventeen and was old enough to sign his first contract, which he was offered four days after his birthday. Although it was not nearly as much as the teenage talents are getting now, Liverpool's new signing went from £42.50 to £400-a-week – a massive 840% wage rise – and received a £5,000 signing bonus. The new deal was set out to rise to £500 in the second year and £600 in the third, but his rapid success meant that those numbers were soon dwarfed by his incredible earning potential.

Owen treated himself to a new car, a Rover Coupé, and, ever the generous lad, he took his parents and his little sister on holiday to Spain. But the most exciting thing for the youngster was his promotion to training with the first team and his new squad number: 18.

Throughout his childhood Owen had always been a No. 9, but with Robbie Fowler the man in possession of that shirt the new Boy Wonder had to settle for 18. Owen was just delighted to be part of the squad, as he told the press, 'When the manager presented me the No. 18 shirt with my name on, it was the best thing that has happened to me.'

That manager was Roy Evans, who told reporters, 'If you are good enough you are old enough. Michael is in the frame because big games won't bother him. He has a similar temperament to Robbie Fowler.'

To help him negotiate his contract, Owen had taken on Tony Stephens as his first, and, to date, only agent. Stephens already represented Alan Shearer, David Beckham, Dwight Yorke and David Platt in an impressive stable of talent, and would later become part of the massive SFX organisation. As well as Owen's Liverpool deal, Stephens helped secure a boot deal with Umbro and the newly professional footballer soon began doing more endorsements: Tissot watches, Jaguar cars and Walker's Crisps were among the early products Owen was associated with and in time he even had his own Cheese and Owen flavour to rival Gary Lineker's Salt and Lineker.

Even as he entered the big boys' arena off the pitch, Owen was still in the Liverpool youth team, and he was in the side that took on Manchester United in the FA Youth Cup. Attempting to defend their trophy, Owen and his teammates, now including Steven Gerrard, lost 2–1 to their great rivals at Anfield. Owen opened the scoring with a penalty early in the second half, but the visitors fought back through a spot kick of their own and a late winner.

Owen continued to catch the eye playing for the England Under-18s and scored two goals and made one more as they beat Scotland 4–1 at Bury. He was working his way into the Liverpool manager's plans and was called up to the reserve team. Evans told the press, 'This is just the start for Michael. He has been in my thoughts for some time.'

With Fowler and Stan Collymore the only fit senior strikers in the squad, Owen's chance was looming ever closer, but he had his own fitness battle, as his manager revealed. 'Michael is a goalscorer, just like Robbie,' Evans said to the press. 'But he has not figured in our plans recently because he was recovering from an ankle injury. We've been monitoring his progress and he was always going to be considered once he was available.'

A fully fit Owen was included in a Premiership squad for the first time, away to Sunderland on 13 April 1997. At first he assumed he was just travelling to Roker Park for experience and told his mum and dad not to bother making the long journey into the northeast, but, when he found out he was in the squad, Owen phoned his parents to give them the good news.

By the time the young footballer found out about his place on the bench, there was no way that his folks could get across to Sunderland in time for kick-off. They offered to come for the second half, but Owen told them not to bother. Fortunately, they didn't miss his debut. Liverpool took control of the game through a first-half Fowler goal and one from Steve McManaman just after the break, and, even though Paul Stewart pulled one back, Owen wasn't required.

He was surplus to requirements again in the next three games, and didn't even make the bench for the Merseyside Derby or a home defeat to Manchester United, which severely dented the Reds' title hopes. Liverpool revived their flagging chances with a win over Tottenham, but, with Fowler suspended, Owen returned to the squad for a trip to Selhurst Park to play Wimbledon.

On 6 May 1997 Michael Owen did make his Premiership debut, and marked the occasion with his first senior goal for Liverpool. With only ten reserve appearances to his name, Owen was brought on to try to save a game that was drifting away from the Reds and taking their hopes of a first Premiership title with it.

Liverpool needed two wins from their last two games to have any hope of catching Manchester United, and they were trailing to Jason Euell's header at the break. The Reds failed to strike back early in the second half and Owen had just been told to warm up when Wimbledon scored again, through Dean Holdsworth. With Liverpool 2–0 down and desperate for the three points, Evans took Patrik Berger off after fifty-nine minutes and put his teenage striker upfront with Collymore in a bid to change things up.

In the seventy-fourth minute, Owen did just that when Stig Inge Bjornebye slipped the ball in behind the defence. Liverpool's new No. 18 ran onto it and applied as cool a finish as a Premiership veteran when only 17 years and 143 days old. It was the type of goal he had already scored hundreds of time in his fledgling career and there were plenty more to follow, but unfortunately no more in that game, and Liverpool's title drought continued.

Having lost 2–1, the Reds were out of the running for top spot, because they were five points behind Manchester United with only one game left. The disappointment in the squad was in stark contrast to Owen's joy at his goalscoring debut and he was the only Liverpool player to leave the pitch with a smile on his face.

Despite playing for only half an hour, Owen created plenty of chances for himself and his teammates, and the press were excited by their first glimpse of the striker in the Premiership. But his manager was too upset by the end of title bid to take any positives from the game, Evans told the assembled media, 'Young Michael made a difference. He has done well through all the ranks. It doesn't surprise me that he can go on today and not look out of place, but you can't have a bonus after you've lost when you needed three points.'

But the Wimbledon manager, Joe Kinnear, admitted how much Owen's performance had worried him. He said, 'The only time we had any real anxiety in the match was when young

Michael Owen came on and scored his goal. Then we had to defend for our lives. They threw everything at us.'

Everybody was keen to find out more about the new kid on the block, and the press managed to get a few words out of him. 'It's gone really well for me,' Owen said at the end of his first professional season. 'I'd love to play upfront with Robbie Fowler at some point. I felt ready for the first team. It's a shame the chance didn't come sooner, then maybe I'd have had a longer spell in the side. I've scored goals whatever team I've played in, and I'm confident I can do it for the Liverpool first team.'

With only one league game left of the season, there was little time for Owen to be eased into the side, but after his dazzling debut there were a lot of people calling for the young striker to start the match away to Sheffield Wednesday. Evans was more cautious in his approach, however, saying, 'We must be sensible. This game is about a team performance, not placing all the responsibility on a lad of seventeen.'

The Reds needed three points at Hillsborough to guarantee a second-place finish and a spot in the Champions League for the following season, but their last game of the campaign was symptomatic of the whole season and, with the match there for the taking, they missed a plethora of chances and it finished 1–1.

With Fowler suspended and Berger still injured, Owen made his full debut alongside Collymore, but the partnership lasted only forty-five minutes as Evans changed things at the interval. Two years after becoming the most expensive player in the British game, Collymore was substituted at half-time leaving the seventeen-year-old Owen upfront with the veteran John Barnes, and it proved to be Collymore's last appearance for Liverpool.

Liverpool created more chances in the second half but when the first goal came it was Wednesday who got it. O'Neill Donaldson dispossessed Mark Wright before beating David James from just inside the box, with a quarter of an hour to go. Owen had twice been denied by excellent saves from Kevin Pressman and had also seen a shot come back off the post with the keeper beaten, so it was of little surprise that Liverpool's new Boy Wonder played a part in the equaliser.

McManaman played a through ball in behind the defence and Matt Clarke, on to replace the injured Pressman, rushed out of his goal to claim it before Owen could get there. Unfortunately for the keeper, his momentum carried him out of his box as he gathered the ball, and he was sent off for handball. Having used all their substitutes, the Owls were forced to put striker Andy Booth in goal, and his first act was to pick the ball out of the back of the net after Jamie Redknapp curled home the free kick from the edge of the area.

With seven minutes left, playing against ten men and a very inexperienced goalkeeper, Liverpool should have been able to make good their advantage, but the home side stood firm and the Reds finished fourth in the table, level on points with Newcastle and Arsenal but with a poorer goal difference, and they were headed into the UEFA Cup, rather than the Champions League.

The manager was understandably disappointed. 'It's totally devastated us because finishing second was something we desperately wanted to achieve,' Evans said. 'And, right now, we have to look back and think our season's not been all it should have been. We created enough chances in the second half to have won three or four games. But how many scoring opportunities can you miss without being punished?'

Having surrendered the league in the previous match, and now given away the Champions League place that had been theirs for the taking, the Liverpool players were understandably upset – except for Owen. After his dazzling thirty-minute cameo against Wimbledon, the teenager had shown he belonged in the Premiership – outshining Collymore in his first start, creating chances and his team's goal – and he was delighted with his performance.

The press were also impressed. Journalist Mike Ellis wrote, 'The one bright spot for Evans was the performance of whiz kid Michael Owen. The teenage ace consistently showed the energy and exuberance that put his more experienced teammates – especially Collymore – to shame.'

Despite Liverpool's disappointing end to the season, Owen was delighted to have made his first appearances for the Reds, and overjoyed at claiming his first Premiership goal, but before he could enjoy a summer holiday the striker joined up with his young England teammates.

Having made his Liverpool debut, Owen was one of the better-known players in his country's squad at the World Youth Under-20s Championship in Malaysia. He scored in each of the group games in Johor Bahru as the young Lions sailed through Group F with maximum points following wins over Ivory Coast, the United Arab Emirates and Mexico.

In the opening game against the Côte d'Ivoire Owen scored a fifth-minute penalty in a 2–1 win. Danny Murphy was the star of the second match, as the then Crewe Alexandra midfielder scored the first three goals in a 5–0 win over UAE. Owen lobbed the keeper for the fourth to keep his strike rate up, and he scored a magnificent solo goal to beat Mexico 1–0, securing England's progress to the knock out stages. In the last sixteen, they faced Argentina, who had slipped to a surprise 4–3 in their final group game against Australia and thus finished second in Group E.

But Australia's luck proved unfortunate for England as

Argentina maintained their impressive World Youth Championship form and went on to win the cup for a third time. Inspired by Juan Roman Riquelme and Pablo Aimar, the South Americans took a 2–0 lead into the break, and, despite Jamie Carragher's goal early in the second half, England couldn't find an equaliser and their tournament was over.

The silver lining to this particular cloud was that Owen would get an extra week without football before the start of a long season that would come to an unfortunate end one year later in Saint Etienne.

Before the new season started, the Liverpool manager made some changes to the squad, which had finished fourth in the Premiership. Collymore found himself surplus to requirements and on his way to Aston Villa. And, with such an exceptional young talent as Owen on his hands, Evans decided to replace the gifted but temperamental former Nottingham Forest striker with a more seasoned pro, and in came Karlheinz Riedle from Borussia Dortmund.

Fast approaching his thirty-second birthday, the German international had enjoyed a glorious career. He was a member of the World Cup-winning West Germany squad in 1990 and scored one of the penalties that knocked England out on that unforgettable evening in Turin. He had played in Italy for Lazio, and it was his two goals in a devastating five-minute spell that had won the European Cup for Dortmund in May, as they beat Juventus 3–1. But Riedle moved to Liverpool for one last challenge to give a suitable end to his fine footballing story.

Despite his goalscoring end to the previous season and a good pre-season, Owen still couldn't expect to be starting ahead of Fowler or Riedle, but his chance for the future looked great, since it seemed Riedle would be around for a only season or two. Owen's short-term future took on a much brighter complexion when Fowler picked up an ankle injury before the opening day, giving the youngster another opportunity to impress. Facing Wimbledon again, Owen made it two from two at Selhurst Park, as he scored a seventy-first-minute penalty in a game that finished 1–1.

With Fowler still sidelined, Owen got his second of the season two weeks later as he hit a fifty-second-minute goal against Blackburn at Ewood Park, in another 1–1 draw. And the young striker's fiery streak was revealed for the first time in his professional career in early September as Owen was sent off while captaining England Under-18s at Rotherham. There were only twenty minutes on the clock when Owen lost his rag. The Liverpool lad had been kicked all over the pitch from the start and, when he retaliated with a head butt to yet another foul from the Yugoslavian defenders, he was rightly shown the red card.

Owen wasn't so sure, and later professed a little innocence. 'They played a man-to-man marker and, every time I got the ball, he knocked me down,' he said. 'I lost my temper for a split second, jumped up and caught him in the midriff. I realised I was stupid. It was debatable whether I should have been sent off, but it was still stupid.'

There was reason to celebrate a week later as Owen scored six minutes into his European debut against Glasgow Celtic. It was a proud day for the whole Owen clan, as many of his Scottish relatives came to watch the game at Celtic Park. Owen's form impressed his family and also the manager – so much so that Evans decided to drop Riedle when Fowler returned from injury and the youngster kept his place in the team and lined up alongside 'God' for the first time. Liverpool weren't enjoying as much success as Owen, however, and their UEFA Cup journey was finished in the next round by Strasbourg, 3–2 on aggregate.

Even after he had firmly established himself as a first-team regular, it took Owen until November to score a professional goal at Anfield. Playing against Tottenham, the Reds had turned on the style in the second half to score three unanswered goals before Owen applied the *coup de grâce* in the eighty-eighth minute to make it 4–0.

There was more good news for Owen the following week as he joined the full England squad for training at Bisham Abbey. Unavailable to play due to the ban he picked up for his sending off against Yugoslavia Under-18s, Owen was called up by England manager Glenn Hoddle to rub shoulders with his heroes ahead of their game against Cameroon.

'Michael has not looked out of place here this week,' Paul Gascoigne said at the time. And the move by Hoddle added noise to the as-yet whispering calls for the youngster to join the World Cup squad for the tournament in France the following year. Owen was taking it all in his stride, as ever.

'I hope I can get into that squad sooner rather than later,' Owen said in *The Times*. 'I don't expect to be in it, but if I am doing well for Liverpool and scoring goals for Liverpool, then who knows what the England manager might be thinking?' Having only just played his way into his club side, Owen was already looking to the next target, with the confidence and dedication that would see him rise to the top of the world game.

As well as the success *on* the pitch there was an increasing amount of interest in English football's hottest young star *off* the pitch, but Owen wouldn't let it change him. 'Since the season began, people tend to recognise you a bit more,' he continued. 'But I still keep my feet on the ground. I still live at home near Chester and I intend to stay living at home. I value my family more than anything. I have still got the same friends. I would like to think I haven't changed too much. I wouldn't change now. I have always wanted to be a footballer. I have always prepared myself for being a footballer.'

His preparation was paying dividends: his involvement with England brought opinion from the great and good of the game, and Owen was making a great impression on his teammates, such as the Liverpool and England skipper Paul Ince. 'I think Michael has every chance of playing in the World Cup,' the midfielder told the press. 'Age doesn't come into it. Glenn gave Rio Ferdinand his first cap last Saturday and he's only nineteen. Nowadays people tend to go overboard because some of these players are so young, but Michael's a very good prospect.

'A lot can happen in the next six months. Players can get injured or lose form and there's a whole bunch of strikers competing for a place in the squad. As long as Michael keeps his feet on the ground – and I'm sure he will – he has every chance for France if the goals keep coming. The most important thing is that he keeps doing the business for Liverpool, and that applies to all of us.'

The goals did keep coming for Liverpool's bright new talent and, although he had been forced to wait for his first professional strike at Anfield, Owen soon had plenty more to go with it as he hit a hat-trick in the next match, against Grimsby Town.

It was Owen's domestic cup debut, and, facing the second-division side in the League Cup, he got off to a great start in the competition, as history appeared to repeat itself. On Fowler's League Cup debut four years previously, he had scored five, as Liverpool thrashed Fulham, and, although the new hotshot didn't score quite as many, the omens were good for the future.

With Fowler out, suspended, Owen was paired with Riedle, but it was the young Englishman who again caught the eye. In the twenty-seventh minute Owen followed up Jamie Redknapp's shot, and tucked away the loose ball when the keeper failed to hold onto it. His second came just before the break after he converted his own spot kick, and Owen saved the best till last, as he curled the third into the top corner from outside the area after fifty-seven minutes.

'Tuesday was the best experience yet in a Liverpool shirt,' Owen told the press, after scoring his first professional three-goal haul. 'To wrap my hat-trick up with my first goal at the Kop end was magnificent. Now I hope I can score a few more hat-tricks. Glenn Hoddle's encouraged me to enjoy the experience of training with the England squad and hopefully I can now push my way into the team. I think I could do a job for him.'

Training with the England squad had given Owen a huge boost. His attention was fully focused on forcing his way into the World Cup squad, and he knew how to do that: by scoring more goals for Liverpool. 'You aren't asked to go to train with England just for the ride,' he added. 'They're looking for future internationals, and if they don't see you in that mould they wouldn't invite you. I'm confident of my own ability and I think I could do a job in France. Glenn Hoddle's said he'll give a few people their chance, and if he's thinking of taking me to the World Cup finals I hope he'll give me that chance before the summer. I'm hopeful of playing and showing what I can do.'

Owen had shown what he was capable of for Liverpool many times since the start of the season, and Evans was no longer sure which of Fowler, Riedle and Owen was his first-choice strike duo. 'We have three major strikers now,' the Kop boss told the press. 'And they are in no particular order. Michael's taken his chance. We said before the season started that we'd take care of him, nurse him along, but he's changed all that. He wants to play all the time.'

On the eve of his eighteenth birthday, Owen was once again

paired with Fowler as he continued his fine form at Selhurst Park, with a goal in the 3–0 win over Crystal Palace. Liverpool were already 1–0 up through McManaman when Owen outsprinted Andy Linighan and beat the Palace keeper twelve minutes into the second half.

The goal took Owen to nine Liverpool goals as a seventeen-year old, and his first twelve months as a professional had proved to be quite busy. 'A lot's happened to me in the last year,' Owen admitted to the press. 'It seems a long time ago since I signed my pro contract on my seventeenth birthday. The highlight was my debut and scoring. When we lost at Wimbledon it meant we weren't going to win the title but it was nice from a personal point of view. I didn't expect it [the success] to happen this quickly, but I wasn't surprised when it did.'

With his typical dedication to football, Owen refused to paint the town red on his eighteenth birthday – a goal against the Eagles was good enough for the young striker. 'I'm having to put a family party on hold this weekend but the best way to celebrate my birthday is by scoring,' he continued. 'I'm meeting with the Under-21s afterwards. We're 2–0 down from the first leg so we have to try and claw that back.'

His first game with the England Under-21s was in the second leg of a crucial European Championship play-off against Greece. The Young Lions had lost the away leg 2–0 and, although they won the return 4–2, they were out on the away-goals rule. It was a good night for Owen on a personal level, though, as he once again scored on a debut with his sixtieth-minute strike. It proved to be his one and only Under-21s cap but it helped the Liverpool forward to complete his record of playing for England at each of the representative age groups.

Owen was enjoying a rich winter in front of goal and made it four from four with the opener in each of the next two games.

He tapped one in at the far post to beat Coventry 1–0 at Anfield, and got the ball rolling with his forty-sixth-minute strike against Leeds on Boxing Day. Fowler added two late goals to beat the Yorkshire side 3–0, and the Reds won 2–0 away to Newcastle to finish the year in a good position.

Liverpool were out of Europe, but fourth in the league, into the quarterfinals of the League Cup and with the FA Cup yet to come – so there was still plenty to play for. Owen had scored ten goals in all competitions since the start of the season and had trained with the England team – 1997 had been a good year, but 1998 would be even better.

The year in which Michael Owen would announce his arrival to the footballing world started in poor circumstances as Liverpool crashed out of the FA Cup to Coventry. A matter of weeks after dominating the Sky Blues in the league, Evans's team lost 3–1 at Anfield.

Coventry manager Gordon Strachan was wary of the Liverpool strikers before the game 'I've never seen anyone better for his age than Owen,' Strachan told the *Daily Mirror*. 'George Best was just before my time, but there aren't many great players in British football that I haven't watched since then. Owen is better than the lot of them – for someone aged eighteen, this boy is quite phenomenal. Owen's pace is phenomenal, much faster than he seems on television and so is his finishing. He also appears to possess a great footballing brain: Owen and Robbie Fowler are quite a handful.'

Strachan's team managed to contain the threat of the young English duo, but Newcastle were unable to repeat the feat four days later in the League Cup quarterfinal. Kenny Dalglish's side kept things tight for ninety minutes at St James' Park, and, with the game goalless, it went to extra time. There was woe for the

Liverpool legend as he saw the Kop's new heroes carve through his defence twice early in extra time to make it into the semifinal.

Five minutes into extra time Owen raced onto a Fowler through ball and chipped Shaka Hislop. Eight minutes later, Fowler got one himself after good work by Redknapp, and the Reds were closing in on some silverware. Owen was delighted and his performance was all the more remarkable considering his preparation for the game. 'I've been ill all week,' the striker told reporters. 'I don't know if it's flu or food poisoning but it took a lot out of me and I was feeling the effects late on. I'm enjoying this competition and I seem to be doing all right up to now. Getting a goal tonight was great for me. I didn't dream of anything like this for this season. To play as many games as I have and to keep my place has been brilliant.'

The games were coming thick and fast for Owen and two weeks later he scored again to beat Newcastle at Anfield. Jason McAteer released Owen in the inside-left channel, and the youngster took a couple of strides forward before stroking the ball past the advancing Hislop and into the top corner of the goal. The game finished 1–0, and despite the result Dalglish couldn't fail to be impressed by the new Prince of the Kop, as the Newcastle manager said, 'Owen had no right to finish like that.'

With six wins and a draw in their last seven league games, the three points put Liverpool level with Blackburn in second place, five points behind Manchester United, and it wasn't just the improvement of Liverpool but also the ever-more influential involvement of Owen that was the subject of the post-match press conference. As Evans said of his prodigy, 'It was a great finish by Michael but he's always capable of doing something like that. He may be only eighteen, but he's passed the stage when you talk about his potential – he's a player now. If he maintains his progress and keeps his feet on the ground he's looking at a career which could span the next fifteen years.'

Always keen to improve, Owen had been spongelike since his Premiership debut, soaking up tips and tricks to maximise his ability. 'I'm always learning,' he said to the press. 'I watch Robbie and Karlheinz and I think I've definitely improved. They recognise I'm a young lad and they help me and make me feel comfortable. I'm playing with and against world-class players every week so there has to be improvement. When you get into the Premiership, results are all-important, so games can be quite physical. Perhaps, when they see I'm only small, they think I'll not be able to handle it, but I can give as good as I get. I'm not going to just lie down and let them trample all over me, although that doesn't mean I'm going to start kicking.'

It was Owen's sheer ability that was marking him out as a target for the hatchet men, and that talent also brought a call-up to the full England squad. He was playing golf at the time the squad was due to be announced and, ignoring the etiquette of the game, he kept his phone on in the hope that the call would come from Liverpool coach Doug Livermore. 'I knew the squad was being announced,' Owen told the *News of the World*. 'And, although you are not supposed to use mobiles out on the course, I switched mine on for a short while. When Doug rang, it was a truly amazing feeling for me. Then the phone went another twenty times in the next ten minutes, so I had to switch it off. My golf went to pieces. I was a couple of holes up on my dad and he managed to pull them back. Eventually I was able to compose myself to win the round and take the money off him again.'

With the World Cup just four months away, Owen was included in the twenty-four-man squad for a game against Chile. There was no room for his Liverpool teammate Fowler in the squad, and the thought was that Hoddle wasn't a fan of

Fowler's off-pitch 'Spice Boy' image, but there were no such worries about the younger Liverpool striker. 'Owen has been nigh-on perfect when he's been with us – at all levels,' the England manager said. 'Just from looking at him, he seems to have exactly the right temperament.'

That attitude was to the fore as Owen celebrated his call-up with a brace against Southampton in a 3–2 loss at home. The young striker was absolutely superb that day, but his teammates weren't up to scratch and the defeat effectively ended Liverpool's title aspirations. Despite the league defeat, Owen was understandably excited to be part of the England squad for the first time. 'I'm absolutely delighted,' said the England new boy. 'It's no secret my ambitions have always been to play for Liverpool and England. At this stage of my career it's vital for me to stay fit, keep learning and keep my feet on the floor. It's wonderful to be selected and, just as at Liverpool, all I can do is continue to let my football do the talking and leave it up to Roy Evans and Glenn Hoddle to decide whether or not to select me.'

The two managers had only good things to say about the new kid on the block. 'Michael has come a long way in a short period of time,' Evans told the press. 'This is recognition of what he's done for us. Whether or not he plays next week, it's another step for him. Glenn obviously feels he's good enough now and I agree. It seems he's somebody you can't hold back. We're always aware of the danger of burn-out and have left him out on occasions, but he doesn't take too kindly to that. Even so, I didn't expect him to play so many games in his first season.'

Owen's attitude had won him many admirers, including Hoddle. 'From the first day he came in to train with the England squad for a bit of experience a couple of months ago, he did not look out of place and he did not feel out of place,' the Three Lions' manager said to *The Times*. 'He seemed to know that there is a time to show no respect to the older players and that that is in the hour-and-a-half of a football match.

'Sometimes you can be in awe of people and your natural performance will not come out. This kid avoided that, but after the game the nice temperament came back again. What he is doing week in and week out at Liverpool suggests that he might be capable of getting into the final twenty-two in four or five months. But I need to find out whether he can do what he is doing in the Premiership against the best defenders in the world. That is a different league – a different level.'

One man who knew all about scoring at every level was Ian Rush, and the Liverpool great had mixed feelings about Owen's England call-up. 'I'm so pleased for Michael and his family. I've known them for a long time and anyone who's seen him play this season will recognise he's ready for the ultimate step,' the Welsh legend told the press. 'Yes, I wanted him to play for Wales. I could see Michael and Ryan Giggs giving us a massive boost. But Michael always insisted he was English, even though he's spent most of his life in Hawarden and still lives there.

'With hindsight, you could say he's made the right decision picking England because he could be playing in the World Cup Finals at the age of eighteen – and that was never going to happen with Wales. I didn't think he'd make the breakthrough so quickly for England because of the fierce competition for places. But he has, and good luck to him.'

As he has so often insisted, Owen was never eligible to play for Wales, and that would soon become an irrelevance as he was selected to start against Chile at Wembley. 'It's all come very quickly for me this year,' Owen told the press before the game. 'And I would be lying if I said I won't be nervous when I start the match tomorrow. But I feel ready. I'm confident in my ability to do well. I don't think age comes into it. The manager's said that if you're good enough you're old enough, and hopefully I come into that category. I suppose there is a bit of pressure on me, but I haven't got anything to lose. A lot of people are bringing my age into it, but for some reason I don't really see myself as a young player coming into the game.'

With only thirty-three appearances for Liverpool, he was light on experience and, at eighteen years and fifty-nine days, he became the youngest England international of the twentieth century, breaking Duncan Edwards's record, which had stood since 1955, by 124 days. Since he had played at Wembley twice before – against Brazil and Germany in his schoolboy days, and scored on each occasion – the omens were good. Owen also scored on his debut at Under-15, -16, -18, -20 and -21 levels for England, but sadly he couldn't repeat the trick against Chile.

Owen lined up in a three-man attack with Coventry's Dion Dublin and Manchester United's Teddy Sheringham, but his debut was completely overshadowed by the performance of Chile's young hotshot Marcelo Salas. Salas, who was twenty-three, was on his way to Lazio in a £13 million move, and his two goals decided the game as the South Americans won 2–0.

The debutant was realistic in defeat. 'It wasn't a good team performance,' Owen said. 'But I feel I did all right. I could have been a lot better, but I could also have been a lot worse. I had one early chance, which came to me quite quickly. I hit it with the outside of my foot, but maybe I should have given it some power instead.'

His fourth-minute effort had been well saved by Nelson Tapia one-handed, but, despite not getting on the scoresheet, Owen was England's one bright spark in a game where Hoddle possibly experimented too much. The manager accentuated the positive. 'I thought Owen acquitted himself very well,' Hoddle said after the match. 'He's only eighteen, but he's shown he can get off markers in the last third of the pitch. He performed as well as anybody against a very organised Chilean side, who were tough defensively.'

The then Birmingham boss and TV pundit Trevor Francis felt the young striker had proved his international quality, and deserved to go to the World Cup. 'You can put Owen on the plane for France right now,' Francis said.

And England's new star proved he could still do it for Liverpool in his next match, as he scored his first Premiership hat-trick to round off a remarkable week. Buoyed by his successful international debut, Owen returned to domestic action full of confidence, and Sheffield Wednesday were the unlucky opposition as he bagged three at Hillsborough. More praise flooded in for Owen as Owls boss Ron Atkinson admitted to underestimating the young star, saying, 'Owen's much better than I thought – and I thought he was very good. All his goals were outstanding.'

Liverpool came back from 1–0 down after six minutes to go in level at half-time, but they then fell 3–1 behind before Owen hit two in seven minutes to make it 3–3. With five goals and his England bow in the space of seven days, it had been a week to remember for Owen and it was then that his World Cup dream started to become more tangible.

'I know Glenn Hoddle wouldn't have picked me against Chile if he hadn't had me in mind for the World Cup,' Owen told the *News of the World*. 'So I was determined not to be ignored. In the match straight after the international, I scored a hat-trick in a 3–3 draw against Sheffield Wednesday. It was one of my most important performances of the year. It was my way of showing that playing for England had not gone to my head and I was in no way complacent. That probably sums me up. I'm not outwardly aggressive, but there is a steel inside me which makes me want to keep on reaching new goals.'

As Owen's fortunes continued to rise, Liverpool's were taking a downturn: beaten at home by Southampton, and then drawing with Wednesday, the Reds were knocked out of the League Cup by Middlesbrough and then drew with Everton as Fowler's damaged knee ligaments put him out of action for the rest of the season and the ensuing World Cup.

Losing their leading scorer as results were going against them wasn't great news for Liverpool, but it meant that Owen was all but assured of a place in the team for the rest of the season, and it took another striker out of the running for the England squad. The injury had served as a reminder to Owen how fragile footballers' careers are. 'Robbie's injury was a big shock to me,' Owen told the *Daily Mirror*. 'You think to yourself "that could happen to me" and it does scare you. World Cups don't come along often and Robbie's going to miss that now. It's a devastating blow but that's what football does to you sometimes.

'What's happened to Robbie is a reminder that you've got to take every game as it comes, enjoy it to the full and do your best because it might be your last for a year or so. It was a major blow for me, and the team, to lose someone of Robbie's ability. We had formed a reasonably good partnership and it was improving game by game. We had shared the goals about when he was playing and now he's gone maybe there is a bigger burden on me to score the goals. But his replacement, Karlheinz Riedle, is capable of scoring so I don't think it's too big a burden.'

In the first game after Fowler's injury Owen scored a penalty as Liverpool lost 2–1 away to Aston Villa, and scored the winner a week later as the Reds beat Bolton 2–1 at Anfield. It wasn't just Liverpool who were struggling with injuries, however, and when Owen joined the England squad for the game against Switzerland in Berne they were without several first-team regulars.

All the pre-match focus was on Owen and whether he would start alongside Shearer for the first time, building on the half an hour they had played together at the end of the Chile match. 'It was a lot different to playing in the Premiership,' Owen said of his England debut. 'A lot of the time, you've got two man-to-man markers and a sweeper, whereas in the league you often find a flat back four.

'Everything was much more organised. It was much harder to get round the back of the defence. The defence is much tighter and much quicker. It was a great experience and hopefully I will have improved as a player because of that. I'm learning all the time. At my age, I don't think you can stop learning. I don't think what I've already achieved will really sink in until I've finished my career. The shirt from my first cap is up on my bedroom wall. I thought I did all right. A lot of people said I played really well, but I'm not sure about that. I suffered from a bit of nerves, but I think that's only natural.'

Owen again refused to be overawed in his first overseas international, but in the build-up to the match at the Wankdorf Stadium the England manager made a statement that would later be the source of constant ridicule. 'I think when you create as much as Michael does, it's hard to be a born goalscorer,' Hoddle said. Generally interpreted to mean that the lad who scored ninety-two goals in a season was not a 'natural', these words would be remembered with amusement as long as Owen continued scoring.

What Hoddle really meant was that Owen's game was not all about goals, as he elaborated in a separate interview. 'He likes to attack players with his face up so that he's aware of what's going on around him,' the England boss said to reporters. 'What

Michael has is a dying art. There aren't many players in this country who can run with the ball as quickly as he does. He's got control and pace and he can run off the ball to create space as well as run with the ball. He's pretty unique, really. He's a striker who attacks people with the ball. You normally find wingers like Ryan Giggs doing that. He's got the ability to go quickly at opponents right down the middle.'

One undisputedly natural goalscorer was Gary Lineker, who was another member of the growing army of Owen fans. 'Owen is an awesome talent,' the former England striker said to the press. 'Even at my peak, I never had the trickery or pace he's got. Glenn Hoddle says he probably won't get as many goals as I did because I was a natural scorer and there's far more to Owen's game than just that. Owen's the sort of player who can come on for the last twenty minutes and change the game, and that could be mighty useful in the World Cup.'

Natural or not, Owen didn't find the back of the net against Switzerland, and was replaced by Sheringham in the second half. Decimated by injuries the England team struggled on their way to a 1–1 draw, and there were very few positives for Hoddle to take from the game.

April started brightly for Owen, as he was announced as the Professional Footballers' Association (PFA) Young Player of the Year. His nineteen goals so far in the season, fourteen of which came in the Premiership, and the promising start to his England career had seen Owen come out on top of the vote by his peers. The Liverpool striker beat Southampton's Kevin Davies, and West Ham's Rio Ferdinand into second and third place respectively.

Owen was making headlines for all the wrong reasons five days later as he was shown a red card at Old Trafford. He'd opened the scoring after thirty-six minutes, but was running around like a madman, and even clattered into Peter Schmeichel – which certainly isn't sensible when you're five foot eight and less than 11 stone. Owen unsurprisingly came off second best in the collision with the Great Dane, but he still hadn't learned his lesson and caught Ronny Johnsen very late and was justifiably sent off.

The referee, Graham Poll, was left with no other choice following Owen's reckless display. Poor Johnsen was taken to hospital and Manchester United took advantage of their numerical superiority to rescue a draw, 1–1. Fortunately, Owen saw sense after his anarchic afternoon and has never been sent off since.

Owen kept scoring for Liverpool as he took his total to twenty-one for the season against Coventry. He earned his third England cap as a late substitute against Portugal, and it was his electrifying performance against a tiring defence that truly showed he was ready for international football. England were leading 3–0 against arguably the best team not to qualify for the World Cup, when Owen replaced Sheringham with thirteen minutes left. In that short time the eighteen-year-old made a big impression as he twice went close to claiming his first England goal, and even had what looked like a legitimate penalty appeal turned down.

After missing just one match, against Chelsea, through suspension, Owen finished the season with a flourish. He scored in the 5–0 thrashing of West Ham, and the 4–0 demolition of freshly crowned Champions Arsenal at Anfield, and, despite losing 1–0 to Derby on the last day of the season, Liverpool finished third in the league. A clear distance behind Arsenal and Manchester United, the Reds were destined for another attempt at the UEFA Cup the following season.

Having started the season with the ambition of starting a dozen

Liverpool games Owen had played forty-four times for the Reds, starting forty-one matches and scoring twenty-three goals. In the Premiership he had scored eighteen from his thirty-six games, to share the Golden Boot with Dion Dublin and Blackburn's Chris Sutton. He was named PFA Young Player of the Year and Carling Premiership Player of the Year. He forced his way through the England Under-21s and into the full team despite being just eighteen years old, and he was part of the squad travelling to Morocco for England's World Cup warm-up matches.

Owen's future looked indisputably bright, and Liverpool's all-time leading goalscorer was already worried about his records. 'When Robbie Fowler first came into the Liverpool team I said he was capable of smashing all my scoring records,' Ian Rush said to the press. 'That still applies because he's only twenty-two, but now you can add Michael's name to the list because he's four years younger. Liverpool are very fortunate to have two strikers so young and gifted. It must be frightening for the rest of the Premiership because the best is yet to come from the pair of them.'

With plenty of room for improvement, it was frightening how good he could become, but in the World Cup in France Michael Owen would show just what he was already capable of.

3

A STAR IS BORN

'The elation was unbelievable. I saw my mum and dad sitting by the halfway line and ran towards them jumping with joy, I knew they were really proud of me and I just wanted to share that fantastic moment with them,' he told the *News of the World*. 'I wouldn't swap what I've got now for anything. Dreams really can come true.'

Michael Owen went into the 1998 World Cup as an enthusiastic and incredibly talented eighteen-year-old but he left the tournament as a national hero and a household name across the footballing world. His goal against Argentina took him from anonymity to global acclaim and by the time Owen stepped off the plane back in England his life had been changed for ever.

He wasn't even in the starting line-up for England's first game in France but his ability to turn a game on its head with a well-taken goal and frighten the life out of the opposition defenders with his sprinter's speed forced Glenn Hoddle's arm, and by the knockout stage Owen was one of the key players in the side.

Owen was selected as part of the squad for the World Cup warm-up matches in Morocco, with only three caps to his name. The Liverpool striker's dazzling cameo against Portugal had put him in the running for a place in the team, behind the established pair of Teddy Sheringham and Alan Shearer, but Owen still had competition for his place in the final twenty-two from Coventry's Dion Dublin and the north-London-based duo of Tottenham's Les Ferdinand and Ian Wright of Arsenal.

The grandly titled King Hassan II Cup got under way with a match against the hosts Morocco, and Owen was on the bench as the manager chose Dublin and Wright in attack. For Wright it was a chance to prove his fitness after missing the run-in to Arsenal's Double-winning season, but, unfortunately for the former Crystal Palace striker, his hamstring wasn't up to the test and his World Cup dream was over before it had begun. But one man's misfortune is another man's gain, and Owen replaced his striking rival after twenty-five minutes, scored the only goal of the game after fifty-nine minutes, and with it he booked his ticket to France.

At just 18 years and 164 days old, Owen became England's youngest goalscorer – a record later beaten by Wayne Rooney. He took a pass from Steve McManaman and displayed his selfish instinct in front of goal by shooting rather than passing to Dublin, who was arguably better placed. It is that hunger for goals that makes Owen such a great goalscorer, and, as his first goal for his country, it was a very important strike, and very well timed with the World Cup just weeks away.

With the amount of pressure on players to perform at the World Cup, it was important that Owen should not have to carry any extra anxiety into the tournament. As composed and seemingly unaffected a young player as Owen was, he was still relieved almost beyond words by claiming his first England goal, and the joy and relief were visible on his face as he wheeled away in celebration.

Owen was left out of the starting team two days later, as England faced Belgium in their second and final game of the Casablanca mini-tournament. He replaced Phil Neville at half-time and joined Ferdinand upfront, but neither side could find the back of the net, and after ninety minutes the game went to a penalty shootout. The organisers of the four team event introduced spot kicks to eliminate draws and to add a little excitement to proceedings, and Owen bagged his effort from twelve yards but England lost 4–3 on penalties and finished second in the table behind France on goals scored.

After the two games in Casablanca Hoddle took his squad to La Manga for a now notorious break ahead of the summer's big tournament. All the trouble started when the manager told Paul Gascoigne that he would not be one of the twenty-two players in England's squad. The mercurial midfielder known as 'Gazza' had struggled for form and fitness; many believed he was past his best, but he was a big-game player having excelled in Euro '96 and Italia '90, and was the only man in the squad with World Cup experience. Gazza didn't take the news well and allegedly smashed up Hoddle's room before going on a destructive rampage around the resort.

As the flawed Geordie genius was dismissed to World Cup history, Owen's adventure on football's greatest stage was just beginning, and he was named in the squad at Dublin's expense. Owen was selected as one of four strikers along with Shearer, Sheringham and Ferdinand, but wasn't content just to be part of the squad, and his focus immediately turned to forcing his way into the starting XI.

The good luck that had started with Robbie Fowler's season-ending injury and continued with Wright's dodgy hamstring continued when his immediate rival as Shearer's strike partner was pictured in a Portuguese nightclub at 6.45 am. The image of Sheringham boozing, smoking and chatting up a blonde in the early hours, just days before the biggest tournament of his life, gave the press all the ammunition they needed in their campaign to get Owen into the team. Hoddle was understandably upset with his striker, and said, 'I'm very disappointed with Teddy. He's the one who's going to lose out in the end.'

With the natural timing that he best displayed in his ghosting runs to the far post, Owen was signing a new boot deal with Umbro as Sheringham faced Hoddle's ire. 'There are so many pitfalls that you've got to be careful,' Owen told the assembled media. 'Footballers are always in the spotlight and I believe they have to be more professional outside the game. I don't drink and I don't smoke. I can't go out and do what normal eighteen-year-olds do, but I know a lot of them would like to be in my position. Sacrifices come with the job and I wouldn't change my life.

'I've been spending as much time with my family as I can. All players have a responsibility to act professionally. I don't feel I do anything that would affect my performance. I've always wanted to be a professional footballer and have watched how they behave and speak in interviews, as well as what they do on the pitch.'

The new contract was for £5 million over six years, and included possible bonuses for winning the World Cup or the tournament's Golden Boot, and he would be facing fierce competition from his captain Shearer, who had a similar deal with the same company. In light of the behaviour of some of Owen's international colleagues, the sportswear firm's spokesman was asked about the off-field behaviour of their two big England stars.

Umbro's director of sports marketing, Martin Prothero, revealed at the press conference, 'We can't afford to invest if a player's going to conduct himself in a manner that's going to embarrass us off the field. In most contracts there are disgrace-related stipulations that mean if the player does something detrimental to the company image he'll face financial penalties. The good thing about Alan and Michael is you are 99.99 per cent certain they will never be used.

'Shearer and Owen are very similar. Both are incredibly cool under pressure and their lifestyles are exactly as you would wish. We are most interested in Owen's on-the-field performance and we're confident nothing will blow him off course away from the field.'

Owen and Shearer have displayed almost angelic behaviour off the pitch and have both been perfect role models throughout their careers. Their shared hunger for goals and drive for perfection on the pitch has infected their private lives and helped keep them focused on both sides of the white line. There was little for Umbro to fear off the pitch, so they would just have to keep their fingers crossed and hope that Owen could get some game time, and show the world what he could do.

Owen told the *News of the World*, 'I have always thought I was capable of playing as an international, so to pit yourself against the best in the world should bring out the best in me. It was nice to get off the mark for England against Morocco and, hopefully, I can get a few more. I want to score in every game I play. I think I could play my natural game alongside Shearer and, hopefully, that will be good enough for Glenn Hoddle. Defenders will be trying to wind me up in the World Cup, but the best answer is to score goals against them.'

One added bonus of his new sponsorship deal was the stellar

treatment handed out to the top players, and Owen now had boots made to measure. 'I'm getting faster as I'm getting bigger,' he said. 'The boots have been made to the exact millimetre and will help improve my balance.'

Before he could think about using his new boots to help pick up the Golden Boot, Owen had to get into the starting XI. 'First and foremost I must try and get into the team,' he told the *Sunday Mirror*. 'My initial aim is to score as many goals as I can, and if I should become leading goal-scorer it would be a great achievement. But for the time being all I am thinking about is helping England win the World Cup.'

With the hype surrounding his going into the tournament, Owen wasn't worried about becoming a marked man. 'Maybe there will be a few players waiting out there for me,' he went on. 'But it doesn't bother me who I play against. Pitching yourself against the best internationals should bring the best out of any player. I have just got to go out and play my natural game – the manager knows what I can do at club level and I don't see why I should change.'

Hoddle knew exactly what Owen could do and he was very impressed by the youngster's approach on and off the field. 'There's a new breed of youngster that will understand what coaches are doing and will eventually get rid of the old school,' he told the *Scotsman*. 'Just because things have happened for a long time does not make them right. Michael Owen and Rio Ferdinand have nothing to lose. They're just kids and the pressure is on the likes of Alan Shearer and David Seaman, not Rio or Michael. If you're going into a World Cup without that feeling then you can get the best out of yourself. We won't be putting any pressure on those two young lads.'

It was a good thing Hoddle wasn't putting any pressure on his starlets, because the media were working themselves into a frenzy as the squad moved on to France and took up residence in La Baule, Brittany. Having left the distractions of La Manga behind, England's bright young hope was still asked questions about his chances of starting. 'I want to be in the XI,' Owen said in *The Times*. 'I wouldn't say I'm really confident. Teddy and Alan have proven very successful for England, so I would say those two are favourites. If you put me on the spot now, I would probably say he will go for Teddy, but I still have a chance. I think I am ready. It remains to be seen who the manager picks, but no team starts with the same XI it finishes with. But I'm like anyone, I would prefer to start rather than come on as sub. I would be disappointed if I wasn't in the starting line-up, but that's not to say I would throw in the towel. Everyone's ambition throughout the squad is to play and to start.'

Owen's chances were given a boost after he started England's final warm-up game. The match against Caen was an unofficial affair played behind closed doors, and allowed Hoddle to pair Owen with Shearer once more. Some people doubted whether this new partnership could ever be as successful as the famous SAS partnership. Shearer as the archetypal English No. 9 – direct, powerful, fearless and great in the air – was well suited to playing alongside Sheringham, a player who liked to 'drop off' into the space between the opposition midfield and defence get the ball on the deck, and play with his head up to see the game ahead of him and quite often play in his strike partner as he did to such success in Euro '96.

Owen has often been criticised for playing too much with his head down, due to his sometimes selfish attitude in front of goal, and that brought concerns that the new partnership would be less of a double act and more of two great one-man shows playing simultaneously. With two such impressive goalscorers as Owen and Shearer playing alongside each other, it became very important that they didn't duplicate each other's movements, making the job much easier for the defence, but rather made supporting runs to work the defenders – forcing them to run in different directions. Fortunately for England, the strikers at Hoddle's disposal were blessed with good footballing brains.

'I started against Caen with Shearer and it works fine,' Owen told *The Times*. 'At the start of the season, a lot of people were saying I couldn't play with Robbie Fowler at Liverpool. But if you are intelligent enough, all you need to do is play with them once to know their runs and how they play. Every striking partnership needs working on, but if you are intelligent about it, you can learn an awful lot in the first game.

'I thought I played well against Caen. I didn't score. Paul Scholes scored but I was through one-on-one at one point and a fellow dragged me back, which would have been a clear sending-off in the World Cup. Maybe I would have got on the score-sheet if it was the World Cup. I know I have had a lot of praise recently but it has got to the stage now where I just want to get out there and show people what I can do.'

Owen was replaced by Sheringham near the end of the match at the Stade Michel d'Ornano and, with six days before the World Cup opener against Tunisia, the press went into overdrive with the Owen/Sheringham debate. But the coach was giving nothing away. 'Ronaldo likes to collect the ball and turn to run at defenders,' Hoddle said in the *Daily Mirror*. 'You can see Owen do that because there are a lot of strings to his bow. He brings us a different dimension. He can start and influence the game. But if he comes on via the bench he can give us something different to anything we've got in the squad.

'At this moment he is being educated in international football and he will develop through this World Cup. He has to develop better awareness at this level and learn how to get off the hook if he is being tightly marked. He has two major assets – genuine pace with the ball and without it, but he also has good movement way beyond his age. Pace with good movement is rare. A lot of strikers I've worked with have electrifying pace, but they don't know how to use it. He has the smell for it.'

With his nose for goal and direct running the young striker was flattered by Hoddle's opinion. 'I think I've still got some way to go before I get to Ronaldo's level,' Owen told the assembled media. 'It's great to hear Glenn compare me to him. Obviously, there are some similarities in that I like to run at people with pace, although there's a lot of hard work to be done before I can really be mentioned in the same breath. But I'll be working on it – I'm learning all the time. I want to get started and show people, show the rest of the world. I feel I'm ready but it remains to be seen whether the manager starts the game with me. But if you put me on the spot I would say that Teddy and Alan are proven and they are favourites to play.'

As the opening match against Tunisia drew closer the debate intensified, with the great and good of the game all more than willing to throw in their twopenn'orth. 'He has exceptional pace and balance and is a constant threat to opposing defenders with his willingness to run at them,' the then manager of Blackburn Rovers, Roy Hodgson, said of Owen.

'Owen's eagerness, his aggressive confidence and his terrific pace could enliven any team,' added Manchester United's Alex Ferguson, without going on record as to whether he'd pick the youngster ahead of one of his own players.

The experienced and well-travelled Dave Bassett didn't sit on the fence, however, and told the press his thoughts: 'It's got to be Sheringham because he's the one with the experience that's needed at this stage of the competition. We're playing for real now, and Teddy's well-documented indiscretion in Portugal should not affect his selection chances. It's what players can do on the pitch that counts now, and I think at this particular moment in time Teddy is the best choice to play alongside Shearer. But I'd certainly stick Owen on the bench to utilise him as soon as it becomes necessary.'

For all Bassett's cautious approach there were plenty of former pros keen to see Owen given his chance, and the World Cup-winning goalkeeper Gordon Banks was one of the most notable advocates of the 'give youth a chance' brigade in England, but the Liverpool lad's meteoric rise had brought him to the attention of bigger fish overseas.

Johan Cruyff said in the *News of the World*, 'Owen is a great talent. I think we will hear a lot about him in the future. He is young but I would not hesitate to put him into the team. In the Premiership he has shown no signs of feeling any pressure. It's been no problem for him. He is very relaxed for such a young player. In fact, he's remarkably relaxed for such a youngster.'

But even for all the talents of the England squad it wouldn't matter who was picked, according to the Dutch maestro: 'I don't think there's any chance that England can become world champions,' Cruyff went on. 'They have a fairly good team but I think that the continentals and the South American countries play that little bit smarter. And in a great tournament like this you need to be very smart. England will make sure we'll see some great attacking games but I don't think they will have a role of any significance in these world championships. I see a lot of football and English soccer is the most fun to watch. That's because they take risks and make mistakes.'

According to the national press Hoddle made a mistake by not selecting Owen or David Beckham in his starting XI, but it didn't cost them against Tunisia, as England comfortably beat their North African opposition 2–0 in Olympique Marseille's

Stade Velodrome. Hoddle's team lined up in his preferred 3–5–2 formation, with Tony Adams, Sol Campbell and Gareth Southgate in front of David Seaman. Darren Anderton, David Batty, Paul Ince, Paul Scholes and Graeme Le Saux completed a five-man midfield, and Shearer and Sheringham were once again together upfront. Shearer opened the scoring in Marseille with a header just before half-time, and although Owen made history in the eighty-fourth minute, becoming England's youngest ever player at a World Cup, it was Scholes who sealed things late on with a fine strike from outside the area.

With only six minutes to impress against Tunisia, it was of little surprise to anyone when Owen was on the bench again for the next match. The only change to the team was in the back three, where Gary Neville replaced Southgate, but, having won the opening game so comfortably, they found things turning out very differently against Romania.

Owen had come on in Marseille only to save Sheringham for the next game, but, when he was sent on with seventeen minutes remaining in Toulouse, it was to try to save the match. Coventry's Viorel Moldovan had opened the scoring early in the second half, finishing with aplomb after Gheorghe Hagi set him up six yards out. As the game went on, it remained 1–0 and Hoddle was forced to bring on his young striker as England chased the game.

It made sense to bring on the quickest player in the squad to try to exploit a tiring defence, and the breakthrough came ten minutes later, when Owen was on hand to bury Shearer's cut-back. Owen came close again when he hit the post from twenty-five yards in injury time, but it was not his day to be the hero. The points were headed Romania's way and, following on from Moldovan's opener, it was another Premiership player who stole the headlines.

Chelsea's flying full-back Dan Petrescu ran onto Constantin Galca's pass and held off his clubmate Le Saux with his right arm before slipping a left-footed finish through Seaman's legs from close range in the ninetieth minute. With Owen's long-range effort the closest England came to an equaliser, they lost the game 2–1 and would have to win or draw their final group game to progress to the next round.

'The two goals we gave away were schoolboy stuff,' Hoddle said. 'The defending was poor. If you give away stupid goals like that at this level you're going to get punished. Now we know what we've got to do against Colombia.' The coach was understandably upset after seeing his side slip to defeat against the unfancied Eastern Europeans, but any team containing Hagi would always be a threat.

Everyone agreed that the one positive from the match was the performance of Owen. 'I told him to go out and enjoy himself and see if he could get that goal,' Hoddle said. 'And it went his way.' The eighty-third-minute strike made Owen the youngest player ever to score for England at the World Cup finals, but he took little consolation from his goal in defeat.

'You can't describe the feeling for a striker when he scores,' Owen told the press after the game. 'But I'd rather draw 1–1 and not score. I'd have liked to've celebrated scoring my first World Cup goal but the team comes first and the feeling was of deep disappointment. There was real disappointment in the dressing room afterwards but we've got to pick ourselves up really quickly and look to the next game. We're still confident of going through. It was a reasonable performance, but we gave away two bad goals and have to make sure we don't do that again.

'When you come on for twenty minutes at the end there's not too much pressure on you. If you can turn it on in those circumstances then great, but no one expects miracles of you.

It's a pressure-free thing. But the manager said if you get the chance you've got to try to take it – and it would be great to stay in the side. Every player who's not playing at present wants to come in and show what they can do – and then hopefully get to start the next game. If I play on Friday then I'll be confident of scoring. You're not born to be a striker if you aren't confident of scoring.'

But his place in the starting XI for Friday's game against Colombia was by no means certain, as Hoddle kept his cards very close to his chest and refused to say whether or not Owen had done enough to edge out Sheringham. The British public had made their decision, though, and they were far less reserved than the national coach. The roar that accompanied Owen onto the pitch in Toulouse was almost as loud as the celebrations that followed his goal ten minutes later.

As the final group game drew closer it seemed Hoddle was going to give in to public opinion, but ever his own man he revealed it had always been his intention to play Owen against the South Americans. 'I've always felt that it would be possible that Michael would start against Colombia, whatever happened,' the manager revealed. 'Even before we got to the tournament, I felt that Colombia played very square at the back, with a flat four, and against that sort of system is where Michael's pace can be so useful for us. He's come on and scored against Romania and so now if we start him his confidence is going to be sky-high.'

For the game in Lens, Hoddle brought in Owen and David Beckham for Sheringham and Batty and, with the best eleven players together for the first time, the fans were rewarded with England's finest performance of the tournament. They completely outplayed Colombia from start to finish and won 2–0, with first-half goals from Anderton and Beckham.

'What an experience that was!' Owen told the press after the game. 'It's the biggest match I've ever played in and there were some nerves at the start. But the confidence of the players has never been affected, not even after Monday's defeat. We believe we can win the World Cup and this victory has only helped to improve that feeling. Some of the lads in the dressing room were talking after the game about wanting revenge over Argentina.'

The effect of the loss to Romania became apparent when England finished second in the group and knew they would face Argentina in the next round, while Romania went through to play Croatia. The highly rated *Albicelestes* ('White and Sky Blues') was one of a handful of sides with real hopes of winning the tournament and very daunting opponents for that early stage. The striking prowess of Gabriel Batistuta, the creative genius of Juan Sebastián Verón, and Roberto Ayala's staunch defending formed the spine of the side that was looking to topple Hoddle's side.

The former Tottenham and Monaco midfielder was in the team that lost out to Diego Maradona's infamous 'Hand of God' goal at the World Cup quarterfinals in 1986, and he was keen to make a new generation of Argentines suffer for his heartbreak, but first he praised his victorious team.

'I'm absolutely delighted with that performance,' Hoddle told *The Times*. 'We really could have won by four or five goals if we had put away even a few of the chances we created. Of course, the object is to qualify for the last 16 and we have achieved that in style tonight. It was a controlled performance that was superb creatively and in defence. None of the players deserved less than eight out of ten. We had always earmarked this game for David Beckham and Michael Owen because we thought that the Colombian back four would be susceptible to Owen's pace and that Beckham could free him with his passing.'

Owen didn't manage to get on the scoresheet against Colombia but he did enough to stay in the line-up as Hoddle stuck with the same eleven for the knockout stage. Having both made their first starts at the World Cup in Lens, the two new darlings of the British media, Beckham, aged twenty-three, and Owen, who was eighteen, were to head to opposite ends of the nation's affections after their actions in St Etienne. It was a game that will live long in the memories of both Owen and Beckham, although for very different reasons, and, fortunately for the Liverpool lad, 30 June 1998 was his date with destiny.

Speaking before the game, Owen was in philosophical mood, with no comprehension of how this one match would change his life for ever. 'I just try to treat it like another game, as if I'm playing for Liverpool's youth team,' Owen said in the *Daily Mirror*. 'That's the only way you can treat it. The manager picks you for the England squad initially for what you do for your club and if he thinks that's good enough then there's no reason why you should change your game. I try not to think about it to be perfectly honest. It is harder to play at international level. You don't get as many chances and the quality is better so you've got to be on your game.'

There were a lot more chances than were to be expected against Argentina, and Owen certainly made the most of them. After the general inevitability of the group stages the tournament exploded into life when Kim Milton Nielsen blew his whistle to start the game. There was more action in the first quarter of an hour than in most of the matches at the World Cup to date, and the action really got under way with five minutes on the clock, when Diego Simeone tumbled over Seaman's outstretched arms. Simeone was clearly looking for the contact and the referee gave the decision his way, booked the goalkeeper, and pointed to the spot. As one of the finest goalscorers in Serie A, Batistuta was expected to score, and he did just that, although Seaman managed to get his hands to the ball as it crossed the line.

Argentina had been defending very deep from the outset, clearly petrified by Owen's pace, and with very good reason. Barely four minutes after going behind, England were level. Scholes sent a looping pass for Owen to run onto and as the youngster entered the box he fell under Ayala's body check. There was some argument as to the amount of contact, but, running at the speed that Owen was, it is very difficult to maintain balance after a collision, and even harder to get a decent shot away while struggling to stay upright.

Just as Simeone had gone looking for a penalty at one end, Owen had gone looking for one at the other, running across the defender and falling under the inevitable impact. Nielsen again pointed to the spot, and Shearer drilled his penalty into the top corner, for his third goal of the competition. Having manufactured the equaliser with his lightning pace it was time for Owen to take centre stage and score the goal that will stay with him for the rest of his life.

There were just sixteen minutes on the clock when Owen scored the third goal of the game, but, unlike the two penalties that had come before, this was a goal of beautiful magnificence that will burn brightly in the memories of all who saw it. Loitering just inside the opposition half, Owen received Beckham's pass in behind the Argentine midfield, and, after controlling the ball brilliantly with the outside of his right foot, he accelerated towards the opposition goal. Only six minutes after conceding a penalty for bringing him down, the South American defenders were still too scared to tackle the youngster. Ayala and his central defensive partner, José Chamot, backed off and Owen surged forward. As the swift striker approached the box he knocked the ball past Ayala, and from a standing start the defender had no hope of stopping Owen.

Scholes moved towards the ball as it came past Ayala, but Owen had run so far now that he had no intention of stopping and he paid no attention to the shouts of the Manchester United midfielder as he closed on the ball and clipped it goalwards from just inside the box. Owen's right-foot finish sailed past Carlos Roa, into the top left corner of the goal, and the youngster wheeled away in celebration. He ran and ran and was mobbed on the halfway line by his teammates just in front of where his family were seated in the crowd.

Against two seasoned campaigners from Italy's Serie A, Owen had turned the game on its head with two runs at the opposition defence in the space of six minutes. By tormenting Lazio's Chamot and Ayala of Napoli, Owen had shown he could perform against some of the world's best defenders, and, by doing it in the second round of the World Cup finals, he had shown he was a man for the big occasion.

By clipping the ball into the back of the net at the end of his amazing run, Michael Owen had announced his arrival on the world stage, and propelled himself into the realms of footballing superstardom. But the game was far from over and, with little more than quarter of an hour gone, there was plenty of time left for the game to go either way. Unfortunately for England, it drifted away from them with two incidents either side of the break.

In first-half injury time, Javier Zanetti levelled the scores from a cleverly worked free-kick routine, and in the forty-seventh minute Beckham was sent off for retaliating to a foul by Simeone. The Argentina captain brought Beckham down and as the Manchester United midfielder lay on the floor he flicked out his foot and caught Simeone on the back of the leg. The Danish referee sent Beckham off as Simeone collapsed theatrically to the floor, and England were forced to play the remainder of the game with ten men.

Hoddle's side defended valiantly, despite Argentina's numerical advantage, and even had chances to win the game as they piled forward every time there was a corner or free kick around the box. It was from an eighty-first-minute corner that England thought they had won the game, but Campbell's headed 'goal' was disallowed for Shearer's foul on the keeper. As Owen and some of his teammates mobbed Campbell in celebration, the opposition took the free kick and broke quickly. Verón surged dangerously into the England half, but Anderton came to the rescue with a vital interception and the other players recovered to relieve the pressure.

England managed to keep the opposition at bay throughout the second half and the tie headed to golden-goal extra time. Owen had a chance to win the game at the end of the first fifteen minutes, but the new superstar couldn't reproduce his first-half heroics and he shot over the bar after breaking free of the defence. With neither side able to break the deadlock, the game drew inevitably to penalties.

The hardest, cruellest way to exit an international tournament, the spot-kick lottery had accounted for England in 1990 and 1996 as the fans remembered all too clearly. Bobby Robson and Terry Venables had been in charge of the teams beaten at the Stadio delle Alpi and Wembley, but one consolation for Hoddle was that his side at least weren't facing the most efficient of footballing nations, Germany. When it comes to penalties, though, Argentina had a record as impressive as Germany with the same total of four wins from five shootouts at major tournaments, and, unfortunately for England, they were soon to improve that record.

Shearer scored England's first, to level the scores, before

Seaman maintained his impressive penalty-saving form, shown over the years for Arsenal, by stopping Hernan Crespo's effort. Ince's shot was saved, and the next three were scored before Owen stepped up. Having played so well throughout the 120 minutes, England's No. 20 was an obvious choice to take one of the spot kicks, and when the manager asked him he wasn't going to back down.

Displaying none of the nerves he must have been feeling, Owen ran up and smacked the ball into the top corner. It actually brushed the woodwork as it went past. No keeper could have stopped it – it was a perfect penalty. With the game tied at 3–3 after four kicks each, Ayala stepped up for Argentina. Despite being run ragged by Owen early on, the experienced centre-back had long since regained his composure and made no mistake with his attempt.

So Batty strode forward knowing that he had to score to keep England in the tournament, and, much to the amazement of Kevin Keegan and the disappointment of a nation, his effort was saved. It was by no means a poor penalty, low and hard, but it was just far enough out of the corner for Roa to get behind it and secure Argentina's quarterfinal showdown with Holland.

'We are almost distraught,' Hoddle said in his post-match press conference. 'It's a bitter, bitter pill to take. Even with ten men we set up so many set pieces we could have won it. It was unbelievable. You couldn't ask more from the players. I don't know if it's destiny. Everything just went against us but it's not a night for excuses.

'I don't deny that the sending-off cost us dearly,' he went on. 'It was a mistake but these things happen in football. I'm not denying it cost us the game.' The press were certain that it had cost England the game: TEN BRAVE LIONS, ONE STUPID BOY, ran the *Daily Mirror* headline, as they and the other tabloids laid the blame squarely at Beckham's feet. But Owen and the rest of the players were united behind their teammate.

'All that stick David is getting it not deserved,' Owen told the *News of the World*. 'I know what he's going through because I was there myself. It's not a nice feeling. He made a mistake, but he will learn from it. Nobody in the England camp blames him.' Owen had seen how much Beckham was suffering and empathised strongly with his future captain. But the feeling throughout the rest of the footballing world was of disappointment, as the World Cup was now robbed of one of its brightest talents – Owen was heading home.

'That's the sad thing,' Hoddle said. 'He would have become even more known worldwide if we'd have continued in this tournament.' The current manager wasn't the only England coach to be impressed by the eighteen-year-old. Bobby Robson was quoted in the press as saying, 'Owen is a genius. His pace is frightening and they couldn't handle him. His goal was one of the best of the tournament.'

Terry Venables said at the same time, 'Owen's goal was sensational.' And it wasn't just the English who were getting caught up in Owen-mania. A STAR IS BORN, read Italian headlines comparing his impact to Pelé's international arrival at the 1958 World Cup in Sweden. And the Brazilian superstar was himself impressed by the youngster.

'The way he moves, the way he dribbles, the way he controls the ball, remind me a lot of young Brazilian players,' Pelé said, quoted in the *Daily Mirror*. 'He has that Latin style which is certainly not typical of English players, and that is what has surprised me most about him. For me Michael Owen is one of the nice surprises of this tournament. He showed the form that everyone has been speaking about, and he showed it in a grand fashion before the world audience. He has a very bright future and I am personally looking forward to seeing him mature into one of the sport's top stars. England should be proud to have a player of this calibre, with such tremendous talent.'

Bobby Robson compared Owen to one of Pelé's countrymen. 'Owen reminds me a bit of Ronaldo because he is already generating the same excitement and expectancy among supporters at a tender age,' the former England boss said in the *Daily Mirror*. Talking of the player he had brought to PSV Eindhoven, he added, 'Ronaldo is a bigger lad who might win more in the air and, at the same stage, he probably had more in the way of dribbling ability, feints and twists. But the way Owen runs at defenders and terrifies them with raw pace, puts him right up there among the most exciting teenagers we've seen for a long time. He's easily the best English discovery since Gascoigne.'

More praise came from a more unlikely source, as the favourite son of the country he scored the 'Wonder Goal' against revealed. 'Owen is a real talent. He is one of the three players that have impressed me most,' Maradona said before listing Owen alongside Rivaldo and Dennis Bergkamp as the best performers at the World Cup.

Owen had signed a new boot deal just days before the tournament started, but with his profile soaring there was talk of how much money he could earn in the next year. Early estimates put the combined revenue from advertisements, endorsements, book deals, wages and the boot deal somewhere in eight figures, when barely eighteen months before the young striker had been a YTS trainee on £42.50 a week.

Rachel Anderson, a football agent, said in *The Times*, 'For advertisers he is too good to be true – handsome, well mannered, loyal to his schoolgirl sweetheart and a brilliant player. He can easily earn £10 million this year, but should take his time and wait for the most lucrative and prestigious deals.'

His life truly had changed for ever. Not even a regular at Anfield before Fowler's injury, Owen had forced his way into the England team and, barring injury, would be one of the first names on the team sheet for many years to come. Although his first World Cup outing had ended in disappointment, at the tender age of eighteen, football's newest superstar would have many more chances to impress on the grand stage.

4

GLOBAL SUPERSTAR

'I'd be lying if I said that I found all the attention easy,' he told the *Daily Mirror*. 'But people want to know about you, so it's something you have to accept. It's hard at times with all the attention. There are occasions already when I am getting fed up with it. But I've got to get on with it and accept that it comes with the job – and I am learning to live with it.'

Michael Owen's success in France had taken him to another level of fame, and things were bad enough before the tournament. 'Me and Danny Murphy went to McDonald's,' Owen said in May 1998. 'Never again. Not to somewhere like that. You don't mind signing autographs, but when there's hundreds of them lining up, you end up staying about an hour and a half. You don't show anyone that you want to go home, but you do think, "I'm not doing this again." It's part of the job, but an hour's a long time.'

Post-World Cup it would have been a lot longer than an hour, but Owen was more intelligent than to try to grab a quiet burger at the golden arches. The youngster's success in France had made Owen the nation's new pin-up and there was sudden interest in his girlfriend. Owen said, 'I love Louise and we are both very happy. But I'm only eighteen and I've no plans to get married. I wouldn't even consider anything as serious as that for at least another five years.'

The young footballer was in no rush to tie the knot, but he still took his girlfriend away with him and his family to America for a holiday. The paparazzi followed Owen all the way to Orlando, where they took plenty of pictures of the youngster relaxing at Disney World, at the beach and by the pool. The pictures were all over the tabloids and, as his friends let him know of the publicity back in the UK, Owen began to realise how much his life had changed.

It wasn't just the fans and the photographers who were taking more interest in English football's new star: Europe's biggest clubs had spent the second half of the summer trying to prise Owen away from Liverpool. There was talk of £50 million bids, and the top football agent and wheeler-dealer Pini Zahavi said to the *Daily Mirror*, 'When I spoke with Liverpool chief executive Peter Robinson a year ago about Owen I was told he was not for sale. There was unofficial interest from Milan and they would not have hesitated in paying £27 million in fee and salary. His price has gone up after what he has done in this World Cup. But if ever such deals were worked out it would be my advice to make sure he was paid most of it when he was older. Too much money too early can have a disastrous effect on young players.'

As well as AC Milan's reported interest, there was plenty of other talk about Owen's heading to Italy. 'Owen is the player of the future and we tried to sign him before the World Cup finals,' said Luciano Moggi, the general director of Juventus.

Lazio were also fairly determined pursuers, but Liverpool weren't interested in selling and Owen had decided to stay at Anfield, committed to the club that had given him his breakthrough and unwilling to move away from his tight-knit family at such a young age. But, even without leaving Liverpool, Owen had to endure some big changes at club level that summer as Gérard Houllier came in as joint manager alongside Roy Evans.

After four years in sole charge of Liverpool the boot room boy had been unable to bring the club the league title they had craved so much since their last win in 1990. And, having seen the great work done at Highbury by Arsène Wenger, the men in charge of the club decided to bring in a top Continental coach. Houllier had taken Lens from the French Second Division to the top flight and even into the UEFA Cup, before winning the French title with Paris St Germain and then becoming technical director of the national side.

Houllier became manager of France in 1992, but, after they failed to qualify for the 1994 World Cup, he resigned, returning to his post as technical director, where he remained until joining Liverpool. And, when France won the World Cup in 1998, Houllier was honoured with a special medal to commemorate the fantastic achievement, a lovely trophy to take with him to his new job in England.

The Frenchman had worked in Liverpool before and even classed himself as a Reds fan after spending a year as an assistant at Alsop Comprehensive School in 1969/70, as part of his degree at Lille University.

Houllier's first task was to rid the Reds of their 'Spice Boys' image and make them a more disciplined and professional outfit. The days of players getting blind drunk every weekend were drawing to a close as England increasingly fell in line with the rest of Europe and their more health-conscious approach to sport. In came more stretching, better physical conditioning, more attention to diet and preparation and eventually an increased standard of football throughout the country.

With Robbie Fowler not expected back on first-team duty until Christmas, Liverpool had signed the South African striker Sean Dundee, from Karlsruhe for £2 million. So, heading into his second full season, Owen was the first-choice forward at Anfield and he was more than willing to take the goalscoring responsibility on his young shoulders.

'I've been grateful that Robbie's been around the training ground, to watch him and learn from him throughout my career so far,' Owen said at a press conference to announce his contract with Tissot watches. 'He's been a great help to me and we will certainly miss a player of his calibre, but I had the most appearances upfront last season and it didn't go too badly. So, even though Robbie's injured at the moment, I'm confident that we can still go two better this year than our third-place finish last season. Liverpool are built on success, so finishing second or third just isn't good enough.'

The Merseysiders had a promising pre-season, and Owen was among the goals wherever they went, which only increased the public's affection for the new Boy Wonder. 'Things have been pretty crazy since the World Cup,' he told the *News of the World*. 'Especially when I was away with Liverpool for the pre-season matches. There were always a few hundred people hanging around the lobbies of our hotels. Many of them were young kids shouting my name. It was all harmless fun. All they wanted was an autograph or the chance to say hello. Some of the more cheeky girls

Young Michael worked hard at school but it could never compete with his passion for football – soon fulfilling every schoolboy's dream by playing on the hallowed pitch at Wembley.

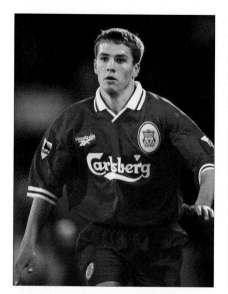

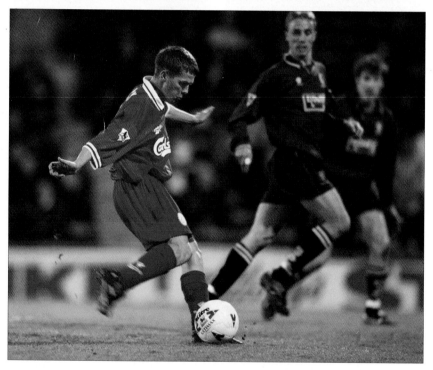

Owen made his Liverpool debut against Wimbledon in May 1997 as a seventeen year old, coming on as a sub and scoring.

Lightning fast, deft and always spinning off the shoulder of his opponent, Michael's skills were evident long before he wore the red of Liverpool, but they helped him to joint top scorer in the Premier League and PFA Young Player of the Year in 1997/98.

'That' goal! – the unforgettable moment young Owen burst into the world's consciousness with a heart-stopping individual strike against Argentina in the 1998 World Cup.

Owen picked up the 1998 BBC Sports Personality of the Year award, and met HM The Queen. As his profile rose at Liverpool, Michael became a figure whom sponsors would pay big money to be associated with; one of the earliest was Umbro, along with Jaguar cars.

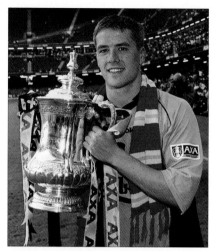

Having scored both goals against Arsenal in a 2-1 victory, Owen celebrates with the FA Cup in 2001. Against Alaves he helped win the UEFA Cup and, along with the League Cup, shared in a historic Liverpool treble.

While Owen slots home his hat-trick in the 5-1 drubbing of Germany in September 2001 (*top*), scores against Brazil in the 2002 World Cup (*left*), and in Euro 2004 against Portugal (*above*), England failed to deliver in any of the major tournaments between 1998 and 2006.

Owen and Liverpool captain Steven Gerrard celebrate the League Cup victory over Man Utd in 2003 – but for Owen, the modest Liverpool attainments that season reinforced his growing longing for the chance of greater prizes elsewhere.

asked for a peck on the cheek – which, to be honest, I found a bit embarrassing.'

At a friendly tournament in Ireland, Liverpool beat local side St Patrick's and then Leeds, who had knocked out Lazio, to win the Carlsberg Trophy at Lansdowne Road. Owen and Steve McManaman both scored in the 2–0 victory over the Yorkshire side, and, despite the midfielder's influential match, it was Owen who received the man-of-the-match award. The striker was obviously embarrassed to take the plaudits, not for the first time since St Etienne, and Liverpool's joint manager Evans was concerned about his protégé. 'I think it gets to him that he's being picked out from the rest of the lads all the time,' he said.

The dressing room banter was that Owen was a dead cert for the man-of-the-match award in every game no matter what, and the young striker took it all in the light-hearted manner that it was intended. But in an interview with the *News of the World* he was keen to emphasise the part his team colleagues had to play in his success. 'People should realise that I am involved in a team game,' Owen said. 'All the fan worship is fine, but I am aware that without the help of all my team-mates from both Liverpool and England, I would not have the chance to be at the centre of all this fuss and attention.'

Owen was sure that he wouldn't let the attention detract from his on-pitch performance, and so he was very careful about which of the hundreds of possible endorsement deals he would put his name to. 'Everyone seems to want a part of me at the moment,' he admitted. 'It's nice to know I'm doing things on the football pitch which made people think so highly of me. I must be doing something right. Of course I am enjoying it – I would be a fool not to. I love my life the way it is and I wouldn't want to change any of it for a minute. It gives me a real buzz to hear my name being chanted and to see people queuing up to meet me. But there has to be a limit. After all, I am a professional sportsman, not a pop star, and as such, I've got to make sure I am physically and mentally prepared to play football at the highest level.'

Umbro had the foresight to sign Owen before the World Cup, and Peter Draper, head of Umbro, predicted big things of their new star. Speaking in the *Mirror*, he said, 'Owen could become the first soccer billionaire – anything is possible. He is also suitable for any marketing contract with a leading multi-national company because he has the right image.'

Of all the deals offered Owen's way the most significant had to be his new five-year contract to stay at Liverpool. Worth a reputed £20,000 per week, it bound him to Liverpool into the next millennium and he had never even thought about leaving. 'I had a clause in my last contract which said that I could renegotiate when I had played for England in a competitive international,' Owen told the press. 'I've spoken with the board recently and I'm pleased to have extended my contract until 2003. As I've said all along, all I want to do is focus on my football and hopefully help Liverpool bring more silverware back to Anfield.'

Roy Evans was overjoyed to have kept his young star at the club. 'Michael was already under contract for a few years,' the joint Liverpool manager said. 'But it was important to reward him for the progress he's made. And we've done that without going out of our wage structure to do it. It's important to keep players at a sensible level – if that can be done these days. But we're delighted with Michael's commit-ment to the club.'

Owen was fully committed to Liverpool, and couldn't wait

for the season to start. Having worn No. 9 throughout his early career, he had been given John Barnes's old No. 10 shirt for the new campaign and it was the same number he would dominate for England over the next decade. With his new shirt and his new contract, Owen was desperate to prove he was no flash in the pan, and his first chance to prove that was away to Southampton on 16 August.

The man responsible for marking Owen at the Dell was Ken Monkou, and he predicted a tough year ahead for the youngster. 'This is going to be the make-or-break season for him,' the Dutch defender told the press. 'He's going to find life much harder because the whole world knows about him and expects so much from him. Coping with all the attention is going to be the toughest lesson of all. What Michael has achieved is nothing short of fantastic. But he's only done it for one season. He's got to perform for three or four years before he'll be at the same level as Alan Shearer and Dennis Bergkamp.'

Monkou insisted that having faced Owen once, when Southampton won 3–2 on Merseyside, he would be better equipped to thwart the youngster's threat. 'During our last game at Anfield,' he said, 'I was quite happy to shepherd him out to the wing. But suddenly he had cut back inside, knocked the ball between us and was away. The lad was so quick that I just couldn't risk a challenge in the box. I had to let him go and he went on to score.

'That's Owen's greatest asset. He makes defenders' minds up for them. It's almost as if he's asking, "Dare you tackle me and risk giving away a penalty, or can you afford to let me go?" But I was given a valuable lesson that day and I don't intend to get caught out again this time.'

For all his good intentions, Monkou failed to stop the

Liverpool livewire, and Owen crossed for Riedle to score the first before he claimed the winner himself in the second half of the 2–1 victory. It was the perfect way to remind people of his footballing ability as the season got under way, and there was plenty more to come.

Playing Newcastle at St James' Park, Owen scored a first-half hat-trick, as the Magpies were beaten 4–1. All three goals came in a devastating fifteen-minute spell as Owen showed up England captain Alan Shearer in his own backyard. The timing was as perfect as Owen's finishing as he joined up with his international colleagues the next day.

After watching Owen score three on Tyneside, Glenn Hoddle described the Liverpool lad with abundant praise. 'He's the top striker in the country at the moment,' the England manager said at a press conference. 'He's the most feared. His finishing is second to none. What he did against Newcastle was sensational. He could have scored five in the first half. The way Michael's performed since the World Cup, he's done everything right.

'Every player gets benefits from experience and by playing in tournaments. And Michael is growing – strength-wise, mentally and technically. He's always been mature off the pitch. Now he's maturing on it, too. What I really like about him is the fact that he's so single-minded throughout the ninety minutes of a game. He's businesslike all the way through. Then he comes off, goes on the telly and is really laid back and enjoying himself. You need a touch of arrogance and self-belief to create the problems he does. That's what he has, even at his tender age.'

Speaking ahead of England's opening European Champion-ship qualification match, Owen was delighted with the compliment. 'There are some great strikers in the country,' the prodigious goalscorer told the press magnanimously. 'Alan played against us yesterday and he's one of them, of course. He didn't have as much service or as many chances as me but he's proven himself over the years and I'm sure if he'd had the chances I had yesterday he would have scored as well.'

Owen's meteoric rise to becoming his country's top striker brought big changes to his lifestyle, but he was prepared to take the rough with the smooth. 'There are downsides, although I'm loving it all at the moment,' he added. 'I know that for some people these things are hard to come to terms with. I can't do certain things that I used to do a few months ago. When I used to go shopping in town, I'd be recognised by only half a dozen people. Now I'd have to go in disguise. It's hard when a part of your life's been taken away from you. But I'm not complaining because I always wanted to be a top-flight footballer.

'I didn't realise exactly how big things had become until I got home from the World Cup in the early hours of the morning and there were hundreds of photographers waiting outside my house. But I hope it goes on. You'll only lead a normal life if you fade away as a player, and I don't want that to happen.'

There was no sign of his fading away, and he was still focused on the quest for unattainable perfection. 'No player's ever going to be the finished article. There's always scope for improvement,' said the England No. 10. 'I still feel young. I've achieved a lot in a short period of time. But I've still got so many achievements to come. I haven't won anything domestically yet, so I hope this is the year that we can do that at Liverpool.'

His club ambitions had to wait, as Owen lined up alongside

Shearer for his country. Trying to qualify for Euro 2000 in Holland and Belgium, England were in Group 5 alongside Sweden, Poland, Bulgaria and Luxembourg. Hoddle's team got off to the worst possible start to the campaign as they lost 2–1 away to Sweden. Without a win in Stockholm for sixty-one years and with no win over the Scandinavian side anywhere since 1968, England had history against them but they were by far the better team on paper and they dominated the opening exchanges, taking a 1–0 lead through Shearer after just two minutes.

But England faded away and were beaten by two goals in three minutes after half an hour, and Paul Ince was sent off for receiving two yellow cards. Owen had been booked for an ugly late challenge on Patrik Andersson after six minutes and once again there were questions raised about his temperament.

His manager was wary of the Liverpool lad's sometimes reckless tackling. 'I think Michael was full of frustration again,' Hoddle said after the game. 'The last times we've seen him do it, frustration has always been a key element and he's got to learn how to respond. It's an old saying, but two wrongs don't make a right, and he's got to count to ten.

'Sometimes we can get carried away and expect too much of him. He's still a youngster and I think that sometimes, with all the hysteria, too much is heaped on his shoulders. He shows maturity on and off the pitch but, like any other player, he's going to have to learn pretty quickly – especially at international level, where referees handle games differently to the Premiership.'

Back in the league, things were going well for Liverpool, and Owen helped his club back to the top of the table in his fiftieth competitive appearance as they beat Coventry 2–0 at Anfield. Patrik Berger and Jamie Redknapp scored the goals, but Owen had two efforts ruled out for offside and his good form looked set to last.

The England man got another goal when Liverpool travelled to Slovakia to play FC Košice in the UEFA Cup, winning 3–0, and travelled to Old Trafford determined to make up for his aberration during his last visit. 'I was sent off and I blame myself for that,' Owen said. 'I may have cost the team two extra points, even though they did well to hang on. I now hope to put that right. Everyone makes mistakes in their life and I made one there, but it was a learning thing for me.'

Owen had little opportunity to make amends during a 2–0 defeat and things weren't much better with England as they continued to struggle through their qualifying campaign. Hoddle's team followed up their 2–1 defeat in Sweden with a dour 0–0 draw against Bulgaria at Wembley. Like the rest of his teammates, Owen failed to make the breakthrough despite playing ninety minutes against the Balkan side, but four days later the opposition were a little less solid defensively and the young striker got his fourth international goal.

Facing Luxembourg away, Owen scored after nineteen minutes, of a 3–0 victory, and, after England had dropped five points in the opening two games, it was vital that they get a win on the board to make the table a little healthier, with the next qualifying game not until March. England weren't looking great, but Owen's position in the national team was growing more secure as he had played from start to finish in each of his country's last five games.

The goals against Luxembourg showed signs that Shearer and Owen were developing as a partnership, but until that game the deadly duo had appeared to nullify each other somewhat against Sweden and Bulgaria. Both men were very focused on the goal and used to being the focal point of the attack wherever they played. The two goalscorers just needed more time according to Owen. 'If we work at it, we can always put it right,' he said at a press conference. 'People said that Robbie Fowler and I couldn't play together at Liverpool, but we have a pretty decent record.

'Some pairings click quicker than others, but you always have to work at it. I think Alan and I have all the makings of a successful partnership. The manager thought we played too flat in Sweden and we've been working to correct that. It's not really for either one of us to change more than the other. It's up to us both. We're both capable of dropping off and playing the killer ball just as much as we are of scoring a crucial goal.

'Alan helps me all the time. Some people might let a young player go and make mistakes and then tell them afterwards what they were doing wrong. But he's tried to stop me making them in the first place. As for me, I don't think that I'm under any more pressure than I used to be. I won't score goals like that one against Argentina every week and no one in their right mind would expect that. I'm still confident. I still expect to score in every game.'

Owen certainly had a better chance of scoring when he was actually playing matches, and that wasn't the case back with Liverpool, as Houllier and Evans decided to rest the young striker for the UEFA Cup tie with Valencia. He was missed in a 0–0 draw with the Spaniards but he came back refreshed and scored four goals in his next game.

Nottingham Forest were the unfortunate opponents who had to contend with a revitalised Owen, and he opened the scoring at Anfield after ten minutes as the Reds went on to win 5–1. 'Whether it was right to leave me out is debatable,' he said. 'A lot of people have said what they think about it, and the managers decided to give me a rest. On this evidence it looks as if it's paid off. But I'm young and I want to play in every match.

The managers know that. If it was felt that I was tired, fair enough. But I feel fine, myself, and I want to play. I was told it was in my best interests; if that's what the managers think, then that's the decision.'

The men in charge defended their team selection. 'England won't rest him,' Evans said. 'So someone has to look at the situation, and we've been given that task. It's not nice sometimes, because you may suffer with a result. Obviously he doesn't just have the burden of Liverpool on his shoulders, but England too. There's been a lot of stuff heaped on Michael's shoulders that I don't think should be.

'Michael never doesn't want to play, like any kid. It's a game of football and if we said to him, play every day, play twice a day, he'd do it. But we are custodians of his talent. During the week, he'd looked really tired, so we took him out of one game. We may have paid the penalty because we didn't get a great result against Valencia, but it's not about one week: it's about ten to twelve years.'

Liverpool squeezed past Valencia on the away-goals rule after drawing 2–2 in Spain, but the busy year caught up with Owen as he limped out of Liverpool's League Cup defeat at home to Tottenham. He scored after eighty-one minutes but then pulled his hamstring and faced a spell on the sidelines for the first time since his breakthrough at Selhurst Park eighteen months before.

A lot happened while Owen was out, as Roy Evans left Liverpool, after the Reds had slipped to twelfth in the Premiership, leaving Houllier in sole command at Anfield. When it became apparent that Houllier was available in the summer, the people in the Anfield boardroom decided that he was too good a coach to let slip through their fingers and they hired him. It would have been very harsh to sack Evans after he had guided Liverpool to a third-placed finish the season before, and there may well have been repercussions for replacing such a popular figure. So Evans and Houllier were given joint command of the club.

During the four months that Owen had two managers at Liverpool the responsibility moved increasingly onto Houllier's shoulders and Evans's position became ever more untenable. When results then started to go against the Reds and they dropped to mid-table, the board needed a scapegoat and it was Evans who was shown the door.

While recuperating, Owen also missed an England game for the first time since his debut, as Hoddle's side beat the Czech Republic 2–0, but he returned to the Liverpool team for a trip to league leaders Aston Villa. With the managerial upheaval at Anfield, it was more important than ever that Owen and his teammates turn things around on the pitch. 'We've to put a string of results together,' Owen told the press. 'Three or four wins and we'll get back into the top six. The only way we can get out of this is through teamwork. Everybody has to fight and dig in. No one person will get us out of this. Bits of individual magic will help, but it's a team thing. It's not nice to be in a run like this, but we do believe we can get out of it. We have to keep the confidence in our ability to get up there.

'If we beat teams like Aston Villa we can get back in the championship race. It may or may not be a good time to play Villa. It could work that it keeps a bad run going – or it could get everybody working together and motivated because we're playing the top side.'

Liverpool were clearly fired up at Villa Park and went 2–0 up in the first seven minutes. Villa hit back to bring it back to 2–1 and 3–2 but Houllier's team showed great resolve to win 4–2. Owen came closest to scoring with an audacious lob in the thirteenth minute, but his goals weren't required, as Fowler continued his rehabilitation from injury with a hat-trick.

The manager was delighted with the response of his players after his first game in sole charge. 'Paul Ince came to see me and said that, on behalf of all the players, he wanted me to know I had their full support,' Houllier said. 'That meant something special to me. But words can be cheap and it is actions that count. Well, they have backed up the words by what they have done on the training ground and what they have done on the pitch. They have shown me they want to do it for this club. They have shown me they are proud to wear a Liverpool shirt.'

It was the first defeat Villa had suffered that season, and, coming at home in their thirteenth game, it showed that Liverpool were turning their massive potential into results at last. All the players were keen to get stuck in and Owen once again revealed his 'striker's tackling' as he went in quite crudely on Stan Collymore, which earned his former teammate a red card when he retaliated. Collymore had previously gone in hard and late on Steve Harkness, a challenge that received a yellow card but probably warranted a red, and that may well have played a part in Owen's ugly tackle, but it highlighted the spirit and togetherness in the Liverpool camp.

Strange, then, that Owen was talking of a desire to try his luck in one of Europe's other big leagues. 'Of course I'd like to play in Spain or Italy, but the German Bundesliga also attracts me,' Owen said in an article in *Kicker*, a German football magazine. 'It is one of the best leagues in the world and I always follow it on television. But for now my job at Liverpool fulfils me. It's a great club but unfortunately we are playing anything but well at the moment. That's probably why Roy Evans left the club and it makes me very sad. But that happens in professional football and life goes on. I'm trying to adjust to all that has happened to me as well as I can, and I've learned to judge my performances realistically. That's why I can live with criticism. Nobody has to tell me whether I am good or bad. I know it myself.'

The game against Villa showed how dangerous the partnership between Owen and Fowler could be, and Owen was confident they could get better together. 'I didn't even think Robbie had lost any sharpness the moment he returned from injury,' Owen said. 'He was absolute quality out there in this match. Together, we can score a lot of goals. We can work as a partnership together, no doubt about that.'

Both the strikers kept scoring, and Owen got two in two games at the end of November to take his total for the season to twelve from just twenty-one games. The younger of the youthful duo grabbed one against Celta Vigo as Liverpool lost 3–1, and then another against Premiership strugglers Blackburn, which meant that, in the thirty-nine games the pair had featured in together, they had contributed thirty-two goals.

Fowler had eighteen of those and Owen fourteen, but it showed that a partnership that many thought wouldn't work out was proving to be quite devastating. 'It's beginning to be something like one goal a game between us when we play,' Owen said to the press. 'We don't often both seem to score in the same game, but one goal between us is a good return, surely. It's a decent record, and it's certainly not something I would expect people to knock. People keep wanting to say we can't play together, but we've produced goalscoring figures like that.

'We've been working together on the training ground, but it

can only really be tested properly in matches. That's the main thing, that's what makes any partnership really work. You can work on the training ground, but only matches really work. You learn game by game, and the partnership with Robbie just keeps improving.'

Both strikers seemed to play in the same way with an almost obsessional hunger for goals. Although Owen relied on his extra pace and Fowler had a more instinctive ability to poach goals, there were many similarities between them and there was a chance that their overlapping skills would nullify their dual threat. But the duo's hard work on the training ground was showing great reward on the pitch and the manager was delighted. 'It's a good partnership,' Houllier said after the Blackburn match. 'I enjoy watching them. They worked very hard for the team off the ball and are very modern strikers. They have worked on their game so they don't go for the same ball. When one goes forward, the other hangs back. They are always looking for each other and they are taking up good positions and working on their runs.'

The ability for the two bright young English talents to forge such a promising partnership led to suggestions that the Liverpool duo should be paired on the international stage, too. Their success was in marked contrast to Owen and Shearer's fledgling international double act, which often appeared laborious. 'People have said that,' Owen added. 'And I know there are things about Alan's game that I don't know yet. But everyone forgets that I only get to train with Alan occasionally and play alongside him for England a few times a season. Obviously, a partnership with Robbie will improve much quicker because we're working on it every day. It's funny the way people say that I can't play with Alan Shearer. It's obvious it's going to take a bit longer for us to work up an understanding.'

Shearer may not have brought the best out of Owen and vice versa, but, alongside the Geordie striker, the Liverpool lad had done enough at the World Cup in France to be named the BBC Sports Personality of the Year in 1998. It had been an incredible year for Owen, and, coming on the eve of his nineteenth birthday, it was a fantastic present, and led Owen to look retrospectively at all he had achieved in the past twelve months. 'My life changed after *that* goal,' he said in the *News of the World*. 'Even now it's all people want to talk about when I meet them for the first time. It's something that will be with me forever. Even if it's the only thing I do in my career, it's not a bad thing to be remembered for, is it?

'The strange thing is, that while I was being compared with Ronaldo and Pele in the summer, a few months later I was being told I wasn't worth a place in the England side after the friendly against Bulgaria at Wembley. That has taught me how important it is not to get carried away by all the praise and glory. It has brought its downside. There's more pressure on me to do well on the football field, but I can live with that. It's harder off the pitch. I can't say I enjoy the intrusion into my private life.'

It didn't take Owen long to get his first goal as a nineteen-year-old, as he scored against Sheffield Wednesday, and he grabbed three more in his next two games as he finished his incredible 1998 on a high. One came in the 3–1 Boxing Day win at Middlesbrough, and he got two more two days later when Newcastle were beaten 4–2 at Anfield.

Entering the New Year, Owen already had thirteen Premiership goals to his name, sixteen in all competitions, and any fears that the goals would dry up were quickly banished as he scored in the FA Cup third-round win over Port Vale. It was his first appearance in the famous old competition, and he marked it with a goal as in so many of his other debuts. Having started the year, as he finished the last, he set out his aims for the season.

'Like any footballer, I'm ambitious to win things and if I can do that with Liverpool, I'll be the happiest person in the world,' Owen revealed in the *News of the World*. 'If I'm here for the next twenty years and winning things, I'll be delighted. My big ambition for 1999 is to win the League championship with Liverpool, if not the League, the FA Cup. People say I've done this and that in my life, but the truth is that I haven't really got anything to show for it in terms of honours.'

His FA Cup dream was soon ended as the Reds lost to Manchester United at Old Trafford in the fourth round. Owen did maintain his 100 per cent record in the competition with the opener after three minutes, but the Red Devils hit back to win 2–1.

Owen was in fine form and also scored in the 7–1 thrashing of Southampton, and the win over Middlesbrough. But Liverpool's form was incredibly inconsistent as they suffered away defeats to Coventry and Charlton.

On 2 February 1999, Glenn Hoddle was sacked as England manager. The former Monaco midfielder's position had become increasingly precarious since he published his World Cup Diary in 1998, which undermined his relationship with a number of players, but most notably that with David Beckham. The straw that broke the camel's back came when Hoddle made some rather ill-advised comments regarding disabled people and reincarnation.

With only eight days between Hoddle's departure and England's next match, there wasn't enough time for the FA to secure a full-time replacement, so Howard Wilkinson took temporary charge for the match against World Cup holders France. The former Leeds manager made some interesting decisions for the match due to a number of injuries, and even called up thirty-five-year-old Lee Dixon. The Arsenal right back hadn't played for his country for more than five years, and, although he played well alongside his clubmates Tony Adams, Martin Keown and David Seaman, it was still regarded as very much a backward step and was greeted with mirth in the media.

Owen once again started alongside Shearer but neither of them could find a way through the experienced defence as the visitors kept a clean sheet and England lost 2–0 to *Les Bleus*. The press at Wembley took it as a sign that Wilkinson wasn't up to the job permanently, and increased their vociferous calls for Kevin Keegan to take control. The former European Footballer of the Year eventually bowed to public opinion and took the job on a part-time basis, while continuing in his role as manager of Fulham.

Keegan initially took the reins for just four games – the World Cup qualifiers against Poland, Hungary, Sweden and Bulgaria – but in May he decided to leave Fulham and assume full-time control of the national team. Owen didn't play under the new manager until September, due to injury, and whether or not that lack of game time had any effect on the relationship between the pair is uncertain, but it is clear that Keegan had very little confidence in the diminutive striker and Owen didn't enjoy his time under the passionate but somewhat unpredictable manager.

The England forward was still very happy at Liverpool, though, and was determined to stay there despite the attentions of foreign clubs. 'I'm staying at Anfield,' Owen said in the *Daily Mirror*. 'We are building for the future and we'll be challenging for the title. I want to be a part of that. It's flattering to be linked with a club like Lazio but I am very happy here at Liverpool and I want to stay here. I don't know where the stories are coming from. I even saw something saying my dad had gone to Italy. He would never do that, and it wasn't nice to read it.

'I have always said that if Liverpool were successful, and they were winning on the pitch, there would be no better place for me to stay. In an ideal world, I would stay there all of my career and be winning the championship every year. But if they don't do anything in four or five years, and they are not looking as if they are going to, it might be time to look elsewhere. I'm not giving up. Hopefully we can start winning things soon.'

Despite Owen's goals, the Reds were looking at another trophy-less season. Out of Europe and both domestic cup competitions, they were also well off the pace in the league. Owen continued to trouble opposition defences and added to his tally in a home draw with West Ham and an away defeat to Chelsea. But injury struck to halt Owen's latest hot streak, as he limped off in a 3–2 loss at Derby and had to miss England's next game.

It was the second time in the season that Owen's hamstrings had given him problems, and, as was the case back in November, he was out for only a couple of weeks and once again missed an England game as Paul Scholes scored a hat-trick in a 3–1 win over Poland at Wembley. It was Keegan's first game and the crowd were chanting his name before the end as the Three Lions made light of Owen's absence.

Owen returned to action a couple of weeks later, and was back in the scoring groove with one at Forest in a 2–2 draw. But a week after that his season was over as he limped out of the match with Leeds at Elland Road. The young striker didn't even complete the first half as he once again had trouble with his hamstrings. At first it was thought that Owen would be sidelined for only a couple of weeks as on the previous occasions, but after a scan it became clear that Liverpool's No. 10 would be out for three months, with a torn hamstring.

'Naturally, I'm disappointed to be injured,' Owen told the press. 'But I have complete confidence in the medical team at Anfield and I know that they will have me back playing as soon as possible.'

The injury was initially viewed as something of a blessing, since it would give Owen a serious break for the first time in his fledgling career. Having had the World Youth Championship in the summer of 1997 and the World Cup in 1998, the precocious youngster had been playing almost nonstop football for three seasons. Since making his debut against Wimbledon in May 1997, Owen had featured in eighty-five of Liverpool's ninety-one games as well as playing thirteen games for England and one for the Under-21s. But all that was to change with the beginning of what Owen has called his 'injury nightmare'.

All the recurring hamstring problems that the Boy Wonder had over the next three years can be traced back to an insufficient recovery following the injury Owen sustained against Leeds in April 1999. Somewhat prophetically, his manager spoke at the time of his intention to avoid future complications. 'The scan has revealed damage to the hamstring and the tendon,' Houllier said. 'The doctors say it is an injury he has had before and I am very aware that I do not want it to become a chronic problem for him during his career. For him to come back he will need a complete healing period. It will take six weeks to recover from it. And then it will take another six weeks to build up the strength in the leg again.'

Owen's recuperation was a source of dispute between Houllier and the club physio, Mark Leather, and Leather eventually left the club halfway through pre-season. Before he departed, he had been at odds with the manager regarding the amount, or lack thereof, of strength work Owen was doing on his injured leg. Without a physio to consult, Owen's convalescence faltered and when the new season started the fleet-footed forward had insufficient strength in his leg to sprint as he had previously, and the inevitable breakdowns followed.

The striker finally put the problem right following the World Cup in 2002 as he underwent a specialised programme of leg exercises to strengthen the damaged muscles, but until that point Owen was sidelined far more often than Liverpool, England or he himself would have liked.

At the tail end of the 1998/9 season, Owen missed Liverpool's last seven league matches, as well as three England games. Manchester United won the league, finishing one point ahead of Arsenal, and Liverpool finished twenty-five points behind the Champions, in seventh. The Reds' 'transitional' season was highlighted by the fact that they would not be in Europe the following season, after finishing below West Ham and Aston Villa, only two points ahead of Derby County.

Owen missed the friendly against Hungary in late April, and the two European Championship qualifiers against Sweden and Bulgaria in June. Keegan's side drew 0–0 with the Swedes at Wembley and 1–1 in Bulgaria as England continued to make hard work of their qualifying campaign.

Despite missing almost 20 per cent of the league season, Owen still finished as the Premiership top scorer and shared the Golden Boot with Jimmy Floyd Hasselbaink and Dwight Yorke, who had also scored eighteen league goals. Injury had robbed the youthful attacker of claiming the award outright, but, despite his sad end to the season and Liverpool's poor campaign, Owen could look back on a successful year in front of goal. A Golden Boot winner after playing in only thirty games, he had followed up his incredible World Cup debut with twenty-three goals from forty appearances in all competitions.

After attracting so much attention the previous summer, Owen had cemented his position as England's most dangerous forward with another bagful of goals, and if Liverpool were to keep his services they would need to improve – fast.

5

HAMSTRUNG

'I t's been a difficult season for me,' he said. 'In for two games, missing two games and then a lengthy period out with niggly little things. But I've played in twenty-five games for Liverpool, which is not as bad as I thought and everybody else thought. I've just played in two consecutive games for the first time in a while and hopefully I'm now looking forward to playing a lot more.'

Michael Owen had a tough year with injuries, but as it drew to a close things were looking up, and he could begin to look forward to the European Championship. 'Everything seems to be slipping into place now, my fitness, strength, stamina,' he added. 'I'm pleased with my own progress. Running in straight lines hasn't been too much of a problem but it's the twisting and turning, awkward movements where I've come unstuck in the past. I know when I did my hamstring first at Leeds, it was a major tear and I was running fast and straight, but that hasn't happened since – it's all been minor strains and pulls. Getting

93

kicked each week isn't a problem – that happens all the time and is part of the game; it's pushing off at different angles that has been the problem and that has been so much better.'

The season began badly for Owen as he reported for pre-season under a cloud after suffering his injury problems at the end of the previous campaign. Following the sacking of the Liverpool physio, Owen visited Dr Hans Müller-Wohlfahrt, a German hamstring-injury specialist, for further tests and treatment. And with this expert extra attention Owen felt he would be ready to play again soon, so that was what he told the press. 'The German specialists have given me a personalised exercise schedule to ensure all my leg muscles are developed in a balanced way both now and in the future,' said the injured teenager. 'I've played a lot of football over the last few years and been relatively lucky with injuries, but the most important thing, now I have a serious one, is that I get myself 100 per cent fit.

'I'm hoping to be fit for the start of the season but I do realise there's a difference between fitness and *match* fitness. I'll be guided by Liverpool's medical and training staff. They'll know when it's right for me to start playing again.'

Owen didn't make it back for the start of the season but Liverpool beat Sheffield Wednesday without him as the plethora of new signings settled in quickly. Houllier had been very busy in the transfer market, recruiting the best part of a whole new team. In came Sander Westerveld, Sami Hyypia, Stéphane Henchoz, Didi Hamann, Emile Heskey, Titi Camara, Rigobert Song, Erik Meijer and Vladimír Šmicer, while the same number of players saw their Anfield careers finished as Houllier put his mark on the Liverpool squad.

Gone were Steve McManaman, Paul Ince, Øyvind Leonhardsen, David James, Karlheinz Riedle, Rob Jones, Jean-Michel Ferri, Tony Warner and Bjørn Tore Kvarme, so, when Owen returned to the first team, it was in a very different XI from those of his last appearance. Of the new players, the one man whom Owen bonded with most quickly was Hamann. The German midfielder shared Owen's twin loves away from football of horses and a round of golf, and, from the moment the former Newcastle player walked into the training ground with the *Racing Post* under his arm, a close friendship was formed.

The Reds missed Owen's attacking threat in their next two games as they lost 1–0 to both Watford and Middlesbrough, but the young superstar was staying busy away from the pitch. Playing on the worldwide notoriety that he had developed in the last tournament, Owen was recruited by the team behind England's bid for the 2006 World Cup. The Liverpool attacker handed the proposal to the FIFA president Sepp Blatter, and shared his thoughts with the world's media. 'It's a real honour to be here today to present my country's World Cup bid,' Owen said. 'The last time we staged a major tournament [Euro '96] I sat on the terraces cheering on my home country, and then two years later it was fantastic to be in the same England team flying off to a World Cup, having a great time. I've played in one World Cup and it was the most memorable occasion of my life, and to play in the World Cup in England would be a dream come true.'

England eventually lost out to the German bid, but Owen was well received and could easily carve out a career as a football ambassador when his playing days are over. Another possible career, which presented itself while Owen was on the sidelines, was that of acting. He was signed up by the BBC to play himself in a children's television show called *Hero to Zero*. Owen played the role of mentor to a young boy who is having problems at school and at home. 'I used to love watching programmes like that when I was a kid. It'll now be great to be part of one,' he said at the time.

Owen narrowly missed an ironically symmetrical return to action at Elland Road, as Liverpool won 2–1, but, nearing full fitness, he was selected for the England squad to face Luxembourg and Poland, and was then named in the Liverpool squad to face Arsenal. Four and a half months after tearing his hamstring against Leeds, Owen was overjoyed to return to action at Anfield. With only two brief appearances in the reserves since his injury, Owen was coming back a little underprepared in his manager's eyes. 'It's a bit too soon for Michael, and he knows that,' Houllier told the press. 'But at the same time, for himself and for the club and for his country, we need him, and we'll maybe need to rush his comeback a bit sooner than we would want.

'From a medical point of view, everything's fine, and there's no risk in him playing. But we'd like to graduate his comeback, give him a slow build-up to full fitness. It would be a mistake putting him on against Arsenal, but we don't have the time or the games to take things slowly. He could be on the bench and he might get ten minutes, but it would be against my better judgement. He can create a spark because of his speed, and we need that. And I can see why England need him, too.'

Owen came on late in a 2–0 win over the Gunners, and, although he wasn't among the goalscorers, he was delighted to be back playing for his club, and he followed that up with a rapid return to action for his country.

With only one cap since the match in Luxembourg eleven months previously, and only a handful of Premiership minutes since May, Owen was understandably left on the bench, but that didn't stop him grabbing his first senior goal at Wembley. Desperate for three points after their woeful start to the qualifying campaign, England were 5–0 up at half-time. Owen replaced David Beckham after sixty-four minutes and put the cherry on the top of sweet victory, curling home right-footed from outside the area in the last minute.

It was his first goal for five months and Owen was thrilled to be back. 'It was a great feeling to score,' he said. 'I haven't scored a goal for about five or six months so it was a great feeling to get back on the pitch, especially playing in an international at Wembley. I've scored for the junior teams here before but never for the senior side at Wembley. I don't think I've played many games here, but having said that it's just marvellous to score.

'Confidence is high now,' Owen continued, turning his attention to the big clash in Warsaw. 'Wednesday is a great game to go into. We expected to beat Luxembourg and we expected to score a few goals in the process. Poland will be a different game, but if you can do what we did against Luxembourg, before going into what we know is the "biggy" next week, then that's great all round. So, it was an important victory and the lads did well.'

Owen put in an impressive twenty-five-minute cameo, but his club teammate Robbie Fowler was developing a fearsome partnership with Alan Shearer and it was difficult to tell who would start against Poland. Fowler had helped the England captain to a first-half hat-trick, but Keegan still had encouraging things to say about Owen. 'It was just a nice way to round things off for him,' the manager said of the substitute's first Wembley strike. 'I was always going to give him thirty to thirty-five minutes, but what a tremendous goal! You'll go a long way before seeing a better goal than that. I don't know if he'll play against Poland, but if he is selected I wouldn't have any doubts that he's fit enough to give it his best shot.'

Keegan decided to use Owen as a substitute again for the crunch tie but neither he nor any of his teammates could find a way through the stubborn Polish defence, and the game finished 0–0. The result left England level on points with the Poles, but ahead by virtue of the head-to-head results between the countries. Having played their last game meant that England's hopes of going to Euro 2000 rested on the results in the last round of matches. Specifically, England needed Sweden to beat Poland the following month to guarantee a second-place finish in Group 5 and a place in the play-offs.

Liverpool's topsy-turvy start to the season continued as they lost 3–2 to Manchester United at Anfield, with Owen making another late appearance from the bench. Days later, he started his first match for five months against Hull City in the League Cup. It was an ignominious match for the Reds, because their participation in the second round of the competition served as a reminder, as if it were needed, of their non-involvement in European football. As their rivals travelled to the Continent or entertained glamorous foreign opponents, Liverpool made the trip to Boothferry Park, where they avoided further humiliation by winning 5–1.

Owen failed to get among the goals, but the match helped improve his sharpness as he showed in his next outing, where he scored two against Leicester. His brace was enough to secure only one point, however, as Liverpool continued to struggle in the league. The League Cup provided no such difficulties, as the Reds competed a 9–3 aggregate victory over Hull with a 4–2 win at Anfield.

Liverpool's dismal Premiership form was then highlighted as they lost the Merseyside derby 1–0 to Everton at Anfield. It was a fractious game, blighted by three red cards, and Owen was very lucky that the ref didn't make it four after the striker's hideous two-footed challenge on David Weir.

And Owen again displayed his youthful impetuosity days later at Villa Park. Aston Villa manager John Gregory had stoked the fires ahead of the game calling Owen a 'baby-faced assassin' and accusing the teenager of getting away with a lot more indiscretions than most due to his angelic off-field persona. 'Owen is a constant irritation to opposing defenders,' Gregory told the *Daily Mirror*. 'And some people think he gets away with quite a lot because he is this Boy Wonder, Mr Squeaky Clean. It is all a question of the size of your reputation and how the public perceives you. In the same way, Alan Shearer escaped possible punishment for a number of years. But in comparison, someone like Vinnie Jones only had to look at an opponent and the referee would be reaching for the yellow card.

'I saw Owen's tackle on David Weir during the Everton game on Monday, and it was a little naughty. Let's face it, Owen is not afraid to get stuck in, and he is also on the receiving end. He was clattered by Leicester's Matt Elliott very recently, but things like that don't stop him putting himself about.'

Owen had upset the Villains the previous season with his run-in with Stan Collymore, and the game between them at Villa Park threatened to get out of hand as nine players were booked and one sent off in a 0–0 draw.

In his next match, the Liverpool goalscorer was once again in the white shirt of England. Having completed their competitive fixtures, Keegan's side had a friendly against Belgium, while Sweden took on Poland in a game that would decide second place in the group and a play-off chance of qualification. The whole of England hoped that the Swedes could do them a favour, and the Three Lions could still get to Euro 2000; Owen was no different. 'I'd be personally devastated if England don't qualify,' he said in the *People*. 'I think everyone in the team would be. But there are a few players who know that if we don't qualify it might mean the end for them. They're not going to be able to play in another World Cup or another European Championship because the World Cup is still three years away.'

It was indeed a last chance for Paul Ince, Tony Adams and Alan Shearer, but, thanks to a 2–0 win for the hosts in Stockholm, England still had a hope of qualifiying for the tournament in Holland and Belgium. The players watched the game together the day before their match against Belgium and they celebrated the next day by beating their possible tournament hosts 2–1.

England were struggling along at 1–1 before Owen came on for the final half an hour and turned the game on its head. It was undisputedly his top performance in an England shirt since his injury. He tormented the visitors' defence at the Stadium of Light for thirty minutes and his manager was very impressed. 'When I put Michael on I thought, "Yeah, that's the player I remember against Argentina in the World Cup",' Keegan said. 'He gave us another dimension. He was superb, doing the things that Michael Owen can do, and that gives everyone a massive confidence boost.'

There was still more to come from the Liverpool lad, but he was pleased with his progress. 'When you come back from injury,' Owen told the *Daily Mirror*, 'it always takes a while to recover your sharpness and eye for goal. And, admittedly, I'm not quite back to my very best. With a few more games behind me, I'll be spot on. I was pleased with what I did against Belgium and what I've done for Liverpool so far since I came back.'

But the big news was the result in Stockholm, and Owen was adamant that the team would be able to seize their European Championship lifeline and qualify through the play-offs. 'To be in with a shout after the Sweden result is brilliant,' he added. 'We all watched the match together and every single one of us was out of our seats when they scored. To still have a chance of qualification, after all that has gone on, is the main thing. Even if it is not the ideal situation, we'll take the play-offs.'

England had to wait a couple of days to find out who the opposition would be out of Scotland, the Republic of Ireland, Ukraine, Slovenia, Denmark, Turkey and Israel, and, when the draw paired them with the Auld Enemy, it gave Owen another chance to talk about his favourite strike. 'My best ever goal was scored against Scotland Schools at Newcastle,' he told the press. 'I wouldn't swap that goal against Argentina for anything, but the schools goal was still my best. I was given the ball on halfway and told to just run at them. I went past about three defenders and cracked it into the top corner.

'It was a great feeling. The TV cameras were there and I was treated like a star for the first time. Anything like a repeat of that would be just fine. If I could score one like that against Scotland in the play-offs, that would be great. In fact, if it just bobbles in off my knee that would be OK by me, I'd settle for that.'

There was still a month to go before the 'Battle of Britain', as it was billed to the press, and Owen's goals were needed to try to get his club season back on track. The youngster grabbed one at the Dell, his fiftieth for Liverpool, but it wasn't enough to beat Southampton and his two misses and a late capitulation meant that the Reds lost 2–1 and were out of the League Cup.

Always level-headed, Owen remained philosophical about his failure to add to his half-century. 'I'm back to near my best,' he said. 'It's always difficult after four or five months out. I'm happy with the way I'm playing; I feel much sharper. You'll always miss chances, but at least I was there to get those chances.'

Liverpool bounced back quickly from the cup disappointment and won four and drew one of their next five league games. Owen failed to get among the goals as his hamstring again forced him onto the sidelines. The England hero limped out of the league match away to Southampton twenty-two minutes after coming on as a substitute but was sure that he would be fit in time to face Scotland. 'I'll be fine for England – there's no doubt about that in my mind,' Owen said. 'I had something like this before during last season and I was only out for ten days. My problem in the past has been my right hamstring and on this occasion I felt a twinge in the left, so I felt it would be best to come off the pitch. I don't think it is too bad and I should be available for England if Kevin Keegan wants me.'

With just three weeks until the game at Hampden Park, Owen's injury was a big issue for Keegan, but to prove his fitness the striker had to get back into the Liverpool team. In Owen's absence Titi Camara had been in quite prolific form, scoring in three consecutive games, and the teenager was worried about getting back into the team. 'I hope I don't have any problems getting my place back,' Owen said in the *Daily Mirror*. 'There is a massive game coming with England and I could do with playing against Derby on Saturday, just to prove to everyone that I am fit and ready to go for England.

'But the manager makes the decision and I can only hope he picks me. I've only been out one week, so that's hardly drastic, and if there was an international tomorrow, then I would be fit for selection. We've got another two weeks before the Scotland game, and there is another Liverpool match before then, so if I get through that unscathed, then I am certainly up for selection.'

Gérard Houllier chose to start Owen in a 2–0 win over Derby and Kevin Keegan had to decide whether or not to start him against Scotland. 'It's really a case of if Michael's fully fit then there has to be a place in the England side for him because he gives you something,' the England manager told the press. 'You saw what happened against Belgium. Suddenly the defenders went back another five or ten yards because they're scared about the pace he's got. That helps other players.

'But you can't ignore the things that have happened, either. Between the World Cup and now is that the lad's been out for a while. He's missed a few games and he's gone out again. He's a young lad and he's very fit. But if you're talking about being match-fit then that's where your slight doubt comes in, because he hasn't played that many games. You could look at it two ways. You could say, "Give us an hour" or "You're probably not match-fit enough to start – what about coming on and giving us something like against Belgium that you did for the last thirty-five minutes?" Let's look at the rest of the training all week and judge it then, but he's certainly trained fantastically this morning. He's always got a lot of enthusiasm and that's never going to go. He always wants to play.'

Owen was determined to start against Scotland, but with only seven starts in as many months there had been questions raised over his fitness. He was bullish when asked about his injuries, however. 'We sort of diagnosed my hamstrings were doing a lot of work to keep my body upright and straight and the muscles around my pelvis weren't working properly,' Owen told reporters. 'So when the hamstrings were asked to run they were already tired from doing overtime. I spend half an hour before and after training stretching and strengthening these muscles and that's an ongoing process I'll do for the rest of my career.'

In the end, Owen got his first start under Keegan, as England won 2–0 at Hampden Park, thanks to a first-half brace from Paul Scholes. Having gained the upper hand in the Battle of Britain, the Three Lions were expected to secure their qualification with a routine win at Wembley and let the Euro 2000 party start. But Scotland had other ideas.

Don Hutchison scored the only goal of the game after thirty-nine minutes, but Scotland dominated the game and probably deserved more. After the defeat, with England safely qualified for the European Championship, Owen was absolutely slated in the press – as the critics declared him to be rubbish in the air, and have no left foot.

It wasn't just Owen who was pilloried in the papers, since the whole team came in for abuse, but it was without doubt the most adverse publicity Owen had received in his prodigious career and he was thrilled to make a goalscoring return for Liverpool in his next match. 'It was a nice way to silence the critics,' Owen said, after grabbing the opener in a 2–0 win over Sunderland at the Stadium of Light. 'I woke up on the morning of this game finding out I wasn't so popular. At least I can say I'm popular again with the Liverpool fans.

'This was a great achievement for us. They have a fantastic crowd who can really make a difference, but winning 2–0 silenced them. At the start of the season we were looking for a Champions League place and top three would be an achievement. There's certainly been an improvement since then. We knew there was quality in what the manager had brought in. The difference is we're starting to play well and understand each other a lot more.'

That understanding had brought a fourth win in a row for the Reds, who were now unbeaten in seven matches, and it finally looked like Houllier's team were getting their act together. But with typically consistent inconsistency they followed up this first away win since September by losing 1–0 at West Ham. It was an especially frustrating day for Owen, who was booked for diving and had a 'goal' disallowed before being substituted, but at least he knew that, if things continued to infuriate him at club level, he had plenty of options elsewhere.

Europe's biggest spenders in 1999 were Lazio, who were linked with a £35 million move for Owen. The Rome-based club's coach added to the speculation with his words of admiration. 'Owen is perhaps the most outstanding young player in Europe,' Sven-Göran Eriksson said. 'He could not have a better school than Liverpool to learn the game, but if he wants to make the most of his ability he must come to Italy.' Owen was in no rush to leave Anfield, and Eriksson would have to wait for his chance.

Liverpool enjoyed a good December as they won four and drew one of their five matches. Saint Michael of Merseyside had a fine end to the year as well, scoring four goals in the last three games, including two at St James' Park, as he found the net on 26 December for the third successive year.

'I don't measure my performances for Liverpool in goals alone,' Owen said after his Boxing Day brace. 'But I have to admit that I'm pretty pleased with what I did out there today. I've just heard that Kevin Keegan was here – and that makes it even more satisfying for me. There are always people watching, but when the England coach is there and you put in a good display it makes you feel better.'

Unfortunately, Owen was far less productive in January due to a fresh hamstring problem. It kept him out of the first game of 2000 against Tottenham, and his absence was felt strongly, as Liverpool lost 1–0 at White Hart Lane. The twenty-year-old was still missing as the Reds crashed out of the FA Cup fourth round at the hands of Blackburn, who were then outside of the Premiership. And, although Owen returned to action in the 3–2 win at Watford, he hobbled off after less than half an hour of the following match against Middlesbrough.

Liverpool were struggling without Owen, and it was hoped he would soon return to action following another trip to Dr

Hans Müller-Wohlfahrt in Munich. But the youngster was justifiably concerned by yet another setback. 'Obviously I'm worried because I've suffered five hamstring injuries,' Owen told the *Independent*. 'But they've not all been in the same area. I've learned now that if you play on when you feel a twinge it can quickly become a pull or a tear and I don't want what happened at Leeds last season to happen to me again. I hope this injury will only keep me out for a week. We have a two-week break now so I still think I can be fit and available for the next game against Leeds.'

The problem soon became of national importance as he spent the whole of February on the sidelines and many England fans were worried that the talismanic attacker might not be fit for the European Championship. But Owen remained confident that he would soon be back in Liverpool red. 'Not only will I certainly be fit for Euro 2000, I shall also be fit to play in Liverpool's last twelve Premiership games,' he said in February. 'I can't believe anyone thinks otherwise. For the next month I shall be exercising regularly and keeping myself fit before stepping it up to start running and kicking a ball later this month. I shall be back against Manchester United – no problem.'

Owen was fit enough to return before that clash but his manager felt it prudent to err on the side of caution. 'The time has arrived when we can no longer play hide-and-seek,' Houllier said. 'We must sort out Michael's injury once and for all. He wants to play, but if we risk him we could be looking at another long injury. What's a month when Michael could give Liverpool so many years?'

With an FA Cup weekend and England game, Owen enjoyed a three-week break and missed only one game, as Liverpool beat Arsenal 1–0. His international manager thought that Owen's spell on the sidelines could work to his country's benefit, come the summer. 'From a purely selfish point of view it could well be that he's fit and firing on all cylinders by the time we play Portugal on 12 June,' Keegan said to the press. 'From England's point of view it could work to our advantage. If he comes back in March and starts to get fit by the start of May, he could really be firing on all cylinders by June. If he's not, then it's a problem for me. It looks bad at the moment but there could be advantages. It's not a question of when I want to see him back. Gérard Houllier is his manager and Liverpool will look after their prize asset in the right way.'

Anfield's prize asset was back in the squad for the trip to Old Trafford, as promised, but, coming on with fifteen minutes left to play, he couldn't find a way through the Champions' defence and it finished 1–1. Owen had one great chance in the eightieth minute as he burst through one-on-one with the keeper, but his lack of match sharpness showed as he curled the ball beyond Raimond van der Gouw and past the far post. 'It's hard when you come on as a sub but I would still expect to score, though,' Owen said. 'It was pleasing to get on for the last fifteen minutes. It's been a long time and hopefully I can build on that.'

The draw left Liverpool ten points behind the Red Devils, looking at another trophy-less campaign. But, with twelve league games left, the Reds were still in with a good chance of a top-three finish and a place in the Champions League the following season. Two more draws, at home to Sunderland and Aston Villa, undermined those hopes but Owen then helped get Liverpool back to winning ways with the first goal in a 2–0 win away at Derby.

It was 18 March and it was his first goal of 2000, as his fitness and finishing had both been affected by some sort of millennium bug, but he quickly made it four goals in three games as Liverpool won five on the bounce to go second in the table. Liverpool beat Newcastle 2–1 at home without Owen, before he returned to make a fool out of the Coventry defence on 1 April, grabbing a first-half brace in a 3–0 win at Highfield Road.

Back to full fitness, Owen had formed a promising partnership with Emile Heskey, signed by Houllier from Leicester City in March for £11 million. The pair had previously played together in junior sides for England, and Liverpool were milking the rewards of their understanding. 'Our partnership is blossoming, and I believe we complement each other perfectly,' Owen told the *Daily Mail*.

'Emile is a great player in his own right. There is no question that he would present real problems for any defender. As a strike partner, he is a dream to play alongside because he is so unselfish and creates so much for you. I have had the benefit of that right through the England junior ranks and at Under-21s level and if we keep producing for Liverpool, we should get the chance to show what we can do together in the senior side. He is a totally different type to me but a contrast in styles often produces the right combination.'

It proved the right combination a week later against Tottenham Hotspur at home, as Owen scored the winner in a 2–1 victory. Coming on 8 April, it was his first goal at Anfield since Boxing Day, and it gave Liverpool a fourth win in a row. Afterwards Owen would talk only of Europe. 'I want to play amongst the elite, and that means the Champions League,' he said at the post-match press conference. 'Playing in the Champions League is something I really want. We've sat and watched Manchester United in their big games and it's made us envious. It's the same for all the Liverpool players. You watch all these top teams and you try to compare yourself to all these players.

'I've played in European nights, UEFA Cup games, and you

can't beat the buzz. You see the United lads when you're away with England and you want to experience what *they're* experiencing. Now we're on the brink of the Champions League and you look around the Premiership and you know that not too many players have appeared in the top European competition. It's the elite, so hopefully we'll get our chance now, but it's down to us.'

Liverpool's future was in their own hands, as they lay second with just six games to go. 'We've been aiming for the Champions League from Day One and now we're second,' he continued. 'But there's still a few good teams behind us making runs. Arsenal have won five straight off and Chelsea have had a marvellous week and they're really finding their form now. Leeds, too, have had a fine season and they're not going to give up without a fight now, even if they've had a few bad results recently. But we're in pole position now and it's up to us to stay there. It's still going to be hard all the way. It's going to be two from four now for two Champions League spots left, so it's going to be hard all the way to the end.'

The run-in proved too tough for Houllier's boys, however, as they suffered a barren-spell in front of goal. Although they beat Wimbledon 2–1 thanks to two goals from Heskey, they failed to score in their last five games and ended up fourth in the table. After a fine run of five wins, Liverpool drew 0–0 with Everton and lost 2–0 to Chelsea, both away, before losing 2–0 to Leicester and drawing 0–0 with Southampton in the following games at Anfield. That dreadful sequence of results meant that the Reds travelled to Valley Parade needing to beat Bradford City to claim the last Champions League place.

The Bantams, however, were desperate for three points as they battled to avoid the drop and they outfought the visitors from start to finish, before completing a great escape thanks to

David Wetherall's headed goal. The joy of the home fans was in stark contrast to the disappointment of the Liverpool players and fans, who weeks earlier had seemed certain of a place in Europe's premier competition and would now have to settle for a place in the UEFA Cup.

The Reds had been in with a chance of third until the final day but finished a miserable twenty-four points behind Manchester United, who retained their title in convincing style, eighteen points ahead of their nearest rivals Arsenal, and it was clear that Liverpool would need to improve drastically domestically if they wanted a first Championship since 1990. Houllier's side had also struggled in the cups: out of the FA Cup in the fourth round and the League Cup in the third round.

Liverpool would banish all thoughts of cup failure the following year as a far fitter Owen would claim his first pieces silverware, but, despite his injury-hit season, in 1999–2000 the young striker still managed to score twelve goals in his thirty appearances, eleven in the League and one in the League Cup, which was a far from embarrassing return for such a disrupted campaign.

But, before Owen could add to his Liverpool tally, he had to contend with the Continent's finest as he travelled to the European Championship in Belgium and Holland.

6

DOWN IN THE LOW COUNTRIES

'We can't look for excuses, we can't blame the fans and the threat to kick us out of the tournament, because as players you have to be totally focused on the game,' he told the press. 'It would be stupid to blame our defeat on anything other than the players, because it was the players who got us knocked out of the tournament. We can't blame anyone else but ourselves. When you come across world-class opponents you have to be on the top of your game. The frustrating thing is, we could so easily have had three wins and now we have to quickly learn to keep a lead rather than throwing it away.'

Michael Owen was right to be disappointed after England were knocked out of the European Championship in the group stages. Kevin Keegan's side threw away a 2–0 lead against Portugal to lose 3–2, and, although they managed to beat Germany 1–0, they then lost 3–2 to Romania after leading 2–1. With only four months until the qualifying for the 2002 World Cup got under way against Germany, it was of paramount importance that Owen and his teammates sort out their defensive problems or they wouldn't even make the group stages of the next major tournament.

After an injury-hit season with Liverpool, Owen headed to Euro 2000 fit and raring to go. Having barely featured in England's qualifying campaign, he was determined to make the most of his opportunities at the tournament in Holland and Belgium. But, unfortunately for him, the Three Lions were well below par and failed to get out of Group A, and Owen had a miserable time as his relationship with Keegan went from bad to worse.

The Liverpool star approached the tournament confident that his injury problems were finally behind him, and insisted it wouldn't be a gamble to select him for Euro 2000. 'I don't see any risk,' Owen told reporters before a friendly. 'I couldn't think of any better preparation. I've played thirty games this season, not fifty like some people or even sixty, and from a selfish point of view for England that's probably better for playing in these championships. It's not as if I've been sitting around losing my fitness all year. I'm fresh to play and I have played in a tournament like this before. So I don't see any problems at all with my fitness.'

Having seemingly recovered from the injuries, Owen revealed how the spell on the sidelines had affected him. 'I'd never been injured before this past year and the psychological side's probably been the worst thing,' he said. 'It also doesn't help when you've had a few niggles since that because, as it was your first injury, you think, "Is it right?" That's natural. If you've had an injury you're going to be worried about it, especially if it is your first one.

'When I came back after my first injury I was a nervous wreck. But when you play a few games you get a bit more confident. I've played the past ten games and have felt more and more confident each time. Every training session and game that I take part in, I think to myself, "Brilliant, you got through that, no problems."'

The England manager had only good things to say about his Boy Wonder at the end of the season, and he was in no doubt as to Owen's fitness. After watching him train ahead of a match against Brazil, Keegan said, 'He's very fit. I see a very sharp lad and there's absolutely no problem with him.'

Any problems that Keegan may have had with the twenty-year-old were not yet apparent, and Owen started the friendly at Wembley. Having not played for England since the dismal 1–0 loss against Scotland in November and without a goal for a month and a half since scoring the winner against Tottenham in early April, Owen was desperate for a good performance, and he gave one against Brazil.

Most people's choice for man of the match, at least for the home side, Owen scored the first goal after thirty-eight minutes – an absolute gem – taking a pass from Shearer, and pulling the ball away from three defenders in the box before unleashing a low shot past the keeper. Throughout the game he displayed the abundant pace, energy and goalscoring instinct of his pre-injury days. But Brazil retained possession with all the effortless grace that is expected from the serial World Cup winners and claimed an equaliser in first-half stoppage time after a mistake by David Seaman.

The game finished 1–1, which was an admirable result against one of the world's very top teams, but England's inability to keep hold of the ball was an obvious negative. The biggest positive of the game was definitely Owen's performance, grabbing his sixth goal for his country and re-establishing himself at the top of the pecking order to partner Alan Shearer. With only one more friendly before the Championship started, it was important for Owen to move ahead of his Liverpool teammates Emile Heskey and Robbie Fowler, and the other contenders Andy Cole from Manchester United and Kevin Phillips, who scored thirty goals in his first season in the Premiership with Sunderland.

'To get a goal against Brazil, the best team in the world, is a great achievement,' a smiling Owen said after the game. 'I'm very happy and it can only help my confidence. I was pleased with the way I played. A lot of people are quick to criticise, but I'm still twenty and have an awful lot to learn, and I've never said any different. Playing against the best team in the world, you're bound to learn an awful lot – with every game I just look forward to being a better player.

'We came off disappointed we didn't win. In the second half I think they were quite happy with a draw the way they were passing it around at the back. That says they were scared of us in certain ways – it wasn't a bad performance by us at all. And there was no problem with the injury, no reaction. I thought my partnership with Alan worked well, although it's always more difficult at international level.'

Shearer agreed that the partnership was looking better, and had plenty of praise for his young sidekick. 'I think the performance from myself and Michael was the best we've played together since Argentina '98 – in fact it was probably even better,' said the England captain. 'We both had and created chances, and it was unfortunate we didn't get more goals in the game. Both of us have to adapt together because we are both goalscorers, so it's important we share the workload, but I'm very pleased with the way the partnership went. We both used the channels and were a real threat to what is possibly the best side in the world. It's important we don't peak too soon – the time for that is when the championships start. The mood's excellent in the camp and the signs are very good.'

Owen was happy, Shearer was happy, and so was Keegan. 'Michael and Alan were very lively upfront when they got the service,' the manager said. 'I saw a lot of good things with them. As regards the first Euro 2000 match, neither of them did themselves any harm. Michael got his goal, and his work rate and link play was good; he looked like he had goals in him. Against Scotland he fell behind the standards he sets for himself but he gave Brazil tremendous problems. Perhaps now we'll look at the positives about him rather than the negatives.'

This barbed comment revealed a lot of what Keegan thought about the youngster. And, much as he seemed to encourage talk of Owen's assets, the manager continued to dwell on those aspects missing from Owen's game. 'He is still a young player who has got a lot to learn,' Keegan told the *Sunday Mirror*. 'If I had to nit-pick he should hold the ball up more. But Michael deserved his man-of-the-match award because he took his goal well and worked hard out there.'

Owen wasn't yet aware of the manager's lack of faith, and spoke fondly of Keegan's kindness. 'The manager said to me before the game that I've not got to prove anything to anyone and to just go out and play my normal game,' Owen said, before outlining his aims for world domination. 'I don't want to be someone who just lives on one thing for the rest of my life – the goal against Argentina. I don't want to be just a normal pro. I want to reach the top so you have to do things against the best teams in the world. I'm the first to say that I have so much to learn. But I'm only twenty and I have a lot of time. You learn quickly playing against teams like this. I would love to be known as the world's best goalscorer. I've had a taste of it all after the World Cup. But you have to reproduce it and keep on reproducing it at this level.'

After his fine performance against Brazil, no one thought

anything of Owen's absence in the following friendly against the Ukraine. It was natural for the coach to try out all of his alternatives ahead of a big tournament, and it was vital that every player should have a chance to stay match-fit. But, when Owen was then left out of the starting XI for the game against Malta, it seemed that Keegan hadn't yet made up his mind as to who would partner Shearer upfront, and the manager was simply giving everyone a chance to impress.

Fowler started with Shearer against the Ukraine and scored the opening goal of a 2–0 win, and Phillips started with Shearer, with Heskey coming on early in the second half for the 2–1 win over Malta. The manager revealed his thoughts to the press. 'Michael's very disappointed not to be playing,' Keegan said. 'But I wanted to take this opportunity to see Kevin. I haven't done it to hurt Michael and I'm not wrapping him in cotton wool. Obviously, it hurts players because playing for England really means something to them.'

It meant a lot to Owen to play for his country. He was disappointed not to be in for the game against the Maltese, but he was still hopeful for the forthcoming tournament. 'I don't know whether today's side will be the same as the team that starts the Championship,' Owen said before the final friendly. 'Teams can change so quickly – Kevin has his chance now, Emile had his and Robbie scored against Ukraine. But I hope I can still persuade the manager and I think I'm a big occasion player. I'm certainly not scared about going into any game at international level against the best players in the world. I can then show what kind of a player I am. It comes naturally to me. I don't fear anyone when I go onto the pitch, and, if I'm picked against Portugal in that first game, I would have no fears.'

Andy Cole had been ruled out of the final twenty-two-man squad through injury, so the remaining five strikers were all travelling to England's tournament training camp in the Belgian town of Spa, with the position alongside Shearer still up for grabs.

As the captain and senior striker, Shearer had a lot of influence over the team selection, and many in the press thought that it would be his opinion that counted when it came to his partner. It was believed that Shearer had enjoyed playing alongside Heskey, and there was talk that it would be Liverpool's cruiserweight and not flyweight striker who would play alongside the Newcastle hit man, although Shearer was also coming in for some stick. Barring a hat-trick against Luxembourg and a few penalties, the skipper had scored only three goals in his last seventeen internationals and had missed two glorious chances against Brazil.

'Everyone has to justify their place, but I can't see Kevin Keegan leaving Alan out,' Owen said in the *Sunday Times*. 'He's the main striker. It's great scoring in friendlies and qualifiers, but the major championships are when you judge a player, and he's done it every time. Emile is a great partner to have. He can go wide, cross and hold the ball up. If you're under the cosh, you can whack it forward and Emile will get hold of it. But I'm not worried about my place. I have always believed in myself.'

As the big kick-off approached, Shearer suffered a knee injury, which caused him to miss five days' training and caused enough concern for him to go to hospital for scans; but he returned, and when he did he lined up alongside Owen. Keegan picked a 4–4–2 formation for the game against Portugal. David Seaman was behind a defence of Tony Adams, Sol Campbell and the Neville brothers – Phil at left-back and Gary at right-back. The midfield had David Beckham on the right, Steve McManaman on the left and Paul Ince and Paul Scholes in the middle, and it was the flame-haired dynamo who made the breakthrough.

England started the game in Eindhoven at an incredible pace and were 2–0 up after eighteen minutes. Scholes grabbed the first after three minutes, and McManaman got the second a quarter of an hour later. It was then that the team and the manager revealed their tactical naïveté by continuing to attack. As Keegan's men poured forward and continued to surrender possession, Portugal worked their way back into the game with two well-taken goals from Joao Pinto and Luis Figo.

Despite offering a good attacking threat, Owen had been guilty of losing the ball far too much during the opening forty-five minutes, and Keegan decided to replace him with Heskey at the break. The confidence that Owen had built up with his goal in the game against Brazil had been slowly eroded by his enforced absence against Malta and Ukraine, and now the manager had ripped away any remaining self-assurance with that substitution.

'When you first get brought off and replaced in a major tournament you ask yourself questions,' Owen later told the *Independent on Sunday*. 'I've been through the game thousands of times in my head, thinking about what I did well and what I didn't do well. One thing I thought is that I was the last person to touch the ball before Figo scored. But at half-time he [Keegan] told me, "You haven't done anything wrong. You're a big part of this team in this tournament. I just wanted to change the tactics and have a different option upfront. I want a different type of player. I think we need to get hold of the ball more."'

Keegan tried to heal the rift the following day by telling Owen he would start in the next game, against Germany. 'He's only young,' the manager said of Owen. 'His day will come, on Saturday.' But the youngster believed that was only because the substitution hadn't proved any more successful and not because of any faith the manager had in him. The second half against Portugal continued where the first left off, with the Iberians in complete control, and England conceded a third goal to lose the match 3–2.

'It's not often you score two goals and come off the pitch losing,' Owen told the Press Association. 'The disappointment was felt right through the team. The pressure is on to win the last two games to qualify – but there is pressure on every game here. I don't think a draw is going to be good enough against the Germans and we have to win it and see how we stand after that.'

After losing their first game, England knew that they couldn't afford any further slip-ups. The manager was man enough to take the blame. 'I pick the team, I decide who plays and how they play, the buck stops with me. It goes with the territory,' Keegan said. 'The players are down, they're licking their wounds, but we have five days to get everyone back feeling we have a chance to go through. It's still in our hands. Despite the doom and gloom, we could even win the group.'

For the game in Charleroi they would be without Adams and McManaman, with Martin Keown and Dennis Wise respectively taking their places, but they could be confident of their chances facing a far from vintage Germany side. Erich Ribbeck's team were not at their best in the 1–1 draw with Romania, and they were still reliant on players whose best days were behind them, players such as Lothar Matthäus.

At thirty-nine, the veteran sweeper was almost twice as old as Owen, and set to win his 150th cap against England; Matthäus had won his first cap in 1980, when Owen was just six months old. It was hoped that the Liverpool youngster's pace would prove incisive against the creaking legs of the German legend, and Keegan was happy to talk up Owen ahead of the game.

'Michael is a proven performer on the big stage and had a

great game against Argentina,' the England manager said. 'He enjoys the big matches, just like a few of the players in the squad do, such as David Beckham and Alan Shearer and at least one or two others. This will not faze him. He's a young man, but he has a lot of experience under his belt for one so young.'

Even after such a fine endorsement of Owen's talents, Keegan warned the striker that another embarrassing half-time substitution could happen if he didn't perform. 'Hopefully, we'll get the right reaction from him,' the coach said. 'But, if he plays for forty-five minutes like that again in a game as big as that, then we will have to change things again.'

Owen made it through the interval without being replaced and even had a hand in the opening goal eight minutes after the break. He flicked on a Beckham free kick and Shearer headed home to make it 1–0. He didn't play much longer after the goal, however, because Keegan put on Steven Gerrard in Owen's place to strengthen the midfield with half an hour left. It was a sensible tactical change in a must-win game, intended to help defend the lead, but it was another blow to the young striker's confidence ahead of a final crucial match.

Fortunately for England, the switch helped to close out the game 1–0. It was a first competitive win over the Germans since the World Cup final of 1966, and meant that a draw against Romania would put them through to the next round along with Portugal, who had beaten the Eastern Europeans 1–0.

Keegan was happy with Owen's performance and insisted as much after the game: 'Michael showed a great improvement. He's got a lively chance of starting against Romania. In terms of confidence, I have no problems with him. He's a bouncy lad and he's in fine fettle. Don't worry. I still feel Michael Owen has something to say in this tournament. What he did against the Germans was good enough for me.'

Owen had dazzled as a substitute against Romania in Toulouse two years previously and he was nostalgic ahead of the rematch. 'Against Romania in the World Cup, we were losing 1–0 and if you are a striker that is an ideal time to come on,' he said. 'I scored and hit the post and if I hadn't done so well against them I probably wouldn't have started against Argentina. Then, people wouldn't have ended up talking about me like they did. I remember after that Romanian game ringing home and it was nice to hear what people were saying, how well I had been playing. I knew that night I had to convince the manager what I can do – and, in a way, I'm still trying to convince the manager now.'

Despite his seemingly precarious position in the team, the opposition were still very wary of the threat the Liverpool lad carried. 'We all remember Owen, because in that game in Toulouse he came on against us and was England's best player, even though he was only on the pitch for fifteen minutes,' Dan Petrescu said in the *Mail on Sunday*. 'We know how fast Owen can be but now we have a tactic to stop him, if he plays.'

The diminutive hit man's place in the team was by no means certain, as Keegan had made so blatantly obvious with his selections and substitutions in the last few games. 'Obviously, Emile Heskey and Alan Shearer are better than me at holding the ball up,' a frank Owen told the press. 'I have different qualities to them. If the manager thinks that their qualities will help to win a game, it's his decision.

'I've got to work on my left foot, my heading, and holding the ball up,' he added in self-analytical mood. 'But not one player in the world keeps every ball that gets played to him, especially being a striker, where you take the risks which you've got to in order to get that half a yard to score goals. I'm not going to go through a game without giving the ball away. But I know I've got to keep hold of the ball sometimes if we're under the cosh. If there's a long ball forward, I've got to get my body in the way and draw a foul or keep possession.'

Romania's chances of progressing to the knockout stages rested on their keeping Owen and his teammates quiet, since, with only one point from their first two games, they needed to win to have any possibility of following Portugal into the next round. Their hopes of beating England were undermined by the absence of their best player, as the mercurial Gheorghe Hagi was suspended for the Group A showdown after picking up bookings in both the opening games.

But, even without Hagi, Romania were too good for England and won the game 3–2. Again, in Charleroi, Keegan's side started badly and went 1–0 down after twenty-two minutes when Cristian Chivu's cross sailed over Nigel Martyn, in for the injured Seaman, and dropped inside the far post. Shearer equalised with a penalty in the fortieth minute and just before half-time Owen rounded the keeper and rolled the ball into the net. That effort was ruled out, wrongly, for offside, but Owen repeated the trick two minutes later and the goal stood.

After being quite comprehensively outplayed, England had fought back to go in 2–1 up at the break, and with a goal to his name Owen was full of confidence, until he got into the changing room. Keegan congratulated his young attacker on the goal and in front of the rest of the squad the coach then went on to tell Owen everything that he was doing wrong.

Romania grabbed a deserved equaliser three minutes after half-time, and Owen was again hauled off with the score at 2–2. As in the Portugal match, that scoreline eventually turned to 3–2 and England were out of the tournament. The final goal came from the penalty spot after Phil Neville made what was best described as a 'suicidal lunge' at Viorel Moldovan in the area. Ioan Ganea dispatched the ball past Martyn from twelve yards and, with only two minutes left to play, there was no time for England to come back.

Many people made Neville the scapegoat, but the fact is that England were guilty of giving the ball away far too easily throughout their three games, and when they did have it they looked entirely devoid of imagination. The only time Keegan's team really looked dangerous was from the set pieces that were consistently excellently delivered by Beckham's trusty right boot.

The England coach failed to look for excuses and admitted that his team had underperformed: 'As a squad we didn't get anywhere near our peak and I take responsibility for that. I never got out of the team the performance they're capable of. I couldn't have asked any more effort from the players and I think David Beckham had a fantastic tournament. But I'm going to continue to pick players who are best for England and then get the balance right. You can't question their honesty and integrity but we don't have a lot of variety on the bench to come on.'

England had relied on honesty, integrity and commitment for far too long, and, playing against a technically superior team who were just as committed as they were, they would always end up second best. Romania went through to a quarterfinal with Italy, while England flew home in disappointment. France eventually overcame Italy in the final to establish themselves firmly as the best team in the world, becoming the first World Cup holders to win the European Championship.

The players came out in support of their manager, and he managed to keep his job despite England's abysmal performances. One man retiring, though, was Shearer, who had called time on his international career. Owen was keen to stake his claim as England's top striker, despite the huge attention that would inevitably come with such a position. 'People say the scrutiny will be on me when Alan Shearer goes but, if that's the case, then I've got twenty-odd caps and feel experienced enough to be able to deal with that,' Owen told the press. 'I've played in World Cup and now European Championship finals and I'm prepared. I'm not going to be running scared of it. I want people to say, "He should be the first striker on the team sheet."

'We're lucky to have two players of the calibre of David Beckham and Alan Shearer and because those sorts of players don't come along every two minutes the spotlight's on their every move. But after the 1998 World Cup I got a lot of attention, so I've had a taste of that already and know what it's like. I don't enjoy being in the newspapers if it's about things I do at home with my family and girlfriend. But on the pitch there are millions of people watching you and everyone wants their opinions about you. It's my job and I can deal with that. No matter what anyone told me, I would always be confident in my ability and what I can do at this level.'

Keegan had a lack of confidence in his young striker, and any faith he did have was undermined by his constant suggestions of how Owen could improve, or, more specifically, what he was doing wrong. Rather than let his players do what they do best, Keegan spent a lot of his time trying to alter the players to fit in with his own game plan. He spent three weeks trying to improve Owen's ability to hold the ball up rather than playing to his electrifying pace and eye for goal.

Fortunately for Owen, he was still just twenty years old and had plenty of time to establish himself as England's first-choice striker. Keegan, however, would soon be out of work. His days as England boss were numbered.

7

CUP KINGS

'This was better than scoring in the World Cup,' he said. 'People talk about the fact that I had a good World Cup and scored a good goal, but it didn't win us anything or get us anywhere. If the game had stopped on eighty minutes, the story would have been how well Arsenal played. People would be talking about how well their defence shackled our strikers and our midfield. Ten minutes turned the story round. It's nice to prove people wrong when they say you haven't got a left foot.'

Michael Owen's two goals in five minutes, the eighty-third and eighty-eighth, had turned around a 1–0 scoreline and meant that it was the red ribbons of Liverpool, and not the red and white of Arsenal, that adorned the FA Cup in 2001. It was the second leg of an unprecedented treble. Gérard Houllier's side had already won the League Cup and would add the UEFA Cup to that haul four days later to cap off a remarkable season.

Owen scored the second with his left foot, and was happy to remind his detractors that he could grab a goal off either peg. It had been a good campaign for the youngster's 'standing leg', as he showed that he was still very willing to learn, and was constantly trying to improve his game.

The season had begun in a flurry of transfer activity as the manager looked to build on the fourth-placed finish in the league the previous year. In came German wing-back Christian Ziege from Middlesbrough, midfielder Nick Barmby from Everton, Borussia Dortmund's veteran defender Markus Babbel and the experienced Scot Gary McAllister from Coventry. McAllister turned out to be the most influential signing, as his cool head helped to control many a game from midfield throughout Liverpool's long season. But it was notable that no more strikers would be joining the Anfield playing staff.

The capture of Emile Heskey midway through the previous campaign had swelled the attacking ranks on Merseyside and, alongside Robbie Fowler, Titi Camara and Michael Owen, it meant that competition for places upfront would continue to be fierce. The youngest member of the Liverpool strike force hoped that his injury problems were now behind him, and he would be able to play a big part in the new season.

'You can never say never with injuries,' Owen said to the press. 'But I hope the hamstring trouble's in the past for me now. Any player can pick up an injury when you play the number of games we do these days. Because of that everyone's more likely to get injured. But I haven't had a hamstring injury now for a long while. I got through the last half of last season without it and then through Euro 2000. I've now completed the hard stuff in pre-season training and it's standing up well so far – touch wood!'

With such a large squad going into 2000/1, Owen would be able to rest more, and hopefully there would be no recurrence of his hamstring trouble. 'There are a lot of games now and that's why the manager's gone out and bought so many new players,' he continued. 'That could help me. He needs to be able to leave players out for some games – that's the idea of building a big squad. People ask why a club signs so many players, but you only had to look at us last season when there were times when we only had one fit striker. That just can't happen again and that's why there's been a determined effort to bring in more players, to give the rest of us a chance not to have to play every game.'

Obviously, given the option, Owen would always choose to play, but it was that youthful zeal that had brought about his injury problem in the first place as he featured in almost every game for two years. 'You prefer to play every game,' he said, 'but the manager makes a decision, and if you're not playing you have to fight like hell to get back in. There's plenty of experience now in the squad and that's given us a great balance. Last season we were among the youngest sides in the Premiership so we've done something to improve that situation.

'The season's here again and the lads who played in Euro 2000 have had only three weeks off. We've to put behind us what happened in the European Championship. It's hard but we've got to do that. We have to be selfish now towards Liverpool and make sure we're successful. England were knocked out in the early stage of the championship but we wanted to succeed as much as anyone one. Now we turn our attention to Liverpool and then to helping England in the World Cup qualifiers. That's my aim now and we have to go into the season with plenty of confidence, if only from looking around the club and seeing so many top players here from so many countries. I don't want to talk about titles or anything like that – we must get off to a good start and have better runs in cups because we certainly didn't do that last term. We must do well in Europe. It's going to be an exciting season and we intend to win some silverware.'

After three full seasons in the first team, Owen had developed a serious hunger for some cups and medals, and this would be the season that Liverpool finally stepped up on that front; but, even before the success, he had not considered leaving Anfield. If Owen had been unhappy on Merseyside there were plenty of other options for him as the big clubs of Europe maintained their endless pursuit of one of the brightest talents of world football. The Real Madrid president, Florentino Pérez, had declared his interest in Owen, and the striker came out to quash the link, saying, 'When you see things like that it means two things. First I can come out and say I'm flattered because it means people think I'm a good player. But on the other hand I'm not happy because I don't want it to cause a problem with Liverpool fans. I imagine some people read that and said they'd sell me for £25 million, but I'd rather everyone was on my side supporting me for Liverpool. From that point of view I wish it hadn't happened because I've never said I would want to leave Liverpool, and I don't want to.'

Owen's manager laughed off the reports. 'I heard a rumour last night that Real Madrid were supposed to be in Liverpool,' Houllier said. 'I can understand that: it's a nice city for tourists! But as far as coming to visit our club, that's not happened. We've struggled to get Michael fit and back to what he used to be, and he is looking very close to it. Any transfer? No chance.'

At least one of his managers appreciated him: Owen was on the bench for England's first game in September, and it was clear that Kevin Keegan's opinion of the little forward hadn't changed since Euro 2000. Liverpool's season began dramatically as they beat Bradford City 1–0 at Anfield, before losing 2–0 to Arsenal at Highbury in a match lit up by three red cards. And the Reds then surrendered a 3–0 lead at the Dell as they let Southampton rescue a point in a 3–3 draw.

Owen got the first and third goals against Glenn Hoddle's side and both strikes came courtesy of his left boot – a point he emphasised by pointing to his weaker foot after each goal. This strange celebration in front of his former international coach showed how much the criticism the previous season had got to the normally self-assured goalscorer, but the improvement in his game wasn't enough to merit selection by Keegan for the friendly against France in Paris.

England lined up in the Stade de France with Andy Cole on his own upfront, and they played well throughout the first half. But France looked dangerous on the break and they eventually hit the net after sixty-four minutes through former Arsenal midfielder Emmanuel Petit. Owen replaced Scholes with eleven minutes to go, and the jilted striker grabbed the equaliser seven minutes later, volleying home Kieron Dyer's cross at the far post.

It was the ideal response to being left out of the starting XI, and Owen was happy to tell the press his thoughts. 'I think I gave the perfect answer out there,' he said after the game. 'I haven't become a bad player overnight but when you come to play the world champions in front of eighty thousand people you're gutted if you aren't playing. It was disappointing not to start but I think the main game you want to be starting is Germany – they're the important ones. Germany is the big one. I think we've done well from tonight's match because France are a very strong side. They are the world and European champions but we don't believe there's such a big gap.'

It was a good result for England and restored some pride after their embarrassing showing in the Low Countries. Owen looked sharp in his brief cameo and was hopeful of starting England's next game, against Germany, but Keegan refused to be drawn on the subject, saying, 'Michael Owen was disappointed and the best way to show that disappointment was to go out there and score a goal. It was a great finish.'

Owen's ambition reached past the big Group 9 clash at Wembley, however, as he wanted to establish himself as one of the first names on the team sheet for years to come. 'The few days before the game were difficult because you don't like being left out,' the Kop idol told the press. 'It's not a nice feeling and it's easy to sulk and wonder why the manager hasn't picked you. But, if you're a professional, you have to lift up your head and concentrate in case you have to come on in the first minute. You still have to be in the right frame of mind. I have been injured so I can't expect to walk into any team, and every player has to keep on improving and impressing – otherwise you won't be in the team. But I want to fill the gap left by Alan, and for many years. I'm an ambitious person, and if I'm playing well I believe in myself. And that means I believe I'll be picked again.'

The motivated tyro returned to Liverpool determined to continue his excellent form and make it impossible to leave him out of the impending big match, and he did just that. Playing Aston Villa at Anfield, Owen scored a first-half hat-trick to put the Reds 3–0 up, and, in contrast to the game at The Dell, Houllier's side held onto their lead to win 3–1. The Germany coach Rudi Voller was in the crowd to view Liverpool's German contingent of Babbel, Ziege and Hamann, but he would have been far more concerned by the England striker's thrilling display. 'I didn't go out there to impress him,' Owen said. 'But scoring a hat-trick in front of him can't have done us any harm. I'm feeling much better now. I go out onto the pitch not even thinking about my hamstring problems now.'

His injury worries seemed a distant memory as Owen made it seven goals from four games, once again opening the scoring at

Anfield. Manchester City were the visitors as Owen took to the pitch for his one hundredth Premiership appearance, and he marked the occasion with his fifty-fourth league goal in a 3–2 win. There was more to Owen's game than just scoring goals, however, and, away to Rapid Bucharest in the first game of their UEFA Cup campaign, the young striker created the only goal of the game for Nicky Barmby. It was Barmby's first goal since he had crossed Stanley Park, and came after Owen beat four defenders and sent a perfect ball into the area for his England colleague to lash home. It was Liverpool's first away win of the season and left them in a great position to complete the job a fortnight later at Anfield.

Owen picked up a back injury in Romania, and was missed in Liverpool's next game as they drew 1–1 with West Ham at Upton Park. Fortunately, the injury wasn't too serious, and the prolific striker was back on the pitch doing what he does best, in the next match at home to Sunderland.

His seemingly inevitable goal came after thirty-four minutes, when he headed in a Ziege cross. It was his second headed goal of the season, the first coming against Villa, and he slapped his head in celebration. For a small man, Owen is very good in the air, but it was clear that the criticism had got to him, as this display showed, and that goal salute was just his way of letting the detractors know that he could in fact use his loaf.

Neither Owen nor any of his Liverpool teammates scored in the next two games as they completed a 1–0 aggregate win over Rapid Bucharest with a 0–0 at Anfield, but they continued their domestic travel troubles with a 3–0 defeat to Chelsea at Stamford Bridge, before all attention turned to the big match against Germany.

In the last game to be played at Wembley before the renovation work began, England were desperate to get their

World Cup qualifying campaign off to a good start against the team that would surely be their fiercest rivals at the top of Group 9. With only the top-placed team in the group certain of a place at the next tournament in Japan and Korea, Owen was committed to making sure it was England. 'It would be a sin,' the young forward insisted in the *Independent on Sunday*, 'for the players that we've got in our country not to be performing on the best stage. I couldn't imagine England not being there. David Beckham, players like that, are just made for the big stage, for the World Cup, it's where they prove what they're all about. It's the place to show what you're made of, isn't it?'

There was still a lot of work to be done before England could think about the Far East, and Owen was vital to that effort, according to Rudi Voller. 'I'm convinced Owen will play,' said the German coach. 'I know there is a possibility that England will play with one striker and Paul Scholes in behind, like they did against France, but I don't think they'll do that. When I went to see Owen against Aston Villa it made us more aware of what he could do. It's very difficult to control him. He's not only very fast and quick but he also scores goals. At the moment he is performing brilliantly.'

As the game loomed ever nearer, it became apparent that Keegan would revert to playing two men upfront, ditching the five-man midfield that had helped England to a draw against the World Cup holders. The final twelve minutes in Paris was the first time Owen had ever played alongside Andy Cole, but he had another chance to work on the partnership against Germany, as the duo started the match together.

With fourteen goals between them already – eight to Owen – as the season entered October, they were certainly the form men. 'They are unarguably the two best strikers in this country at the moment and I don't see any reason why they can't play together,'

Keegan said. 'They can be a fantastic combination. They have a lot of pace, that's for sure.'

Owen was looking forward to starting a game under Keegan, and hoped that he would still be on the pitch at the final whistle. He hadn't completed a full ninety minutes for England for two years, since the game against Luxembourg at the end of Glenn Hoddle's reign. In the interim Owen had won eleven caps, appearing as a substitute in four and being hauled off in each of the seven matches that he had started. 'I don't enjoy coming off and I don't enjoy being a sub,' he told reporters. 'I want to be in that starting XI and I want to play the full ninety minutes. I want to prove I'm the man to take over from Alan Shearer. I'd like to come down to the England squad without picking up a paper, or switching on a TV channel, and seeing "the big debate" between Owen and someone else. I don't feel that way yet. I believe that I've done as much as I can in the first few weeks of the season. I'm playing as good as I've ever played.'

Nobody who was English played particularly well in the last game under the Twin Towers, and Germany deserved their 1–0 win, courtesy of a Hamann free kick that skidded past David Seaman in the pouring rain. The game signalled the end of the old Wembley, and the result brought the end of Keegan's run as England boss. The former European Footballer of the Year's time at the top had revealed the tactical and organisational limitations of a passionate and enthusiastic manager who had done so much at Newcastle and Fulham. Owen, for one, wasn't too disappointed to see the back of him.

With only four days until England's next match the FA appointed Howard Wilkinson as caretaker manager for the game against Finland in Helsinki. The former Leeds boss showed as little faith in Owen as his predecessor and decided to recall Teddy Sheringham to play upfront with Cole. As the game petered out to a 0–0 draw, Wilkinson didn't even summon the in-form Owen from the bench, and the Kop hero was fuming.

Speaking at a press conference before Liverpool's game against Derby, Owen said, 'I think my form is as good as it has been for a long time. I've got confidence in my ability no matter what happens. Even if I'm left out of the side for an international it won't affect my confidence. Nothing can dent that at the moment. The only way to respond to any situation of criticism is on the field. There's no point in me saying I should be playing. The best thing for me to do is to prove it on the pitch. Derby's my next game, and I'll be doing my best there as I always do when I play for England. When you're playing well for your club it makes a big difference. That's very important, no matter what's happening with other things.'

And, despite his impressive start to the season, Owen came in for new criticism, as somebody came to the conclusion that the precocious talent cared only about playing for England. 'I've read letters in the local paper that I only care about England,' Owen added. 'But no one can question my feelings towards Liverpool. I sometimes wonder whether people who say such things have actually been to see me in Liverpool games.'

His dedication to the Liverpool cause saw a seriously concussed Owen taken by ambulance to hospital from Pride Park, after a collision with Derby defender Chris Riggott's knee opened up the back of the striker's head. The skin tore open and blood began to pour out from a wound that needed thirteen stitches to close. After being stitched up, Owen insisted on a return to the ground so he could travel back to Liverpool on the team bus with the rest of the squad. But the effects of the blow were so bad, that he then went to a Liverpool hospital, where he had two brain-scans and was kept in overnight for observation.

Owen suffered dizzy spells, which delayed his comeback, and, in the three weeks that he was out, he missed five games. But Liverpool coped admirably with his absence, as Heskey hit six goals in four matches. The Reds recorded a first league away win with a 4–0 victory at Pride Park, and followed that with four successive home wins over Leicester and Everton in the Premiership, Chelsea in the League Cup and Slovan Liberec in the UEFA Cup. But Houllier's men lost 4–3 away to Leeds before Owen returned to the squad for the away leg against the Czech side.

With a 1–0 lead from the game at Anfield, Liverpool made hard work of the game in Eastern Europe as they came from a goal down to beat Liberec 3–2. Owen put them 3–1 up on the night, seconds after coming on as he gathered Barmby's throw-in and turned it into the net. Liberec got another one back three minutes later, but with only five minutes left of the match they couldn't recover and eventually succumbed 4–2 on aggregate. It wasn't a result to make the rest of Europe take notice but it did put Liverpool into the third round, where they would meet Olympiakos.

Before travelling to Greece Liverpool again demonstrated their Jekyll-and-Hyde domestic form as they beat Coventry 4–1 at home before losing 2–1 at White Hart Lane. Their poor form on the road was undermining their league season and they were now fourth, nine points behind the leaders Manchester United. Owen missed missed England's friendly in Italy through injury, as Pete Taylor took control of the national side.

The former England Under-21s boss had some interesting thoughts on his absent striker though: 'I feel that if Michael had played ten games at Under-21 level, it might have helped him in the long term,' Taylor told the *Sunday Mirror*. 'Michael played one Under-21s game, against Greece, but then he went automatically into the senior team and automatically into the World Cup finals. When you're absolutely flying and playing superbly you can just get on with it, but then you have to face different defences and things might get difficult. For Michael's long-term career it might have been better if he had played ten games at Under-21 level, because the football is so different.'

England lost 1–0 in Turin, but Owen wasn't out for long and returned to the Liverpool line-up for the match against Olympiakos, but he was forced off with a recurrence of his back injury in Greece and faced another spell on the sidelines. Despite the strong links between lower back pain and hamstring injuries, the manager insisted that it was nothing to do with Owen's former problems and was merely a knock. 'Michael got a back injury in Athens, that's why we took him off because he was suffering,' Houllier said. 'It's nothing to do with the serious hamstring troubles he had a few months back, but it is a problem and we will be careful with him. But we do not need to take the risk because if it had gone wrong he could have been out for another three or four weeks.'

As it was, Owen missed two league games, a home win and an away defeat, and the League Cup tie at Stoke, which Liverpool won 8–0. He was left on the bench for the UEFA Cup's third-round second leg against Olympiakos as Heskey and Barmby helped the Reds to a 2–0 win. Owen made his latest return to duty in the 1–0 home defeat to Ipswich Town.

Having missed a couple of games through injury, it was understandable that Owen would take some time to get back up to speed, but after replacing Fowler against Fulham in the League Cup quarterfinal he grabbed his first goal for a month.

While Owen had been on the sidelines, Heskey had firmly established himself as Houllier's first choice upfront, with twelve goals in twelve games, and Owen was now left to battle it out with Fowler for a place alongside the former Leicester striker. And it was obvious to all that neither of Liverpool's home-grown shooting stars would be happy on the bench.

Owen told the *Daily Mirror*, 'I don't just say I'm the best because that is what's expected, I believe it. I have to, because there is no other way you can survive at the top. I know Robbie is the same. I really believe in my ability, and that I should be playing. I am sure everyone understands that desire, because it is the one that drives you.'

But the manager was more concerned with results on the pitch than the contentment of his squad off it. 'I have to make decisions for the club, and not to keep players happy,' Houllier said. 'If they don't like it, then that is their problem.'

Houllier's results were proving good enough for his tactics and team selection to remain beyond reproach, and, although their poor away form left them thirteen points adrift of leaders Manchester United, Liverpool headed to Old Trafford for a game against the Champions and left with all three points, courtesy of Danny Murphy's first-half strike.

It was one year and 363 days since Ferguson's team had last lost a league game at home and it was a great boost to Liverpool's confidence ahead of Arsenal's trip to Anfield. Owen scored the second goal as the buoyant Reds destroyed the Gunners 4–0, and there was a renewed belief that the title dream need not be over for Houllier's men.

But their poor away form once again dealt them a blow and they lost 1–0 at Middlesbrough. Owen was particularly culpable for the defeat, because he missed three good chances during the game, further evidence that his injuries had taken the edge away from his sharpness in front of goal.

Liverpool entered 2001 in fifth place in the Premiership, and, as the transfer window opened across the European leagues,

Houllier took the opportunity to bolster his squad further. The Finnish striker Jari Litmanen joined on a free transfer from Barcelona, and Owen had even more competition for his place in the team.

He was the victim of squad rotation for the first time in his career and it appeared to contribute to his rustiness in the League Cup semifinal, where Owen missed a couple of chances in the first leg against Crystal Palace. In a 2–1 defeat at Selhurst Park the young superstar was well below his best, and he was relegated to the bench for the win over Aston Villa and the 0–0 draw with Middlesbrough.

A hamstring injury flared up for Owen, ruling him out of the League Cup semifinal's second leg, but Liverpool battered the Eagles without him, were 3–0 up after eighteen minutes and went on to win the game 5–0. Houllier's solid defence and rapid counterattacking style had seemed well suited to cup football, and so it proved as the Reds were on their way to Cardiff with hopes of a first trophy since 1995.

Before the League Cup final Owen had plenty of time to get back to form and fitness, and, as well as a playing for a place in the team for the final, he received extra motivation with news from FA headquarters. The men in charge at Soho Square had spent four months searching for the right man for the job, and they thought they'd found him in a Swedish former Benfica, Sampdoria and Lazio boss. Sven-Göran Eriksson was named as Keegan's full-time successor, and Owen was keen to impress the man who had been one of his long-term admirers.

With the great sense of timing that had shone through when he was at his best, Owen found the perfect game to dazzle, as he scored both goals in a 2–0 win over Roma in the Olympic Stadium, a month after Eriksson took control, and with the Swede watching from the stands. It was a great boost for

Liverpool – in the very stadium in which they had clinched their European Cup wins in 1977 and 1984 – and his manager was delighted. 'I knew a week ago he was back to his best,' Houllier said. 'In training and against Sunderland last week he looked sharp and very lively. When he is like that he is always a threat and can score goals. I was very pleased with his performance.'

Owen was also pleased to be firing on all cylinders once more. It was his first start in eight matches, and it was no coincidence that it brought his first goals of 2001, two weeks into February.

The dry spell had clearly affected Owen, as he revealed while speaking to the *Daily Express*. 'When you haven't scored a few goals, you have not been playing to the best of your ability, and then you are injured, a lot of frustration builds up,' he said. 'But I let a lot of that out with the goals in Rome. It was a great feeling to score after the last few months I've had. It is the hardest thing in the world having to shut people up, but I've had a good couple of days.

'All strikers have good and bad patches during a season. Even players like Thierry Henry and Emile Heskey started off the season flying but have gone a number of games without scoring a goal. The people who matter, such as the manager, are always behind you. It didn't bother me that I wasn't scoring goals. I prefer it that I'm there to miss chances rather than not be in the position at all.'

Chances were much easier for Owen to come by when he was actually playing, and, despite the England striker's fine performance in the Eternal City, he still wasn't assured of his place in the team. The next game for Liverpool was in the FA Cup as Houllier's side continued their four-pronged quest for trophies, and Owen was left out as Heskey and Litmanen put Manchester City to the sword. Missing an FA Cup fifth-round tie was of little consequence to Owen, since he was by now well used to being left out; but a week later he found himself on the bench for the League Cup final, and that remains one of his biggest footballing disappointments.

After dazzling against the Italians away, and sitting out the FA Cup tie, Owen returned for the home leg against Roma, where he was well marshalled by the Serie A leaders' defence and missed a penalty. But, despite losing 1–0, the Reds went through 2–1 on aggregate.

Speaking after the Roma match, Owen revealed his thoughts on spending time on the sidelines. 'I understand why the manager has introduced the rotation system, but everyone is quite selfish and wants to play in the games,' he said in the *Daily Express*. 'But I need games now after three weeks of doing nothing. It would be hard to take if you were rotated for a cup final or a big match like this one in Rome. But I want to play – that is all I want to do – yet so does everyone else in the squad. I know you build an immune system if you play. You don't even get stiff or have cramp. You don't get anything. When you play one game and then are out for two weeks, it does nothing for you. You need to be playing, to be fit and training every day.'

Next up was Liverpool's trip to Wales. And, playing against Birmingham City at Cardiff, Owen was on the bench and had to sit and watch as Heskey and Fowler started the showpiece event. Heskey was still No. 1 and Houllier plumped for whoever, of his other strikers, he felt was playing better to start alongside the big man, and, on 25 February 2001, he chose Fowler.

The younger striker sat quietly in the hope that he would still have a chance to play in his first cup final, but Fowler scored after thirty minutes, and, although Owen was happy for the team, he was all too aware that it decreased his chance of running out at the Millennium Stadium.

The game drifted into extra time after Birmingham equalised and, when Houllier sent on his third substitute, Owen realised that he would not get onto the pitch in what was the first cup final of his professional career. Liverpool won the cup on penalties, after Andrew Johnson missed his spot kick, but Owen found little satisfaction in his winner's medal.

There was no time for Owen to dwell on his disappointment, however, as England faced Spain three days later in Eriksson's first game in charge. Owen had endured a torrid time under Keegan and had missed out on the last two England matches as first Wilkinson and then Taylor took control of the national side. But with a new man in charge the Liverpool lad was determined to fulfil his potential as Alan Shearer's successor.

Playing a friendly at Villa Park, Owen was delighted to be picked by Eriksson for his first game, and this faith from the start established the foundations for what was to prove a good working relationship between the young striker and his new international coach.

Eriksson seemed somewhat in awe of the star players in his teams, and it was this that eventually proved his undoing; but, like the four previous managers before him, the Swede started his tenure as England boss with a win and the players, press and fans were happy with the new man. A 3–0 win over the dangerous Iberians was a great result, and, although Owen didn't get among the goals, he still did enough to prove himself worthy of selection.

Even with a first trophy of the season in the bank, Liverpool continued to struggle in the league away from home, and they lost their next game 2–0 at Leicester. They were having no such problems in the cups, however, and as they entered March the Reds were in the quarterfinals of the FA Cup and the UEFA Cup. Thanks to Owen's goals they were swiftly into the semis of both competitions and Owen was confident that the treble was 'on'.

Liverpool drew 0–0 away to FC Porto, before beating Tranmere Rovers 4–2 at Anfield, where Owen got the home team's second; and he repeated the trick four days later, when the Portuguese side came to Merseyside and were beaten 2–0.

'The priority's still getting into the Champions League because we want a few more European nights like this next year,' Owen said to the press after the game. 'But we have a fighting chance in all the cups, so we're going to try to win them all. We're in the semifinals of the UEFA Cup now, which is a great achievement, and the semifinals of the FA Cup – while we've already won the Worthington Cup.'

With two goals in two games to send Liverpool into the semifinals of two competitions, Owen was hitting top form at just the right time. The Reds had made themselves very difficult to beat, and with Owen's pace and finishing there was always the chance of a goal. In short, Houllier had made his counterattacking team perfect for cup football, the League Cup was in the bag and, with the FA and UEFA Cup semifinals looming large, there was the chance of an unprecedented treble. After missing out in the first cup final, Owen was determined to make his mark in any others that might come his way.

Owen continued his fine form against Derby County where he made it three goals in three games with a brilliant strike in a 1–1 draw. It took his total for the season to fifteen, and Owen was very happy to grab another goal as Eriksson watched on ahead of a World Cup qualifying double-header against Finland and Albania. 'Thankfully, I did all right,' Owen said. 'I want to be regarded as *the* England striker. The Finland game's back here at Anfield in front of our own fans. I'm looking forward to it. It's a special ground, a special place.'

England's first competitive match under Eriksson started badly as they fell behind to a Gary Neville own goal, but Owen equalised with his left peg just before half-time and David Beckham scored the winner, rewarding the manager's faith in giving him the captain's armband. Since they had claimed only one point from their first two qualifying games, the win over the Finns was vital to the England cause, as were another three points against Albania. And their red-hot striker was determined to keep his goal streak going. 'I don't want to tell people I can do it. I just want to show them,' Owen said. 'Every time I get an opportunity I intend to show everyone what I can do. The team didn't play brilliantly and neither did I. But I scored and we got three points.

'I think Alan Shearer was exactly the same as me. He scored a lot of crucial goals. If you go back and look at the top strikers, most of them scored goals at vital times. Whenever I set foot on the pitch I feel I'm going to score, especially at the moment. I felt as high as a kite going into the game. In the last three Liverpool games, I've played as well as I ever have for my club. I didn't play as well against Finland, but being a striker is about scoring, and I'm pleased I scored, especially at Anfield.'

He made it five goals in five games, grabbing his tenth for England in his twenty-seventh appearance for his country, as Eriksson's side won 3–1 in Tirana. The two victories helped to get the qualifying campaign back on track after a dismal start, and, with three wins in his first three games, the new coach had started well. But for Owen it was even better, as his goals in successive games strengthened his claims to be England's first-choice striker.

March had been a fine month for Owen and it finished gloriously for Liverpool, as they completed their first league double over Manchester United, for over twenty-two years.

Having already won at Old Trafford in December, the Reds won 2–0 at Anfield to send their fans home in raptures. Owen appeared for only the last two minutes, so it was of little surprise that he failed to get on the scoresheet for the first time in six games, but for once his goals weren't required as Gerrard and Fowler wrapped up a sweet victory.

April was far less fruitful for the twenty-one-year-old, but Liverpool's trophy quest continued unabated, despite Owen's failure to find the back of the net. They made it into the UEFA Cup final after beating Barcelona 1–0 on aggregate, courtesy of McAllister's penalty in the second leg at Anfield. And it took two late goals from Heskey and Fowler to beat Wycombe Wanderers in the FA Cup semifinal at Villa Park, but it meant that Owen could yet have two final appearances in which to make up for his League Cup disappointment.

Liverpool also picked up ten points from five Premiership games to keep them in contention for a Champions League place the following season, and, as the 2000/1 season drew to a close, it was clear that Owen and his teammates still had plenty to play for.

Taking his reputation as a big-game player to another level, Owen showed once again that he could be relied upon to get goals when it mattered, by grabbing nine goals in six games in May. Having endured the League Cup final from the bench, the young superstar was determined to avoid a repeat performance, but, since he was hitting the best form of his short career, there was little chance that Houllier would leave him out.

Owen scored a cracking opener against Bradford City on the way to a 2–0 win, and followed that up with a hat-trick against Newcastle at Anfield four days later. It was clear that the England striker enjoyed playing the Magpies, and by grabbing all the goals in a 3–0 win, he took his total to twelve in six games against the

Toon Army. 'This week could be the best I've had since the World Cup finals,' Owen told the press. But, even with four goals in two games, he refused to take for granted his place in the team. 'I have no idea whether I'll be playing on Tuesday against Chelsea, or for either of the finals – I'll just have to wait and see.'

Three more points would effectively guarantee third place in the Premiership for Liverpool, whose goal difference was much better than those of their rivals. And Owen insisted that the high league finish was the priority, despite the allure of the silverware. 'If we can win one more game we should be in the Champions League,' he went on. 'That was the goal at the start of the season, everything else was a bonus. If we could get into any cup final it was going to be an extra bonus. We've got into three, won one already, but we must finish in the top three. If we don't do that the main aim for the season will be out the window.'

Owen kept the Reds on course for third place with a brace in a 2–2 draw at home to Chelsea, taking his May total to six in three games and making his place in the FA Cup final team a certainty, but his season's highlight was still to come as Owen peaked at just the right time. The Hawarden-raised youngster had always had an affinity for Wales, but the afternoon of 12 May 2001 meant that Cardiff would join St Etienne as cities graced by the Owen genius.

Liverpool were completely and utterly outplayed for most of the match at the Millennium Stadium, but came away with the famous old trophy, thanks to a late double from the Boy Wonder. Arsenal dominated for eighty minutes, but were unable to take their chances as the Liverpool defence stood firm once more. Fredrik Ljungberg finally got the breakthrough after seventy-two minutes, but the Gunners couldn't find a second to put the game beyond doubt.

The Reds hit back with a heavy psychological blow as Owen

hit an equaliser ten minutes later, McAllister's free-kick was knocked down by Babbel and Owen held off Keown to spin and knock the ball past David Seaman in the Arsenal goal. Having worked so hard to get ahead, the Arsenal players' shoulders dropped as they began to think it might not be their day.

An FA Cup final goal is a special thing, and, just like buses that keep you waiting, only for several then to arrive at once, in Owen's case another goal was not far behind. Five minutes later Arsenal won a corner, but Liverpool cleared the danger and the ball fell to Patrik Berger, who sent a beautiful ball down the inside-left channel for Owen to run onto. Lee Dixon was back for the Gunners but Liverpool's No. 10 had too much pace for the old full-back, and Owen was past him in the blink of an eye. Tony Adams tried to get across to the young striker, but Owen shot left-footed before his former England teammate could get to him, and the low strike bounced over Seaman's outstretched hand and into the bottom corner.

Jamie Carragher summed up his teammates' thoughts about Owen and his man-of-the-match performance. 'He is still only 21 and he will say himself that he is still learning the game,' the defender told the *Daily Express*. 'But he has proved without doubt that he has got what it takes. Against Arsenal he was the difference – and that difference was someone who can finish clinically. He had two chances and we won the game. He is a class act, a class finisher. The final showed what he can do.'

With only three minutes left to play, the little striker's goals had won the first FA Cup final to be played outside England – and Owen still refers to it as his greatest day. 'This was better than scoring in the World Cup,' he said afterwards. 'People talk about the fact that I had a good World Cup and scored a good goal, but it didn't win us anything or get us anywhere.

'It was a late goal, but better late than never. It was a case of not giving up. You can go for nearly ninety minutes and not score, and then it happens. That's what makes it all worthwhile. I was pleased with the first goal. It reminded me of the goal against Romania in the World Cup. And for the second, well a lot of people questioned my left foot but I think I've now got double figures with my left foot. The Champions League was the main aim this season. You can say that after winning the cup but there is the UEFA Cup final and the Champions League place still to play for.'

There had been much criticism of Houllier's rotation policy, but it was the fact that Owen hadn't started more than four games in a row throughout the season that had left him fresh enough to grab two goals at the death against Arsenal in the cup final. 'Our play was not good,' Houllier said. 'We were struggling with the heat. But as soon as Michael scored I said we would win it. He has been like that for a few months now. How can you describe him? Unbelievable.'

But there could be little celebration for Owen's unbelievable achievement, since there was still a UEFA Cup final and a final Premiership game to try to secure third place. Owen's goalscoring run had to come to an end, and after eight goals in four games he failed to score in the next game. But that didn't stop his teammates from winning a nine-goal thriller courtesy of a golden goal.

Owen started his second cup final of the season, but unlike in the FA Cup final, where his late heroics saved the day, he was replaced after seventy-nine minutes as the manager chose to strengthen the midfield. Houllier's side had taken an early lead against Alavés through Babbel and were two up through Gerrard after fifteen minutes, but the Spanish side pulled one back in Dortmund and it was 3–1 at half-time thanks to a McAllister penalty for a foul by the keeper on Owen.

Liverpool's defence had been superb all season so there seemed little chance of an Alavés comeback, but that's exactly what happened as Javi Moreno grabbed two in six minutes to draw his team level. Fowler made it 4–3 after seventy-two minutes, before Owen was replaced by Berger in a bid to preserve the lead, but Jordi Cruyff headed a late, late leveller with a minute to go and the final went to extra time.

Owen was once again forced to watch from the sidelines as his teammates tried to settle a cup final in the added thirty minutes, and this time he didn't have to bear the agony of penalties, as the unfortunate Geli headed a McAllister free kick into his own net, winning the cup for Liverpool by a golden goal, 5–4.

It was a dramatic end to an absorbing contest, but any celebration would once again have to be muted, because the Reds still required three points from their last game, against Charlton Athletic at the Valley, to secure third place in the Premiership. And Owen revealed to the press how important it was to him, saying, 'It would be great having a nice break in the summer thinking that we've a load of big games to come in the Champions League next season. The Champions League means a great deal to me. Every top player in the world is playing in it.

'If I want to regard myself in a certain way, I have to play in the Champions League. I've still got a load of years to go and I hadn't won any medals before this season and now I've got two, so I know it'll come. I will play in the Champions League – I just hope we can get it this year.'

Owen sounded fairly motivated ahead of the game but Liverpool struggled throughout the first half as Charlton unexpectedly took control. But the Reds' tight defence stood firm and it was 0–0 at the break. With a Champions League place up for grabs, the players received a serious talking to in the dressing room and came out for the second half with a fierce resolve and won 4–0 with Owen grabbing Liverpool's last goal of the season.

Having won all three of their 'cup finals', the players now had the opportunity to celebrate their success properly, and Owen had a few drinks with the rest of the boys on the coach, and headed out to a nightclub when they got back to Liverpool.

With the League Cup, FA Cup and UEFA Cup in the trophy cabinet, Houllier's side had proved they could beat anyone on their day and by finishing third in the Premiership they would have the chance to take on Europe's finest the following season. It was a great year for Liverpool and the Anfield faithful lined the streets as the team displayed their cups from their open-topped bus parade from the training ground at Melwood down to Albert Dock.

Owen finally had some medals to show for all his goals and promise, but, despite his sixteen league goals, Liverpool ended up eleven points behind champions Manchester United, and he was determined to close the gap the following year. 'The league title is what I want,' Owen told the Press Association. 'Personally I'd want to win the league before trying to conquer Europe. The table never lies and Manchester United have shown they are among the best in Europe. If you win a title over thirty-eight games it proves you are the best team in England and among the best in Europe. We'll look at the championship race next season, but I don't think United will win it by as many points as they have this season. It's disappointing for everyone involved trying to catch them, it's been a non-event from early on, but it will be a lot closer next season.'

Following Owen's explosive return to form, there were the inevitable stories linking him with a move to the Continent, with Italian and Spanish clubs often mentioned as likely destinations, but it was clear where the talented striker saw his future. 'I'm staying at Liverpool for years to come,' Owen said in the *Daily Mirror*. 'The question of whether or not I'll be staying has never really been an issue. Liverpool have told me that they want me, and I'm really pleased about that. I have told them that I am happy to sit down and negotiate a new contract in the summer. I've been here ten years, and the future has never looked as good as it does now. I'm very excited to be part of it.'

He was still an integral part of the Liverpool team, and he had scored twenty-four goals in his forty-six appearances at club level in 2000/1 as well as grabbing three from five for England, but his season still wasn't finished. Owen still had a couple of games to play for his country before he could take a well-earned break.

Sven-Göran Eriksson's side had a World Cup qualifying match against Greece in Athens, which they prepared for by playing Mexico at Pride Park. Owen started both games as he further cemented himself as one of the first names on the Swedish coach's team sheet. The Liverpool striker failed to score in either game, but a 4–0 win in the friendly at Derby set England up perfectly for the game against their Group 9 rivals, and they ended the season on a high with a 2–0 win.

Owen had enjoyed a fantastic season, as he won his first trophies as a professional footballer, and banished any doubts about his 'weak' left foot with the winning goal in the FA Cup final. He had played more games than in any previous season and was confident that his injury problems were finally behind him, but there was still plenty more to come from the Liverpool striker in 2001.

8

HAT-TRICK HERO

'You can dream about scoring a hat-trick but you don't think it's going to come true,' he told the BBC after the game. 'It was unbelievable to come here. No one would have predicted this scoreline, but some of us might have predicted the victory. We're a good team. It's not about me. It's good on a personal note to score a hat-trick, but, had David Seaman not made a world-class save at 1–1, it might have been a different story. Gerrard got a great goal, too. Everyone will get ten out of ten in the papers for this performance.'

Owen was right to be proud of his teammates after they had helped England to a devastating 5–1 win in Munich. It was the first time the Three Lions had beaten Germany away since 1965, and his three goals made Owen the first England player to score a hat-trick against the old enemy since Geoff Hurst in 1966. More importantly, the win closed the six-point gap at the top of Group 9 to three and automatic World Cup qualification was now in sight.

The season had begun in a wave of confidence for Owen at club level as the Reds looked to build on their treble. 'I joined the club when I was eleven and every year we all get excited and optimistic about the start of the season,' he told the *Daily Post*. 'But this season there is probably an inner belief that we can get closer to the champions and do well in the Champions League and in the two cup competitions. There is a real belief we can do better this season. It's not a hope, it's a conviction.'

The manager brought in John Arne Riise from Monaco to replace Christian Ziege, and Jerzy Dudek to replace Sander Westerveld, and Houllier's team quickly added two more pieces of silverware to their already-bulging trophy cabinet, as they won the FA Community Shield and the European Super Cup. Owen was delighted to be part of a successful Liverpool team, as he felt his Anfield efforts had been previously under-appreciated. 'I made my name playing for England, especially after scoring *that* goal against Argentina in the World Cup finals in 1998,' Owen revealed in the *News of the World*. 'People all around the world were talking about me after it. But I never felt the same sort of appreciation from Liverpool supporters.

'Maybe they thought playing for England was more important to me than performing for my club. But achieving something with Liverpool has always been a must – which is why it was so fantastic to lift three trophies for the fans last season. I hope the goals I scored last season, especially the couple in the FA Cup final against Arsenal, helped convince the Liverpool fans how committed I am to the cause and how I want to be part of an even more successful future.'

Part of that future involved playing in the Champions League, and having finished third in May Liverpool needed to see off FC Haka in a qualifying-round tie to ensure their place amongst

Europe's elite. After they had worked so hard in the league to achieve that top-three finish, it was imperative that the Reds shouldn't fall at the last hurdle. But, in the first leg in Helsinki's Olympic Stadium, the Finnish champions were unlucky enough to find Owen straight back in the goalscoring groove, as he grabbed a hat-trick in a 5–0 win.

Following their awesome European display, Liverpool got their domestic season under way with the traditional curtain raiser – the FA Community Shield, played by the FA Cup holders and the reigning champions. For this, Owen and his teammates had to face Manchester United in Cardiff. Back at the scene of his greatest day in football, the young striker was optimistic about getting a result against Liverpool's old rivals and laying down a marker for the coming season. 'I am not predicting we are going to topple United this time,' Owen told the *News of the World*. 'But I feel we are capable of getting even closer to them. We're a good young team. We beat United twice in the league last season as well as the likes of Arsenal, Roma and Barcelona. Where we have tended to fall down is by not beating the so-called lesser teams. The challenge for us is to maintain consistency over a thirty-eight-game season. If we can do that we will give United a run for their money.'

Liverpool won 2–1 in Cardiff as Owen maintained his fine record in Wales. Gary McAllister put the Reds ahead from the penalty spot after two minutes, and Owen added a second after sixteen minutes, but Ruud Van Nistelrooy scored after the break to grab a consolation goal.

Having played a Champions League qualifier and the Community Shield, Owen joined England for their first game of the season. The Liverpool striker started a game on the bench for the first time under Eriksson, but came on at half-time against Holland at White Hart Lane as the Three Lions suffered their first defeat under the new coach, losing 2–0. The home side looked rusty so early in the new campaign, but the visitors had no such problems as their superior technique saw them through.

After he had had a summer without football for the first time in five years, it was no coincidence that Owen had begun the new season looking fresh and sharp. He didn't score for England against the Netherlands but he scored in his third consecutive Liverpool appearance three days later when West Ham came to Anfield.

Owen got both Liverpool goals in a 2–1 win, making it six from three for Liverpool in 2001/2. His great form had carried over from the previous campaign and he was hoping to continue it as long as possible, as well as his fine fitness, as Owen told the *News of the World*: 'I haven't felt a single twinge from my hamstrings for as long as I can remember. I've learned a lot about my body in the last few years and I know what I need to do to get the best out of it. As soon as one match is over, I start preparing for the next one. I have a massage and do warm-down exercises. Hopefully it will keep me injury-free for as long as possible.'

The squad rotation of the previous season played a part in Owen's lack of recent injuries, and he was once again left out of the Liverpool team as they faced FC Haka in the second leg of their Champions League qualifier. With a 5–0 lead from the first leg, the Reds were always in control, and they went on to win 4–1 at Anfield, comfortably progressing to the Group Stages 9–1 on aggregate.

Owen's next match was also in Europe, as Liverpool faced Bayern Munich in the European Super Cup. Bayern were the European Cup holders and the Bundesliga Champions, but, just like so many teams before them, they found that in cup competition Houllier's team were nigh on invincible and they were beaten 3–2 in Monaco. It was Liverpool's fifth trophy of a glorious year but 2001 still had plenty in store for Owen.

With just one week to go before England's World Cup qualifier in Munich, the European Super Cup had given Owen a great opportunity to get used to German opposition and goalkeeper Oliver Kahn in particular, whom he unsuccessfully tried to chip in the first half, before drilling Liverpool's third goal home after half-time. 'We knew Bayern were a very good side, so to beat them is a real triumph for us,' Owen said after the game. 'I also learned something about facing Kahn. He's a very dominant keeper and makes himself look very big when he comes out to confront you. I learned my lesson from that first chance. I know now not to try to put the ball past him high, he's so big. I do know that whoever plays for England will have to be really good finishers, because he's fantastic. I missed one chance and you don't often get a second opportunity. So when it came I was intent on playing the ball past him low, first time, and it worked.'

That lesson was to prove invaluable to England when Owen travelled to Munich, because, with twenty goals in his last sixteen games for Liverpool, sixteen of which had come in the last ten games, the young striker was in the form of his life, and, facing Germany on 1 September 2001, he delivered the performance of his life.

Before the game, Owen summed up how important a victory would be. 'Like all our meetings with Germany, this is a massive match,' he told the *News of the World*. 'I don't have very good memories of the last game at Wembley. It was not one of my best and the mood in the dressing room afterwards was pretty miserable. Then we heard that Kevin Keegan had resigned as coach and we were totally shocked. It was a day we all wanted to forget. Immediately we were being written off as far as the World Cup finals were concerned. It says a lot for the England squad and Mr Sven-Göran Eriksson that we have kept our hopes alive with the victories we have achieved since he took over as coach.'

Between Owen's two German appointments, Liverpool lost 2–1 away to Bolton, and the Boy Wonder didn't score for once, but, as the in-form striker in Europe, he was assured his place in the starting line-up in Germany and he certainly justified his selection.

The whole team were immense in Munich: David Seaman; Gary Neville, Sol Campbell, Rio Ferdinand, Ashley Cole; David Beckham, Steven Gerrard, Paul Scholes, Nick Barmby; Emile Heskey and Owen. Every one of them made his mark on the game but none more so than the Star of St Etienne.

It was by no means the best German team of all time, but, with Kahn in goal and Michael Ballack in midfield, there were two genuine world-class performers. Owen's Liverpool teammate Dietmar 'Didi' Hamann brought familiarity to the midfield, and the giant Carsten Jancker brought plenty of presence to the attack. And it was the big man who scored first, steering home a header from his strike partner Oliver Neuville after only six minutes.

But the home side's lead didn't last long and inevitably, with what was to follow, it was Owen who bagged the equaliser, seven minutes later. Barmby received the ball in the area with his back to goal, and as the keeper rushed out the winger flicked it to Owen, who swivelled and knocked the ball into an empty net. With the scores at 1–1 Owen and Heskey continued to scare the life out of the German defenders and they looked dangerous every time they had the ball. However, neither of them could find another in the first half, but one of their Anfield teammates did.

Gerrard hit an unstoppable twenty-five-yard pile driver just before the break to make it 2–1, and it was this goal that really knocked the stuffing out of the hosts. It was his first goal for England – and what a time to get it!

Behind at the interval, Germany would have to chase the game in the second half, which would leave them even more vulnerable to the pace of Owen and Heskey. The Germans had long made a reputation for themselves in the way they could close out a game after taking the lead, and having taken the lead they were aghast finding themselves behind. The fact that it was home game made it almost too much to bear, and there was much worse was to come.

Just three minutes into the second half, Owen made it 3–1. Displaying all the understanding developed at club level, Heskey chested the ball down for his strike partner, and the little goal machine got there first to knock his second past Kahn, but he was still not finished. After sixty-six minutes Owen once again displayed his impeccable timing, as he raced onto a ball over the top from Gerrard, took one touch and then blasted it high into the net over the falling keeper.

With three goals to his name, Owen leapt into a handspring celebration, as he laid out his joy for all to see. Heskey added goal number five with seventeen minutes left and the German embarrassment was complete. It was only their second defeat in sixty-one World Cup qualifying games and their first on home soil, but for England it was worth more than three points. This was a sign that this team were capable of beating any of the great powerhouses of world football, and gave them the confidence to believe in themselves when the going gets tough.

'This is the stuff dreams are made of,' the manager revealed afterwards. 'I told the players this morning that they were a good team, one that was well capable of beating Germany in their own country, but even I could not have imagined a performance or a score like that. It was incredible. What can you say about Michael Owen? He took his goals brilliantly but this was a victory for the team and I would not like to pick one person out.'

Although Eriksson wouldn't praise any one player more than the others, he did later provide his thoughts on his hat-trick hero, saying, 'Michael Owen is very cold and very quick. If you have that combination as a striker, it is a killer. Everyone recognises what a special talent he is. Michael is such a great finisher.'

Owen's fantastic finishing was clear to everyone who has ever watched that memorable ninety minutes from Munich, but more importantly for England was how the team had performed as a unit. The entire team came from just four clubs, three from Arsenal, three from Manchester United, one from Leeds United and four from Liverpool, three of whom provided the five goals. 'There's no magic formula,' Owen told the *Daily Express*. 'But I think that is the first time we have all really clicked together. It was a special performance by everyone, one of the few times since I have been involved that we really have gelled as an international side.

'We should do well in the next World Cup, but if you look at the age of the team, in five years' time all our players will have reached their peak. That is when I think we can really do well. We have got some of the best players in the world in this team. Everyone knows how good they are because clubs in Italy would give their left arms to have these players.'

To qualify for the tournament in Japan and South Korea, it

was imperative that England remain focused for their next game four days later against Albania at St James' Park. After they had beaten Germany 5–1, people thought it would be a cakewalk against the Balkan side, but, resolutely defending from start to finish, the Albanians were much more difficult to break down than England's previous opponents, and it ended 2–0, thanks to a goal each from Owen and Fowler at the end of each half.

The players were under no illusions as to how difficult it would be against the minnows, though. 'The manager said we would have to be patient and they were going to defend. They didn't disappoint,' Owen said in the *Daily Mail*. 'They defended in numbers and the chance I took was the hardest one of the night. I've played here a couple of times and got on the score-sheet, so it was nice to do it again.'

The six points from two games put Eriksson's side to the top of Group 9 with sixteen points. They were now in control of their own destiny, having looked play-off hopefuls at best a week previously, and they knew that a win against Greece at Old Trafford in October would secure their place in the Far East. But Owen would play no part in the final group game, because he had suffered yet another hamstring injury.

As he returned to club duty, Owen's Liverpool suffered a hangover from their England players' glory, losing 3–1 to Aston Villa at Anfield. Much to the visitors' relief, Owen was named among the substitutes and, appearing with only thirty minutes left, he couldn't turn things around.

Owen returned to the starting XI three days later for Liverpool's Champions League debut against Boavista and, as on so many first games in other competitions – League, FA Cup, League Cup and UEFA Cup – the prolific youngster marked the occasion with a goal, the equaliser, in a 1–1 draw. 'It's nice to score on your debuts in different competitions,' Owen told the press. 'And I have been fortunate enough to do that. I must admit I'd got to an age when I didn't think I'd have another debut. Getting into the Champions League has taken a long time coming – and we intend to do well. We could have done a lot better against Boavista, but there are a lot more games to be played for us to put things right.'

Dynamo Kiev drew 2–2 with Borussia Dortmund in the Group's other match, so the result wasn't too bad, but before travelling back to Germany Owen had to face Everton in the first Merseyside Derby of the season. Having lost their previous two league matches, and with only three points from the opening three Premiership games of the season, the Red half of Liverpool was elated with a 3–1 win at Goodison Park. Owen scored a penalty after half an hour to take his goal haul to thirteen for the season, and it was only mid-September.

It was his ninety-second goal for Liverpool, remarkably his first against the Toffees, but he insisted that fact hadn't been playing on his mind. 'To score in a derby is great, but to be fair I've never thought I've had the best of luck in games against Everton,' Owen told the *Liverpool Echo*. 'It's not as though I'd missed a lot of chances and I've missed a few games with injury. I felt it was just a matter of time before I scored in a derby eventually, so I wasn't getting myself in a hot flush about it.'

He may not have been in a flush but he was certainly red hot. However, it proved too good to last, because he first failed to find the back of the net in Germany, as Borussia Dortmund proved more resilient than their national colleagues in a 0–0 draw, and he drew another blank when playing against Tottenham at Anfield, but at least Liverpool won 1–0. Owen appeared only as a second-half substitute against the Lilywhites but then had to be replaced himself after he suffered a minor tear of his hamstring, and it would be more than a month until he scored again.

Owen continued to be busy during this particular injury hiatus, as he first signed a new contract extension for a further four years on a wage believed to be between £60,000 and £80,000 per week. 'It has never been a thought in my mind about playing for any other club than Liverpool,' Owen said at the press conference. 'And I'm obviously delighted to have signed. I'm only twenty-one and yet this is my fourth professional contract I've signed with the club. They've always been incredibly fair by reviewing contracts early, and this is one of the many reasons there's such loyalty at Liverpool.'

Sven-Göran Eriksson had shown a lot of loyalty to Liverpool's latest 'signing', since taking over as England boss, but he was without Owen's services for the final World Cup qualifying game. Still sidelined by his hamstring injury, the young striker decided to watch the big game as a television analyst, so he was in the ground at Old Trafford as his teammates twice went behind and were dragged through to the World Cup by a monumentally inspirational captain's performance from Beckham, and his crucial last-minute free kick.

Ecstatic to have finally seen England's place at the World Cup confirmed, Owen could begin to think about building on the reputation he had laid the foundations for in St Etienne. But, in October, there was still plenty to play for at club level, where Liverpool were set to be without Gérard Houllier for much of the season.

Still recuperating from his latest hamstring trouble, Owen was merely a spectator at Anfield when Liverpool's French manager was taken to hospital with a serious heart condition. After giving his half-time team talk against Leeds, Houllier was taken to hospital complaining of feeling 'light-headed and a bit odd'. As Owen watched from the directors' box, he noticed that the manager didn't appear for the second half, and spotted that Houllier's wife had also disappeared from her usual seat, but the true scale of the problem didn't come to light until the next day.

At training the players were told that the manager's condition was 'very serious and possibly life-threatening'. Houllier had a dissection of the aorta and required an eleven-hour operation to fix the issue.

Everything was dedicated to the manager for the next five months. The family feel of the club was underlined by the way the fans reacted to the news that the man who had guided them through such a trophy-laden season the year before was now fighting for his life in a hospital bed: they chanted his name at matches, home and away, and unfurled a massive French flag with Houllier's name on it across the Kop.

Two months after the operation the manager began calling some of the players over the phone, and a couple of weeks after that he began regular visits to Melwood, never to do any work, but merely to stay in touch with the club and the players. It wasn't until five months later that Houllier finally reclaimed his spot on the Liverpool bench.

Owen returned to Liverpool action much more quickly than his boss, because his injury kept him out for little more than a month. It had been a very busy and mixed month for Liverpool as they had picked up seven points from three games in both the Champions League and Premiership and had been knocked out of the League Cup while fielding a weakened team. After missing seven games, Owen could be forgiven a little rustiness on his return, but he got the second goal in a 2–0 win over Charlton at the Valley, before going off on the hour mark, and was being lauded as the best striker in the country in some quarters.

Alex Ferguson had begun a debate by declaring his new striker Ruud Van Nistelrooy as the best in Europe, before Arsène Wenger declared Thierry Henry the best in his opinion. Jimmy Floyd Hasselbaink was described as the best centre forward in the world by Claudio Ranieri, but Ian Rush was in no doubt as to who was best.

'They are all great strikers but in my opinion none of them is in the same league as Michael Owen,' the former Wales striker told the *Daily Mail*. 'When Michael is fit then Liverpool and England have one the greatest strikers in the world. In fact, he probably is the greatest striker in the world. Just before Michael's recent injury he was playing the best football I have ever seen him play, just sensational. I am not being disrespectful to the other strikers because they are exceptional in their own right. But Michael is head and shoulders above the rest.'

Stand-in manager Phil Thompson was delighted with Owen's return, and the accompanying three points, which took Liverpool to the top of the Premiership. The good news continued for the Merseysiders as they then beat Borussia Dortmund 2–0 to qualify for the second group stage of the Champions League. Owen failed to score against the 1997 European Champions, but he was elated by the progress Liverpool were making in club football's premiere competition. 'We've wanted this for a few years now,' Owen told the press. 'We won the UEFA Cup last season and really fancied this crack at the Champions League. You can all see how well it's going. There are so many good teams in it; we can't really start talking about winning it. But we felt that last season about the UEFA Cup when there were some really good sides involved, but we ended up managing to beat them to take the trophy.'

There was still a long way to go before the trophies would be handed out, but Owen helped consolidate Liverpool's position at the top of the Premiership with two goals in a 3–1 win over Manchester United at Anfield. It was a position they held for six weeks, and, by the time their short reign at the top came to an end, there was a new reason for Owen to celebrate.

Following the Manchester United game, Owen had missed England's friendly draw with Sweden, but he recovered in time to face Blackburn at Ewood Park and maintained his goalscoring form with one in a 1–1 draw, and another in the 3–1 loss to Barcelona at Anfield.

Before suffering a rare European defeat, Owen was named on the short list for the European Footballer of the Year award, the prestigious Ballon d'Or. 'It's a great honour to be in the running and, yes, it would fulfil an ambition to win an award like that,' the Liverpool forward revealed in the *Daily Star*. 'I've had a good year, but something like this only comes along when your team is doing well and winning honours. I've been singled out, but if I was to be voted first, second or third then it would be just as much down to my team-mates as me.'

Owen found that he had come first before facing Roma in the Italian capital when Houllier phoned to tell him the news, but the new European Footballer of the Year managed to keep the announcement quiet, telling only his parents. The prizewinner was still in good form scoring in the 1–0 win at Derby, and grabbing the opening goal in a 2–0 victory against Middlesbrough. But Liverpool were stuttering a little, and, as well as three league wins – over Sunderland, Derby and Boro' – the Reds had drawn 0–0 in

Rome and at home to Fulham before losing 4–0 to Chelsea at Stamford Bridge.

Owen missed the game with a hamstring niggle as Liverpool suffered their heaviest league defeat for nine years, and the result meant that the Anfield side were knocked off the top of the Premiership for the first time in six weeks two days later. But the club disappointment was eclipsed by personal joy for Owen as he travelled to Paris to pick up the Ballon d'Or as the whole footballing world found out the name of the new European Footballer of the Year.

Only the sixth British player to win the award, Owen joined Sir Stanley Matthews, Denis Law, Sir Bobby Charlton, George Best and Kevin Keegan on an illustrious list. He was the first Englishman to pick up the trophy since 1979 and the first player in England to claim the 'golden ball' since 1968. Owen having only recently turned twenty-two, it was incredible that he should find himself on a winner's list that included such greats as Franz Beckenbauer, Michel Platini and Johan Cruyff, but after the Kop hero's year he truly deserved it.

It was his goals that had humbled the Germans in Munich to get England's World Cup campaign back on track; it was his goals that had claimed the FA Cup for Liverpool; it was his goals that had propelled Houllier's team to trophy success on four other fronts. He had scored thirty goals for Liverpool and six for England, from fifty-four games for club and country (forty-six and eight respectively); 2001 really was Michael Owen's year.

'I could not believe it when I first heard the news,' said the award winner. 'I knew I was one of the five nominated but it was still a shock. There was Francesco Totti, Raúl and David Beckham and they are all fantastic footballers. We've had a great season for

Liverpool, winning five trophies and I'm very happy to win this award too. It's the highest privilege I can win as a player and I'm over the moon to win it.'

The Ballon d'Or is arguably the most prestigious of individual awards available to a footballer. Every year the trophy is presented by *France Football*, the magazine that created the award in 1956. The voting is completed by football writers throughout Europe, selected by *France Football*.

FIFA's World Player of the Year is the young pretender to the Ballon d'Or's position at the top, having started only in 1991. The votes come from the national coaches of the member countries of FIFA, and they tend to be more politically inspired. In 2001 Owen was unlucky not be more highly considered in the voting for the FIFA award but finished eighth as Luis Figo picked up the award.

Owen's Liverpool manager Gérard Houllier, still recovering from heart surgery, added in the *Daily Express*, 'I am not surprised Michael has been named European Footballer of the Year. He is a gifted footballer who will get even better because he wants to learn. He is the first Liverpool player to win and I am very proud of that.

'Michael is a symbol of Liverpool and everything we are trying to achieve. I remember when he came back from that famous victory over Germany in which he was tremendous. I was delighted with his attitude. He is so modest but at the same time you can sense his passion for the game he loves. He does everything right. In training, a team-mate will score a goal in a five-a-side game and Michael will congratulate him as if he scored in the World Cup final. He just loves his football.'

The great and the good were lining up to be quoted, and Geoff Hurst was on hand to give his opinion. 'Michael's not just a goal-scorer,' the World Cup winner said in the *Daily*

Mail. 'He has become a great outlet for the ball-players in the team because of the runs he is making all the time. In Munich, Michael was a threat to the Germans from the word go, even before he scored. The goals were the icing on the cake. It was the performance itself that showed what he is becoming – and that is one of the best three or four strikers in world football.'

The praise and awards didn't stop there either as Owen was voted into a World XI by French newspaper *L'Equipe* and also by readers of French monthly *Onze Mondial*. He narrowly missed out to Zinédine Zidane in the magazine's poll for World Player of the Year, but 'Zizou' was full of praise for the Liverpool youngster. 'I like Michael a great deal. He has had an exceptional year and I have been impressed by him,' the Frenchman said.

Owen was flattered by the recognition from another country's public, as his popularity seemed to develop exponentially. And he felt there was still plenty of time for his footballing talent to do likewise. 'I'm still light years away from my best. It's great to know that a soccer player doesn't reach the climax of his career until he's twenty-seven or twenty-eight,' he told the press. 'I'm not in a hurry to be that old. I'm still a rookie in the soccer world and there are still a lot of good seasons ahead of me. Being a good player was not enough for me and it will never be. I want to get better – there are still a lot of steps to climb to become the best with Liverpool and with England. I know that I can still improve my game. I have to keep trying to improve, because I'm still young. But I want to move on into the next phase of my career now.'

He moved smoothly into that new phase with another milestone as he scored his hundredth goal for Liverpool in the last game of 2001. The Reds had dropped points since Owen picked up his award, losing to Arsenal at Anfield, and, although they beat Villa on Boxing Day without any goals from Owen, he was on hand to rescue a point at the death from Upton Park. Coming off the bench, the award-winner smashed Heskey's cross into the roof off the net with only two minutes remaining of normal time, allowing his team to draw 1–1 with West Ham, and, having waited three weeks since Goal 99, he was understandably overjoyed. 'It's been an incredible year for me,' he said. 'It's the kind of stuff that dreams are made of. Hopefully, I'll get two hundred goals for Liverpool. It's a great milestone to get a hundred goals and I'm very proud to be up there with great names like Roger Hunt and Ian Rush.'

And his stand-in manager was just as happy. 'It's just great that Michael's ended a fantastic year on a great note,' Phil Thompson said in the *Daily Post*. 'It was as if it was written for him. Today he showed that he's not only got pace but his link-up play and all-round game is top class. And he's so young that he'll add things to his game. He'll add more to his game over the next year and will improve with experience. There's no doubt about that.'

Thompson certainly wasn't alone in his admiration of Owen's ability, and Lazio continued to follow the England striker's progress. Having made enquiries as to Owen's availability during the summer, Sergio Cragnotti remained vocal with his intentions. 'I want to buy Owen,' Lazio's owner was reported as saying in the *Daily Express*. 'I wanted to purchase him a couple of years a go. He is a talent, a real champion and a player that I have always admired. It won't be easy to buy him from Liverpool, but we will try because we want to have a competitive team made of champions.'

Liverpool had no intention of selling Owen, but one man on

his way out of Anfield was Robbie Fowler. Previously held in deific awe by the Kop, the instinctive goalscorer had fallen out of favour with Houllier, and especially Thompson, and was on his way to Leeds United in a £12 million move. The 'Toxteth Terrier' was soon replaced though as Nicolas Anelka joined the Reds on loan for the remainder of the season, from Paris St Germain.

Owen was excited by the arrival of the twenty-two-year-old Frenchman. 'It was a shock to find we had signed Anelka because it had not even been hinted at,' he said in the *Liverpool Echo*. 'But it looks a good signing for us. I can vividly remember the goals he scored in helping Arsenal to win the 1998 Double and if he is capable of doing that for us it will be well worth him coming here. Hopefully, that will bring us the goals which can win the title.'

Having dropped to fourth in the table, Liverpool certainly needed a boost. Despite the new signing, they suffered a poor start to 2002 in the league as they drew three games 1–1 against Bolton, Arsenal and Southampton, where Owen got the goal. They also lost 2–0 to Southampton at the St Mary's Stadium, but there was some welcome respite in the FA Cup, as the Reds beat Birmingham City 3–0 with an Owen brace and Anelka's first for the club.

With only three points from four games, Liverpool weren't in the best of form for a trip to Old Trafford, but they rose to the occasion and beat their fiercest rivals 1–0 in their own backyard to give their title aspirations a huge fillip, and not before time. 'We've been going through a bad patch but hopefully winning at Manchester United will get us through our problems,' Owen told the Press Association. 'It may have been just three points, but it could be the result which kick-starts our season.'

It certainly did that. In Liverpool's next eleven Premiership matches they won ten and drew one, claiming a thirty-four-point haul from the thirty-six available, including the Manchester United win. It was without doubt title-winning form, but the 2001/2 season belonged to Arsenal as the springtime goals of Freddie Ljungberg guided them to a second 'Double' in four years, when they won their final thirteen league games to finish seven points above the Reds. As well as pipping Liverpool to the Premiership post, the Gunners also saw off Owen and his teammates 1–0 in the FA Cup fourth round at Highbury.

With only the Premiership and Europe to concentrate on, Liverpool commenced their impressive run of form that took them so close to the title, and to within six minutes of a Champions League semifinal. The Reds beat Leicester 1–0, Leeds 4–0 with one from our man, and Ipswich 6–0 with an Owen brace to show that they meant business, and although they drew three games in a week Liverpool were still well placed at home despite a precarious outlook abroad.

A 0–0 stalemate at home to Galatasaray was followed by a 1–1 derby draw with Everton at Anfield, before a 1–1 in Istanbul had Liverpool bottom of Group B with just three points from their first four games. With matches away to Barcelona and at home to Roma to come it would be hard for the Reds to progress to the knockout stages, but if they could transfer their improved league form to Europe then they would be in with a shout.

But, even if Liverpool weren't heading to the top in Europe, it seemed certain that Owen would, as the European Footballer of the Year was declared as a transfer target by the Real Madrid president. 'We want Michael Owen,' Florentino Pérez said. 'Owen can be one of the world's great players and the best players must play for Real Madrid. In England there are two great players – Owen and Beckham, but Beckham plays in the same position as Luis Figo. With the signing of Zidane, many French people and Arabs became Real Madrid fans. Now I would like to sign an English star.'

Liverpool's big English star was sidelined through most of March with a hamstring injury, but the Reds kept winning in the Premiership, and secured a 0–0 draw in the Nou Camp to keep their Champions League hopes alive. And for their final Group B match the players received a well-timed boost: Houllier returned, unannounced, to take the team talk for the must-win game against Roma in the Champions League; the manager's appearance lifted the troops and they won 2–0 to qualify for the quarterfinals, where they would face Bayer Leverkusen, with a fit-again Owen.

The England striker returned to club action in a 1–0 win over Chelsea at Anfield and was back in Eriksson's team days later. Playing their first World Cup warm-up match, the Three Lions finished off second best against Italy at Elland Road despite Fowler's opening goal. Having missed the vital game against Greece in October, Owen played his first match for his country since scoring against Albania in September, but, fit again, he was straight back in Eriksson's first XI.

Owen got his first goal for seven weeks three days later as he returned to the starting line-up at Liverpool. The second goal in a 2–0 win over Charlton at Anfield, it was a well-timed strike with the home leg against Leverkusen just days away, but the Germans were still scared of the little star following his heroics in Munich. Oliver Neuville was playing in the match against England and he remembered it well. 'Owen gave us nightmares,' the German striker told the *News of the World*. 'After Steven Gerrard made it 2–1 we pushed forward but Owen and Emile Heskey are fantastic on the break. I can only hope next week we will avoid suffering a similar experience. Those three can create chaos for our defence again.'

Playing at Anfield, Neuville's side displayed better handling of that trio, but still lost 1–0 as Sami Hyypia finished from close range after Owen met Riise's corner. Liverpool's lead wasn't enough to go through to a semifinal against Manchester United, however, as they lost 4–2 in Leverkusen. After eighty-four minutes of the second leg, Houllier's side were level on aggregate and still ahead by virtue of their away-goals; but, on a night when everything that could go wrong did go wrong, Owen missed three chances that he would normally be expected to score, and the usually reliable defence conceded a late goal to see Liverpool dumped out of the competition.

Despite an injury scare following the European disappointment – Brazilian defender Lúcio accidentally stood heavily on Owen's foot and the England striker needed an X-ray, but, fortunately, it was only heavily bruised and not broken – the prolific youngster took Liverpool to within one point of Arsenal at the top of the Premiership with the only goal of the game against Sunderland at the Stadium of Light.

Showing remarkable 'bouncebackability' after the Champions League defeat, Owen and Liverpool dug deep against the Wearsiders to keep their title challenge on track, with only four matches remaining. 'We've got a lot of hard games left,' Owen said after securing an eleventh win in twelve games. 'Tottenham away is never easy, and we've got three home games, but we have to win them all to stand any chance.'

However, before Owen could take any more steps towards what would be a first championship for Liverpool since 1990, he had more history to make with his other team. On 17 April 2002, he led out his country at Anfield to become England's youngest captain since Bobby Moore. With Beckham out of action because of a broken metatarsal, Eriksson turned to Owen. 'He was the best footballer in Europe last year,' Eriksson said, explaining his decision. 'And I think he's a very clean and popular one inside and outside England. It's up to him to show that he's also a leader, and I think he is.'

And Owen certainly wasn't understating what it meant to him. 'If you had asked me just a few hours ago to list ambitions,' the new skipper told reporters, 'being England captain would have been one of them. It's something I wanted as a child. I'd love to captain Liverpool, to play in a few World Cups, *win* a World Cup. Then there's the league title and European Cups. Everyone has their ambitions and being skipper of England was one of mine.

'It's obviously a great honour to be named captain. When the manager told me, I was straight on the phone to Mum and Dad and friends and family. It was a complete surprise. People had been naming a few that could get it, but it was a surprise and a pleasant one. Being at Anfield completes it all – in front of your home fans on the pitch you know best. It's something I've always dreamed of – to get it at twenty-two is sooner than I imagined. It's going to be a great occasion.'

Facing Paraguay in a final warm-up match at home before heading for the Far East, Owen didn't disappoint. He led from the front and opened the scoring after just four minutes, somewhat appropriately heading in a Gerrard cross in front of the Kop. England went on to win the game 4–0 and Owen had completed a far better job than the last time he had led out his country, having been sent off against Brazil while wearing the armband at Under-18s level.

As the friendly came at the business end of the season Eriksson agreed to play Owen only for the first half, so as to keep him fresh for Liverpool's run-in. 'I lost the toss-up before the game and so was then delighted when Paraguay decided to kick towards the Anfield Road end,' the new skipper said to the press. 'I knew I was playing forty-five minutes and wanted to shoot towards the Kop. It was then nice for me to get off to a dream start with a rarity from me – a headed goal – and that probably settled a lot of nerves in the first few minutes.

'It was a tremendous honour, one I won't forget in a hurry,' he added in the *Sunday Mirror*. 'I remember, just after scoring the goal, jogging back to the halfway line and thinking, it doesn't get much better than this. All the same, though, I would far rather see David Beckham return from injury and lead the side into the World Cup.'

Owen enjoyed the responsibility, but, like the other players, he was keen to see the usual captain back in time for the tournament in Japan and Korea. For once, however, there were no concerns about Owen's fitness, and, three days after becoming England's second youngest ever captain, he was back to banging in the goals for Liverpool.

Derby were the visitors to Anfield as the history-making forward claimed a brace to win the game 2–0, and consign the Rams to relegation. The three points had a more invigorating effect on Liverpool, however, since they lifted the Reds to the top of the table, although Arsenal were two points behind with two games in hand. With three games left, Owen remained focused on the task at hand. 'We still feel we can win the title and that has to be the next target,' he said. 'Arsenal have the games in hand, but if they slip up then we're there waiting, and they know that. That puts on its own pressures.'

But it was Liverpool who couldn't handle the pressure, and losing 1–0 to Tottenham at White Hart Lane effectively ended their title dreams; and, when Wenger's team then beat Bolton, Liverpool's title was a mathematical impossibility. Never one to dwell on disappointment, Owen immediately set his sights on the next year's championship, and the one after that. 'It was disappointing losing to Tottenham because we'd been on such a good run,' he said at an Umbro boot launch. 'Everyone would love to win the title, and it's a major goal of mine. I'm sure we're going to do it in the next year or two. We've shown a lot of improvement in the last three or four years, and I hope we can keep that going. Every year we've made a giant step forward. You just have to look at the points total.'

The Reds won their last two league games to improve that total further, to eighty points, with Owen grabbing his twenty-eighth Liverpool goal of the season in a 5–0 win over Ipswich. Arsenal won the Double at Old Trafford, after scoring in every Premiership game, and completing a season without losing an away game in the league. Considering all the records that Arsène Wenger's team had broken in 2002, they finished only seven points above Liverpool, who were three points above third-placed Manchester United.

'I still think that it's been a good season,' Owen went on. 'The points total we ended up with could probably win the league next year. That shows just how far we've come. We have such a young side and have grown up together, and I don't think the manager will change things drastically in the summer. He might buy one or two players – but that's in his hands.'

Liverpool clearly needed someone to share the goalscoring burden on Owen, who had enjoyed his most prolific campaign as a professional, with four more goals than the previous season. His twenty-eight goals gave him more than double those of the Reds' next-best marksman, Heskey, who got thirteen; and, if Houllier wanted to improve on second place, they would need to have more options upfront and more goals from midfield.

But, despite Owen's obvious importance to his club, his country and his position as European Footballer of the Year, he still missed out on selection for the Professional Footballers'

Association Premiership team of the season, where his peers paired Henry and van Nistelrooy upfront. 'I don't want to be bitter but, if it had been picked at the start of the year, I would have been in it because of the start I had and the goals against Germany and Albania,' Owen said. 'Players pick for the moment and, at the time they voted, Ruud van Nistelrooy, Robert Pires, Thierry Henry and Craig Bellamy were on fire.'

He may have been underappreciated by his fellow pros, but Owen would have the support of the whole country for the next month and a half as England headed out East for the World Cup.

9

BIG IN JAPAN

'I can look back now and remember the goals I have scored to help to get us here,' he told the *Daily Post*, 'especially the hat-trick in the 5–1 win over Germany, and the two I scored in the finals, against Denmark and Brazil. But I would gladly swap them all for us to have been able to go all the way to the final and lift the trophy. Perhaps in ten years time I'll be able to look back with fond memories at the goals – but, at the moment, they mean nothing because we are going home.'

Michael Owen was right to be disappointed. Playing in a side blessed with talent, he had made it only to the quarterfinals of the World Cup. After his prolific season at club level, he went into the tournament high on confidence, but finished by limping out of England's last game as he once again suffered from his problematic hamstrings.

Due to the ever-increasing popularity of the Premiership in Japan, England arrived at their World Cup base amid an incredible amount of attention, from press and public alike. It was unlike anything Owen had ever seen before, and, although he didn't create as much frenzy among the locals as David Beckham, the Liverpool lad was clearly the second most popular of the England players with the Japanese public.

Throughout the tournament there were people camped outside the England hotel, waiting in hope and expectation of a glimpse of their idols, and, whenever the team coach rolled out for practice or matches, the roads were lined with fanatical supporters. It was the kind of hero worship not seen in Britain since the Beatlemania of the sixties, and, although Owen had been warned of what lay in wait for him and his teammates in Japan, it exceeded his expectations considerably, and that kind of celebrity was one thing he wouldn't miss from his Oriental experience.

After Owen's anticlimactic end to the season, he was part of the squad that Sven-Göran Eriksson took to Dubai. The Swede reasoned that happy players are better players, so he allowed his men to take their respective girlfriends, wives and families with them for what was partly a team-bonding holiday and partly a training camp. This allowed the players to relax a little after their long, hard domestic seasons, but also to acclimatise to the heat and humidity that would be such a huge factor in the afternoon games out East.

Another big factor for Eriksson's squad was the pressure to succeed as the anticipation back home increased day by day. 'Obviously, everyone wants England to do well and wants the players to play well, so there's an expectancy, but if you're a footballer that's what you're paid to do,' Owen said. 'I'm four years older, four years wiser, and it's going to be a great tournament. Hopefully, we can come out doing well. There's quite a lot of experience, even though we're a young side. We've got players from Manchester United, Arsenal, Liverpool who have all done well in Europe and who have all played in massive games before, so I don't think the stage will frighten any of the players.'

One of the players who would be missing out on the big stage was Owen's long-time teammate Steven Gerrard. The two had progressed through the Liverpool youth ranks together, and were now both key players in the England side, but the midfielder was going to miss the tournament due to a troublesome groin injury that required a second operation. 'He's one of the best players in the world, let alone in England, and every team would miss him,' Owen said of Gerrard. 'It's a bitter blow because he would have had something to give on the world stage.'

But in the build-up to the tournament the British media had been more concerned with another injury, as the whole nation was gripped by metatarsal madness. Beckham had broken the second metatarsal in his left foot in Manchester United's 3–2 win against Deportivo la Coruña, when the Argentinian Aldo Duscher caught the England captain late. Beckham's clubmate Gary Neville suffered a similar injury even closer to the tournament and was ruled out, and Danny Murphy was called up as a replacement before he too broke a metatarsal in training.

Following a relaxed week in Dubai with their partners, Eriksson's elite headed to South Korea for some hard graft. Training in the mornings and the evenings so as to avoid the heat of the day, they stepped up their preparation with friendly games against South Korea and Cameroon to ready themselves for the big kick-off. With Beckham still out, Owen continued as captain for the game against the co-hosts. 'We want to win every game,' said the stand-in skipper. 'But if we beat South Korea tomorrow it doesn't mean we're going to win the World Cup, just as defeat doesn't mean we're *not* going to win it. We need to play these matches because we don't get together that often – but it's all about confidence. It'll be a tough game but we're gearing up for the match against Sweden. That's the one which matters.'

With many players looking ahead to the bigger game, the match against South Korea petered out to a 1–1 draw, despite Owen opening the scoring midway through the first half. The captain turned in a rebound after Paul Scholes shot from distance to make it two goals from two matches with the armband. Happy as Owen was to take the responsibility, he was looking forward to Beckham's widely anticipated return. 'Being England captain is a fantastic feeling,' the striker said. 'But I would be happy to hand the armband over to David. He's a vital player to us and we need him fit. I would prefer David to be doing it and I'm expecting him to be leading the team out for Sweden. If he's not, I will be willing and able to do it.'

It was important that England get through the game against the Scandinavians without any further injury problems, and the same was true five days later as they prepared for their appointment with Nigeria by playing their West African neighbours Cameroon. Robbie Fowler rescued a draw with a last-minute equaliser to make it 2–2 before the Three Lions turned their attentions to the serious stuff.

The England team took up their residence on Awaji, a small island at the Eastern end of the Seto Inland Sea, between the much larger Shikoku and Honshu islands. With a golf course twenty minutes away and a manager who allowed his players their freedom, the squad would have plenty of opportunity to relax during the tournament. And with the group England had, facing Sweden, Argentina and Nigeria, they would need to be at their best to progress.

'It is going to be tough,' Owen told the *News of the World*. 'I would even say you could not have picked a more difficult group than this if you had tried. But that doesn't mean we'll be going to the finals expecting to come home early. The way we have performed over the last twelve months, we don't have any need to fear anyone.'

Having played against most of the Swedish side in the Premiership, Owen knew exactly what to expect in the opening match, and he was determined to get some points on the board early on. 'The first game against Sweden is massive, and we can't afford to be beaten,' Owen told the press. 'If we are, we would have to win our other two matches, against Nigeria and Argentina, and that would be asking an awful lot.'

With England set to play Argentina again, there were the unavoidable comparisons with France '98. 'St Etienne does feel like a different world now,' Owen said in the *Daily Mirror*. 'But I didn't want to be remembered just for that goal against Argentina. The last few years have gone very well although it's inevitable that people will think back to Argentina.

'You can't play well in every game and I've had ups and downs and injuries. But four years ago, I'd have settled for being where I am now.'

A lot of that improvement was down to the guidance of Owen's club coach, Gérard Houllier. 'Michael had to improve his left foot,' the Anfield supremo told the *Mirror*. 'He did and I can pick out two games to show the work he's done. In February 1999 we played at Highbury and drew 0–0. He was running down the left, came back on to his right foot and tried to whip it in, but Seaman read it. I said to him: "If you want to be a top player you have to use your left foot. If you have to come back on your right foot, you lose your advantage and the goalkeeper knows what you're going to do." But the second game is the FA Cup Final last year. He knew he had to improve his volleying as well. At Cardiff, the first goal was a volley and the second with his left foot!'

With the improvement Owen had shown since his last World Cup appearance the young striker had become one of the first names on the England team sheet, and that allowed him to feel more at home while away with the squad. 'When you go into a tournament like the World Cup for the first time, you're never sure whether you should really be out there,' Owen told reporters. 'But, once you've met up with the squad thirty or forty times, you feel part of it and relax. I would like to think I've got plenty more to offer, and I'm confident about proving it over the next few weeks.

'There are maybe six or eight teams who will feel they have a realistic chance of being world champions and, potentially, we're one of them. We're a young side whose best football will come in the next few years, but we can make our mark on these finals. If the worse came to the worst and we didn't go far, I don't think a negative scenario would last. We've such a young side that probably our best football won't come for a few years. That's not to say we can't do well in this one, but we do need to get off to a good start.'

England did get off to a good start in Group F, and took the lead twenty-three minutes into the game against Eriksson's homeland, as Sol Campbell headed home Beckham's corner. But, the longer the game went on, the further back the defence of Danny Mills, Rio Ferdinand, Campbell and Ashley Cole dropped to defend David Seaman's goal and the lead. There were far too many long balls forward for Owen and Darius Vassell to chase, and the midfield four of Beckham, Owen Hargreaves, Paul Scholes and Emile Heskey spent most of the time watching the ball sail over their heads.

Sweden got a deserved equaliser just before the hour mark in

Saitama and, even though Owen took the armband from Beckham when Kieron Dyer replaced the midfielder after sixty-four minutes, it couldn't inspire him to score a goal, as he remained starved of possession. England had allowed the pressure to get to them and the sense of the occasion weighed heavy on their shoulders as they retreated further and further into their own half, inviting the pressure onto them. And, in the end, they did well to hold on for a 1–1 draw.

Owen was realistic when he summed up his own performance after the game, saying, 'Unfortunately, I didn't get much of a chance today but I'm sure it'll be better against Argentina.' It couldn't be much worse: the little striker had done next to nothing with the ball, and, despite chasing many a lost cause upfront, he would have to hope for better service against Argentina.

The Liverpool man felt fresh, though, and he was confident that goals would come if he continued to work hard. 'At the moment I feel really sharp,' Owen said in the *Liverpool Echo*. 'I did a lot of good work in Dubai before the tournament and I feel really good. I don't think I can reproduce a goal like the one in St Etienne again but maybe I can produce a tap-in from two yards. I'd settle for that.

'I do believe this England side can play as well as they did against Argentina four years ago. The better the team we play, the more it brings out the best in us. I hope that will prove the case again because Argentina are a world-class team. We are going to have to produce the standard of performance we gave against Argentina four years ago or Germany in Munich to get a result.'

Argentina had beaten Nigeria 1–0 in their opening game and were thus first in Group F, and beating the *Albicelestes* would put England on top of their mini-table. This is usually a great incentive to win a match, but the players needed no extra motivation ahead of arguably the biggest game of the entire group stage.

A rerun of their classic encounter in 1998, with some of the same characters, the game in Sapporo gave Beckham a chance to get revenge over Diego Simeone, and the rest of the players the chance to erase their spot-kick agony. A week is a long time in politics and sport, but four years is still short enough to keep the pain of a penalty shootout very real. 'Certain things like that rest in the memory,' Owen said, recalling St Etienne. 'It would be nice to beat them and get our own back. We can beat Argentina – on our day we can beat any team in the world.'

Juan Sebastian Verón and Ariel Ortega joined Simeone in midfield, and with that much talent in the middle of the park it was no real surprise when Eriksson changed his team to make it more solid in that area. Making just one change from the team that had drawn with Sweden, the manager brought in Nicky Butt to replace Vassell, as Heskey moved into attack.

The build-up to the game also centred on England's other World Cup meeting with the South Americans, when Diego Maradona robbed Bobby Robson's side of a place in the World Cup semifinals in 1986. The Argentinians were stereotyped as cunning, and Owen was asked to what extent he would bend the rules in pursuit of victory. 'I don't think you should cheat but you should be clever,' the Liverpool striker told reporters. 'If you go down without being touched that's cheating. But, if you can try to make someone foul you by enticing someone to get a toe in and they bring you down, then that's not cheating. That's drawing a foul. If some clumsy defender wants to throw himself in front of you, what are you going to do? Let him do it?'

Just before half-time Owen was tripped for a penalty and Beckham made no mistake from the spot. Television replays suggested that Owen had dived, but, running towards goal, he knocked the ball past the defender and invited the challenge. There was certainly enough contact to warrant a penalty and it even opened up a gash in Owen's leg. The nerves were visible as Beckham strode up to put the ball on the spot, and the relief was palpable as he smashed the ball down the middle of the goal and into the net. Afterwards Owen revealed that he had offered to take the kick for his captain, but was rebuffed. 'I asked David if he fancied it and he was really up for it,' the striker said. 'I could see that he was nervous, but at the same time it was important for him to do it – and I knew that.'

The rest of the game was marked by England's superb defensive effort and steely resolve. Owen came off after eighty impressive minutes, looking far more comfortable alongside Heskey than Vassell, as Wayne Bridge slotted in on the left of a five-man midfield. This substitution left Teddy Sheringham, who had replaced Heskey, upfront on his own, and, good though Tottenham striker was, what little pace he ever had was behind him as he played on through his thirty-sixth year. So Eriksson was again criticised for inviting pressure onto his team, but this time they held out and won the match 1–0.

Argentina took the defeat badly and reportedly didn't want to swap shirts, but Owen didn't need a Blue and White shirt – England had the three points and that was the most important thing. But with Sweden beating Nigeria 2–1 the job was far from complete. 'It was a vital victory but it will only mean anything if we go on and beat Nigeria,' Owen said in the *Liverpool Echo*. 'Everything that happened will be pointless if we don't win on Wednesday.

'Obviously we've had a great win and important win. We went into the match knowing what we had to do and we did it. We'd seen the Sweden result earlier in the day and, to be honest, it made us realise even more what we had to do in our own match. This victory puts us right up there now. Getting something from this game gives us a lot of confidence. The longer we're in this tournament, the better we will get. We were disappointed after our first game, but now we feel much better.'

With four points from their first two games, England were second in the group on goal difference and were in total control of their destiny, but having worked hard to reach that position Eriksson's side laboured to a 0–0 draw in their final group game against Nigeria, where Trevor Sinclair came in for the injured Hargreaves. 'The only positive thing to take from the game is that we're through,' a pragmatic Owen told the press. 'But from now on we know we have to win every game, so we need better performances, and I'm sure they will be.

'It was really tough going. Hot, humid and very hard to play in. By the time we came off it felt like we'd played a few matches, never mind one. The humidity was the worst we've played in and if there is an advantage of finishing second it's that we play Denmark at night in the north, where it should be much cooler, rather than down south against another African team in the middle of the day again.'

Owen was replaced fifteen minutes from time in Osaka, after a poor game in which he once again failed to score. Without a goal from his three appearances in Japan, the fleet-footed youngster remained upbeat. 'The bigger the game, the more you want to score,' Owen said. 'Obviously I'd like to score, but, if we progress through and I don't, then I'll be fine about it, as I'll know that I've made a contribution.'

And Eriksson was equally unfazed by the lack of goals from his number-one striker. 'I don't think Michael is disappointed. I think he's happy and is playing better and better. He is becoming sharper,' stated the England coach. 'Of course, we hope that he starts scoring again and he will do that. I shouldn't be at all surprised if his next goal comes at the weekend.'

Right on cue, Owen grabbed his first of the World Cup against the Danes. Eriksson kept faith with the same eleven who had disappointed so spectacularly against Nigeria, and this time they did him proud. Rio Ferdinand opened the scoring with a header that Sunderland goalkeeper Thomas Sørensen failed to keep out after seventeen minutes, and Owen made it 2–0 five minutes later. Butt flicked on a cross from Sinclair and the Liverpool striker got clear of the Danish defence to slide the ball left-footed past the keeper.

Denmark had beaten France 2–0 to top Group A, and send the defending World Cup holders home in shame, but they proved no match for England in Niigata, as Heskey added a third just before the break. The biggest disappointment on the night was Owen's substitution at half-time. Five minutes into the game the Liverpool speedster picked up a groin injury. He battled on until half-time searching for his first goal of the World Cup, and with that, and the game, in the bag he didn't return after the interval.

In the post-match press conference Owen put a brave face on things, but he knew he was in trouble. 'I could have stayed on, I think,' he said. 'I felt something in my groin after a couple of minutes. I haven't had any groin problems before, so I wasn't sure what it was. I played on for forty-five minutes, but when we went 3–0 up I thought there was no point in carrying on and leaving yourself exposed to get an injury for the next game. It was a precautionary type thing and if the scoreline had been goalless then I would have probably carried on.'

If he had continued, he almost certainly wouldn't have been fit to face Brazil in the quarterfinals, and as it was he was barely able to run when he lined up against them. With only four days to recover after the Denmark match, Owen was off training and spent his time getting treatment instead. He was still having intensive deep-tissue massage from the specialist masseur Richard Smith throughout the morning of the game, and it was worth it.

Midway through the first half, Owen used all his experience in front of goal to pounce on a mistake by Lúcio. Heskey put a ball over the top and the defender was too busy concentrating on Owen to pick up the flight of the ball, so, as it dropped in behind the unfortunate centre-back, the Liverpool striker was already onto it and bearing down on the keeper.

Even with his injury Owen had too much pace for the defender to reach him, and England's No. 10 chipped Marcos and the ball nestled into the back of the net. It was 1–0 to England in the quarterfinal of the World Cup, and the fans began to believe that this really could be the year that the inventors of football reclaimed the sport's greatest trophy.

But it wasn't to be: just before the break Ronaldinho ran hard and fast through the middle of the England team, brushing off Ashley Cole, before laying the ball off for Rivaldo's sweet finish. If the defence had remained firm until the interval, it might have been a different story, but conceding so close to half-time had a huge psychological effect. England no longer looked like winners, and four minutes into the second half they were behind.

Again, it was the genius of Ronaldinho that left England reeling, as he lobbed Seaman with a free kick from forty yards; and, although the buck-toothed entertainer was sent off for a tackle on Mills in the fifty-seventh minute, the damage was already done. Playing with a one-man advantage, Eriksson's side still looked clueless, pumping long ball after long ball forward, more in hope than expectation. It was a sad end to a tournament that had promised so much for an incredibly talented squad, but the Brazilians held on easily for a 2–1 win and England were on their way home.

Seaman was distraught after the game, but none of his teammates were blaming him. 'I'm very sorry for David because it will probably be his last World Cup, but I'm sure he will bounce back from this at club level,' Owen said, looking to the future. 'We've got to take as many positive things out of this as we can and move forward in four years time. You can't play at your maximum all the time and I'm glad to be part of such a good side. We're all looking forward to the future.'

With four more years' experience and a fully fit squad, England would be among the contenders at the next World Cup, and Owen thought that the absence of one of his teammates was felt particularly strongly in Japan and South Korea. 'Of course, we missed Steven Gerrard. He could have made a difference for us,' the striker told the *Liverpool Echo*. 'He is a great player now and will be an even better one in the future but this time it just wasn't to be. Things like injuries happen in football and we just had to get on with it. To be fair to everyone in the squad most players pulled through for us and did well. The game is about ifs and buts so things like injuries you just have to accept.'

Owen's groin injury forced him off after seventy-eight minutes of the clash with Brazil, and arriving home he told the *News of the World* just how bad it had been. 'I didn't train all week,' he said. 'Except for the day before the Brazil game. I had treatment every day – for eleven hours a day. When it first happened it didn't feel like a bad injury. But then the next day it just went tight. There was nothing torn. It was just a niggle but I could feel it as I went out to play against Brazil. I could run but I couldn't go flat-out. But it was a game I didn't want to miss. It's not every day you are able to face Brazil in the quarter-finals of the World Cup.'

The young striker had proved his worth to the team despite his injury, but it wasn't their day, nor was it their tournament. Brazil went on to win the World Cup, beating a stubborn Turkey side in the semifinals and a fairly average German side in the final. And, looking at the way the tournament unfolded in Japan and South Korea, England had a great shout of winning the World Cup, if only they had beaten Brazil, which, barring a piece of freakish brilliance, they might well have done.

World Cup holders France fell at the first hurdle, finishing bottom of Group A. Argentina and Portugal had also failed to get through to the knockout round. South Korea then used their home advantage to good effect, beating Italy in the second round, courtesy of a golden goal, and Spain on penalties in the quarterfinals. It was a tournament where big names fell and the underdog flourished. It was just a shame that England couldn't take advantage.

10

ALL GROWN UP

'I thought about the implications before, when I knew my girlfriend was pregnant,' he said. 'But since my daughter was born you don't tend to think about it. You just take life as it comes, really. Who knows what it will be like in the future when she grows up, goes to school and she's known as Michael Owen's daughter? I can't imagine what that'll be like for her.'

Michael Owen did a lot of growing up in the 2002/3 season. As well as enjoying the birth of his first child, the Liverpool starlet had to deal with a new Boy Wonder coming onto the England scene and the revelations about his gambling debts making a splash in the national newspapers. He also managed to rid himself, finally, of the persistent hamstring troubles that had afflicted him for the previous two and a half years.

Owen's penchant for gambling made him the subject of gossip up and down the country after one of the Sunday papers found out that the millionaire footballer had allegedly written a £30,000 cheque to England teammate Kieron Dyer. Over a five-week period in Dubai, South Korea and Japan, Owen played cards with Dyer, Teddy Sheringham, David James and Wayne Bridge, apparently running up quite a debt.

Considering the Liverpool man's basic wage, believed to be £60,000 to £80,000 per week, with an estimated £2.5 million a year off-field earnings on top, it was not a sum of money that would cause him to lose any sleep. But it was a huge amount of money to the man in the street, considerably higher than the average annual wage in Britain.

With another report alleging that over a two-and-a-half year period he had staked a total of £2.2 million with various firms, the millionaire footballer came out to defend his clean-cut image, and deny accusations of a gambling addiction. 'I fully accept that high-profile sports people like me are role models for youngsters and I would never encourage anyone to gamble,' Owen said. 'I've done nothing wrong. I can't believe some of the hurtful allegations that have been thrown at me, especially as they're so obviously inaccurate. I would never deliberately do anything to embarrass my club, my country, myself and, most importantly, my family.'

But, as a horse owner and fan of racing, Owen would continue to enjoy a flutter on the gee-gees. 'This publicity will not stop my love for horses,' he added. 'They're my main hobby outside of football.'

Long before the furore over his betting broke across the tabloids Owen had enjoyed a mixed start to the season. Liverpool made it to November before suffering a domestic defeat, but the normally prolific striker made it to the end of September before scoring a goal in open play. Gérard Houllier had strengthened the squad considerably after the World Cup, bringing in Senegalese duo El Hadji Diouf and Salif Diao and the French midfielder Bruno Cheyrou for a combined fee of £19 million. Diouf was the

African Player of the Year and had impressed at the World Cup, helping Senegal into the quarterfinals on their World Cup debut.

Milan Baroš also arrived from Banik Ostrava. Having initially signed for the Reds midway through the previous season, the twenty-year-old striker had continued to play in the Czech Republic until a work permit could be acquired. With new additions to the front line, Houllier decided not to extend the loan deal that had brought Nicolas Anelka to Anfield, and he also allowed Jari Litmanen to return to his old club Ajax.

But, before Owen could begin work with his new strike partners, he needed to regain his fitness for the new season. 'We've been given three weeks off and I'll rest as much as I can in that time,' Owen told reporters after the World Cup exit. 'Then I'll look forward to another attempt at winning the title with Liverpool. But my first resolution for the new season is to get rid of all the problems with injuries which have affected me in the past.'

To banish his injury problems once and for all, Owen began a series of strengthening exercises on his damaged hamstrings to build them back up to the level they were at before his initial tear at Elland Road in April 1999. On top of all the normal pre-season training, he did a lot of extra work on his legs, and, when the season started with the FA Community Shield, he was clearly not at his best.

Liverpool lost 1–0 to Double winners Arsenal in Cardiff, and although the Reds began their competitive season solidly there were few goals from the usually prolific Owen. He even missed a penalty in the game against Aston Villa. But the Reds beat Villa and Southampton without Owen's goals, and then drew with Blackburn, before the diminutive poacher grabbed his first of the season with a penalty in the 2–2 home draw with Newcastle.

'Of course, I'm pleased to get a goal, but it didn't win us the game,' he told the Press Association. 'So there's a tinge of disappointment there as well. I had some good chances and of course I'm disappointed not to have scored a few more, but I know that if the chances do keep coming then I will score goals.'

It was a great boost for Owen ahead of his first England game of the season, where he once again deputised for skipper David Beckham, who was injured. Having scored in his first two games as England captain, Owen was clearly motivated by the armband, but he couldn't find a way through against Portugal, and the friendly ended 1–1.

Owen was partnered upfront at Villa Park by twenty-one-year-old Leeds striker Alan Smith and, although it was the first time he had been the elder statesman upfront for his country, it certainly wouldn't be the last. Still one of the first names on Sven-Göran Eriksson's team sheet, Owen was now part of a strong squad at Liverpool and found himself rested for the game away against Bolton.

The idea was to keep Owen fresh for the game against Valencia in the Champions League, and Houllier apparently told him that he would play in the Mestella Stadium; but Baroš and Emile Heskey played brilliantly in the 3–2 win at the Reebok Stadium and the manager had a problem. In the end, Houllier decided to drop Baroš, despite a brace against the Trotters, and he paired Diouf with Heskey against Valencia.

As an obvious problem with the rotation system came to light, Owen sulkily sat out the 2–0 defeat in Spain. He returned to the team for the Anfield match against West Bromwich Albion, but Owen wasn't enjoying the rub of the green in the autumn of 2002 and he bungled his second spot kick of the season, to increase the talk of his demise. But his teammates rallied round him, and goals from Baroš and John Arne Riise meant that his miss wasn't costly.

Sami Hyypia was quick to defend his teammate. 'Michael was very unlucky on Saturday,' the Finnish defender told the press. 'He missed the penalty and a couple of other chances and I really felt sorry for him. He's going through a period where the goals aren't going in at the moment but he'll soon turn things around. Everyone in the squad will help him get through this spell.'

Houllier had always stood by his men, and Owen hadn't turned into a bad player overnight. 'I have always supported him – and I always will,' the Frenchman said to the press. 'OK, things aren't going the way he wants them to at the moment, but I don't believe in it being bad luck. Michael's all-round game has improved, he's moving all over the place on the field to create space and he's working very hard. I'm sure that, because of the work he is putting in, he will eventually get the success he deserves. It's just a pity for him that if he had managed to convert most of his chances he would be the Premiership's leading scorer at the moment.'

The rehabilitation had taken its toll on Owen and he wasn't as sharp as usual on the pitch, but as his extra training eased off a level the England attacker was soon back to his best. He didn't score in the Champions League draw with FC Basel, but, after four minutes of the Premiership clash against Manchester City, Owen scored a first goal of the season from open play.

In typical Owen style, he followed it up with plenty more, as he grabbed a hat-trick in the 3–0 win at Maine Road, and the European Footballer of the Year was back to his goalscoring best. His celebrations, especially that for the third goal, belied the calm face he put on things afterwards when asked about his drought. 'The truth is there was not much wrong,' Owen said. 'I wasn't unduly happy about the way I'd been playing. Of course, the thing that was missing was goals. But I've been through spells like this before and I will again. I knew how to deal with it. The most important thing was my self-confidence stayed intact. I don't think I'll ever lose that. And as long as I still believed in myself I didn't see any reason for me to change anything.'

No one doubted that the goals would come again – it was just a question of when. And, after Owen flashed home Danny Murphy's corner from six yards out, he refused to smile, taking no satisfaction from the end of a barren spell that went on too long, having gone eleven games without a goal in open play. It was only when he put a crisp finish to a Steven Gerrard pass that he allowed himself a grin, but having completed his hat-trick late on he wheeled away in a celebration almost maniacal by comparison with his usual efforts.

Liverpool beat Spartak Moscow 5–0 at Anfield to help steady their European course in Group B of the Champions League, before Owen continued his return to form with the only goal of the game at home to Chelsea. The win took Houllier's side to within two points of Arsenal at the top of the table, since the Gunners had started the season in the same phenomenal form as they had finished the last one. But, despite Owen's early lack of form, Liverpool had almost matched the Champions, and with the little man back to his best it was hoped they could really challenge the Londoners for the title.

Points were just as important for England when Owen joined his international colleagues for the start of their Euro 2004 qualifying campaign. Eriksson could count himself lucky that Owen had played his way back to form at club level, when his No. 10 scored the winner after eighty-two minutes. The Three Lions went behind to Slovakia after twenty-four minutes, but Beckham equalised with a free kick before the Liverpool striker's goal spared England's blushes late on.

The match was marred by racist abuse directed at England's

black players, and scuffles in the crowd, and Slovakia proved to be a very hostile environment for Owen and his teammates as they heard gunshots from their hotel through the night, but they returned home with three valuable points and faced Macedonia at Southampton's St Mary's Stadium four days later in another qualifier.

England were a shambles on the south coast and not even Owen could rescue a win against the Balkan side. Following David Seaman's error in the World Cup, he allowed an Artim Šakiri corner to float over his head and into the far corner of the goal without anyone else touching it. Eriksson's side fought back from a goal behind twice to draw 2–2, but Seaman's treatment after the game left quite an impression. The abuse and ridicule that the formerly great keeper got in the fallout from what proved to be his final international game astounded Owen, and in time it will be interesting to see whether the young striker calls time on his own international career, like Alan Shearer, rather than face the possibility of being hounded out by media and public persecution, like Seaman.

Back at club level, Liverpool maintained their hounding of Arsenal with a 1–0 win over Leeds in Yorkshire without Owen, before the hit man returned to grab his second hat-trick of the season in Russia. Spartak Moscow took a shock lead midway through the first half, but Owen's treble meant that the Reds won 3–1 and were now second in Group B with seven points from four games.

It was the first time Owen had scored in Europe for eleven months and his manager was delighted with his return to form. 'Michael deserves special credit,' Houllier told the press. 'It's a tremendous achievement to score a hat-trick away in Europe. A month ago he was getting stick for not scoring. But he has a habit of getting important goals for us.'

Owen got another important goal for Houllier as they returned to league action with a 2–1 win over Tottenham. It took an eighty-sixth-minute penalty from the in-form youngster to beat Spurs but he could do nothing to stop Valencia completing a double over his side with a 1–0 win at Anfield four days later. Rafa Benítez's team had embarrassed Liverpool in the Mestella six weeks previously on their way to a 2–0 win, and the humiliation was completed thanks to Francisco Rufete's shot, which deflected in off Hyypia.

Owen helped Liverpool to recover quickly from the defeat with two more goals against West Ham the following Sunday, as the Reds kept their title challenge on track. It took Owen's tally to ten goals from his last seven starts, and made a mockery of the early-season criticism that he had had to put up with.

Houllier had never doubted him. 'He will have a tremendous season,' the Anfield boss said in the *Independent*. 'Physically he is stronger. He works extremely hard for the team, drops when he has to drop, runs across defenders, runs off the ball when needed. It looks as if his pace and strength are getting there.'

The prolific striker was in unstoppable form, and, although Liverpool's fine start to the season was about to come to an end, Owen continued to score as his club's season unravelled around him.

Liverpool saw their way past Southampton in the League Cup without Owen, before making the trip to Middlesbrough, where their unbeaten start to the league season came to an end. Having won nine and drawn three of their opening twelve matches, the Liverpool players were starting to believe this could be their year. The fans were, too. But Dudek made a huge mistake for the only goal of the game and, by the time leaves were back on the trees, the Reds' title dreams were gone. After all of their excellent early-season form, Houllier's side failed to win any of their next eleven Premiership matches.

It wasn't just their domestic form that suffered, however, as Liverpool found themselves out of the Champions League and into the UEFA Cup after they failed to beat FC Basel. Houllier's side were lucky to get away with a point against the Swiss champions after going three goals behind inside the opening thirty minutes, but Murphy, Vladimir Šmicer and Owen hit back in the second-half to draw 3–3. Sadly, the result left Liverpool third in Group B and out of Europe's premier club competition.

The UEFA Cup provided some welcome respite for Liverpool in the poor run of form as they saw off Vitesse Arnhem with 1–0 wins home and away, courtesy of Owen's goals, but in their league things remained dour. A 0–0 draw at home to Sunderland was followed by defeats to Fulham, Manchester United at home, Charlton and Sunderland.

A League Cup win lifted the Liverpool spirits somewhat and they then drew their next three games – against Everton, Blackburn and Arsenal – to stumble into 2003. There was joy for Owen on a personal level, however, as he told the press that he was to become a father for the first time, with his girlfriend Louise expecting to give birth the following spring. 'I've had a few exciting moments in my career but nothing that compares to how I felt when Louise told me the news,' he revealed. 'We're both really delighted and excited at the prospect of being parents for the first time. We're very much in love, and we get on very well together and have a lot of fun.'

There was little New Year cheer for the Liverpool fans on the first day of 2003, however, as they lost 1–0 in Newcastle. Owen summed up the problem at Liverpool in an interview with the *News of the World*. 'The main thing that is affected when you are on a run likes ours is your confidence,' the twenty-three-year-old said. 'Players are afraid to try anything for fear of making a mistake and sometimes even finding one of your own players with a simple pass becomes difficult. Sometimes you are wary of launching an attack in case it breaks down and you concede at the other end. It is not physical or anything to do with a lack of ability. It is very much a mental thing.'

Liverpool beat Manchester City 1–0 in the third round of the FA Cup to lift spirits, but their form was still patchy as they lost their League Cup semifinal first leg 2–1 away to Sheffield United and then drew 1–1 with Aston Villa at Anfield. Owen got the goal that provided the Reds with their first point of 2003, and the following Saturday they beat Southampton away to record a first Premiership win for more than two months.

Any on-field respite that the victory provided was short-lived for Owen, because it was then that his gambling debts came to prominence through the national press. A spokesman for the player moved quickly to calm stories that had become so exaggerated as to allege that Owen had gambled upwards of £2 million in the previous two years. 'Michael's father, Terry, has confirmed that he opened an offshore betting account two or three years ago and has also used this to place bets for friends and family, occasionally for Michael,' the spokesman said. 'Michael's gambling losses probably total about £30,000 to £40,000 over the last couple of years. Although the sums represent a tiny percentage of his earnings, Michael and his family know how important even £100 is to a normal household. It was not long ago that their family of seven lived together in a tiny house in a North Wales village.'

Owen kept his head down and remained focused on scoring goals for Liverpool, and in their next game the occasional gambler hit the jackpot as his extra-time strike took the Reds to

Cardiff for the League Cup final. As they trailed Sheffield United 2–1 from the first leg, Diouf scored after nine minutes, and, with away goals not counting double until the end of 120 minutes, the semifinal went to extra time.

The little striker got his goal after 107 minutes and he was more than happy to tell the press what it meant to him after the game. 'The headlines about me over the past few days haven't really bothered me but I could have done without them,' Owen said in the *Daily Mirror*. 'The main thing for me tonight was to do my talking on the pitch. And now we are looking forward to going to Cardiff for the final. It is a great place for a final because the atmosphere is so special.'

More important than the gambling stories for Owen, though, was the opportunity to play in a League Cup final, and the memory of watching the 2001 final from the dugout clearly still hit a nerve in the usually affable goalscorer. 'If picked, it will be a great occasion to be involved in,' Owen told reporters after his strike sealed a 3–2 aggregate win in the semi. 'It's down to the manager.'

Houllier clearly felt that he owed his striker for the horrible memory of two years before. 'The last time we reached the Worthington Cup final Michael was in the dugout, so he deserves to play now,' the manager said. 'His attitude was brilliant that day. I will always remember when Jamie Carragher scored the winning penalty: Michael was jumping up, celebrating and punching the air. That tells you something about him.'

But there was still plenty of action before the latest in Liverpool's trips to Wales, as the Reds crashed out of the FA Cup to Crystal Palace, and continued to stutter in the Premiership, while Owen welcomed Merseyside's new Boy Wonder into the England setup.

Liverpool drew 0–0 at Selhurst Park in the fourth round of

the FA Cup, and were confident of beating the underdogs back at Anfield. But the Reds succumbed 2–0 in the replay and were left with just the UEFA Cup and the League Cup to hope for as trophies. In the Premiership, Houllier's side twice came from behind to claim a point from Champions Arsenal at Anfield, and they beat West Ham before drawing with Middlesbrough as the goals began to elude Owen.

The Liverpool striker's latest mini goal drought was in stark contrast to that of his latest striker partner for England. For the friendly against Australia, Owen started but Everton's Wayne Rooney broke his new teammate's record to become England's youngest-ever debutant, when he appeared at half-time at Upton Park after catching the eye with many exciting appearances in the Premiership.

Eriksson's side lost the game 3–1 after making eleven substitutions at half-time, but Rooney made a good impression and appeared more than capable of playing at the international level. 'I can see similarities in our reputations,' Owen said of his new international teammate. 'But not similarities as players. He's probably more mature physically than I am now and he's probably got more hair on his chest – and I'm twenty-three.'

Owen played only forty-five minutes against the Australians, but it was still another game without a goal, and the criticism was building up once again. 'I would be lying if I told you all this leaves me indifferent,' he revealed to the press. 'I'd like to be more consistent, and I have to be. But I'm only twenty-three and at the start of my career. People often forget that because I've been at the forefront for some years now. So I still have lots of things to learn – as well as plenty of time to make progress.'

His latest barren spell lasted only a month, and Owen once again hit top form after grabbing one goal. The breakthrough strike came in a 2–1 defeat away to Birmingham, and Owen scored again in the next game to register his twentieth European goal for Liverpool. His strike in the 2–0 win over Auxerre secured his club's progress into the quarterfinals of the UEFA Cup, and equalled Ian Rush's Liverpool record.

In the next round Liverpool would face Celtic, the side against whom Owen scored his first European goal, and the team that most of his father's side of the family support. 'It's great to have equalled Ian Rush's record, very pleasing,' the striker told the press. 'Anything can happen now. As soon as we came out of the Champions League we fancied that we could do well in this competition. Now a tie against Celtic is a dream for us. I remember playing there when I was seventeen in 1997. I scored and I'll remember that game for the rest of my life. I hope we can experience that atmosphere again.'

Owen's next game was at one of his other favourite grounds, as Liverpool faced Manchester United in the League Cup final in Cardiff. Playing at the Millennium Stadium brought Owen a new happy memory from the country he'd lived in all his life as he scored another late goal to win some silverware. Five minutes from time he struck the ball past Fabien Barthez to make it 2–0 and effectively end the game and guarantee a trophy in what was fast becoming a disappointing season. 'Certain grounds give you a buzz – and the Millennium Stadium is a lucky ground for us,' Owen said after the game. 'I scored twice here when we won the FA Cup against Arsenal a couple of years ago and that was my greatest moment in football. The atmosphere here is incredible. It's a very special place and I'm delighted we've made it even more special with this win.'

The Reds could yet make 2002/3 a success with both the UEFA Cup and qualification to the next season's Champions League to play for, and Owen was determined that they would. 'We must use the win over United to help us move on and move forward,' the goalscorer said after the game. 'We just have to make sure this result kick-starts a run for us now.'

They certainly went on a run in the Premiership, where they won seven out of their next eight games, but Liverpool weren't to repeat their UEFA Cup success of 2001, as they lost 3–1 on aggregate to Martin O'Neill's resilient Celtic side in the quarterfinals. Owen was back in the goals stakes, too, as he scored in wins over Bolton, Spurs, Leeds, Fulham and Everton. He didn't get one against Manchester United but none of the Liverpool players did, as they lost 4–0 at Old Trafford, the soon-to-be Champions exacting harsh revenge for their League Cup defeat.

Owen was on fire and he transferred his goalscoring form to the international stage, grabbing the second goal in England's 2–0 win in Liechtenstein to help give the qualifying campaign a much-needed boost after the dismal 2–2 draw with Macedonia. The victory closed the gap to Group 7 leaders Turkey to two points and, with England's next game against the World Cup semifinalists, they were still in a strong position. 'We expected to win here,' Owen said after the game in Vaduz. 'The main thing was the three points and the main game now is the Turkey game. We knew that was going to be the big one.'

Owen lined up alongside Rooney for the first time in the big match at Sunderland's Stadium of Light, and, although Owen went off after an hour with a back injury and the scores still level, his seventeen-year-old partner impressed everyone in his full debut as England beat the Turks 2–0.

'Wayne did really well,' Owen said after the game. 'I think the Turkish defenders were worried by the pace we had upfront and we knew we could surprise them. It was a shame from his point of view he didn't have many chances, but he had a great game and a goal probably would have capped it all nicely for him.'

There was no trouble finding the goal for Owen at club level, however, and, although Charlton kept him quiet as Liverpool won 2–1, the young striker marked the start of a memorable week with four goals in a 6–0 win over West Brom. Owen's second was his hundredth Premiership goal for the Reds and he dedicated the impressive haul to his soon-to-be-born baby. 'Louise is expecting to give birth on Thursday,' the centurion said. 'And by our next match I'll probably be a dad, so the ball will be a nice present for the new arrival.

'It's a great honour to join players like Ian Rush, Kenny Dalglish and Roger Hunt. I'm told Hunt has the all-time record of 245 League goals for the club. I'm not thinking about that now.'

Owen was more concerned with the impending arrival, and on Thursday, 1 May 2003, Gemma Rose Owen was born at Countess of Chester Hospital, the hospital where both the infant's mother and father had been born, in the very same maternity ward, even. Louise was admitted to the hospital on the Wednesday night; there were no complications and the newest addition to the Owen clan arrived naturally at 3.30 pm the next day weighing a healthy 6 pounds 8 ounces (3 kilos).

'This is the most amazing moment of my life,' Owen told the press. 'I think I was more nervous than Louise. We're very proud parents and look forward to spending time together as a family.'

Making a rare public statement, Louise was quoted as saying, 'This is the happiest day of my life. I'm very tired but delighted. Gemma is absolutely gorgeous.' Owen had rushed from training to be at her bedside but his new baby's excellent sense of timing meant that he didn't need to skip any matches for the birth.

A couple of weeks after Gemma was born, Owen spoke more freely about life as a father. 'People have asked me to compare it to scoring a goal, but Gemma's birth came with an excitement unlike anything I've ever known,' he said in the *Liverpool Echo*. 'I'm not ashamed to say I shed a few tears. In fact I'm proud to say it.

'We were praying for her to arrive on time without being induced because of my heavy football commitments. It's only just starting to sink in for me. I get home from training and realise I have a new baby waiting for me. It's a fantastic feeling. I've watched Louise changing nappies and I've been trying to get the hang of it. It looks a bit technical for me at the moment, but after a few viewing sessions I reckon I'll be ready for it.'

But, with two games left of the league season, Owen's technical prowess was still needed on the pitch, where Liverpool were desperately chasing fourth place and a chance to play in the Champions League the following season. Their hopes were knocked by losing to Manchester City at home, and they headed to Stamford Bridge for the final game knowing only a win would be good enough to get them into fourth.

Liverpool and Chelsea were level on sixty-four points from thirty-seven games, so it was a winner-takes-all clash with a potential jackpot of £20 million for the victor. Despite going ahead through Hyypia, Houllier's side eventually lost 2–1 and would have to play in the UEFA Cup the following season. They had finished fourth, third and then second in successive seasons, but there was to be no league title to complete the run in 2003. Instead Liverpool were fifth, a massive nineteen points behind Manchester United. 'In the previous years we had been getting closer and closer,' Owen told journalists. 'When we started off great this season, I think everyone thought this was our year. We never said it in the press, but I think that was the general feeling around the ground, among the supporters and among the players. Then it went downhill and you lose a bit of confidence in yourself, in the team, in everything, really. Hence we had a lot of bad results.

'If we can restore that confidence, have everyone believe in each other again and get on a good run – maybe we need one or two more players – I think we can win the League in the next year or the next couple of years.'

Owen's form had fluctuated throughout the season from red-hot to ice-cold, and, although he matched his best-ever total with twenty-eight goals – nineteen in the Premiership, seven in Europe and two in the League Cup – he was disappointed with the ones that got away, but he had an explanation for them. 'I've been working an awful lot harder in the gym this season,' Owen said to reporters. 'I had to if I wasn't going to be plagued with injuries for the rest of my career. I've had hamstring problems that I've never quite got over and it's mostly because I haven't put the work in on my legs.

'Trouble is, it's hard to do the weights with so many games all the time. You don't want to do them the day before a game in case your legs get too heavy or the day after because you're tired. So, with match day itself, that's three days you're not in the gym. With two games a week, that's six days at a time you haven't done the training and that's no use.

'So I took a decision that I would bite the bullet and do the weights every day except right before matches. If it means I lose a bit of sharpness, so be it – it's only for one season. But if I don't get my legs sorted now I'll be out for ten or fifteen games at a time for the rest of my career, and I'll never get into a rhythm.'

His fitness was clearly benefiting from the change, as Owen played in fifty-four matches for Liverpool and six for England between August and May, but his season still wasn't over. With a whole month from the end of the league season until England's Euro 2004 qualifier against Slovakia, there was plenty to be done before Owen and his international teammates could take a break. First stop was a week in South Africa.

The trip was a clearly a public-relations exercise, with England heading out to the country hoping to stage the 2010 World Cup, and, although it gave Owen and his teammates the opportunity to meet the incomparable Nelson Mandela, England seemed to take little from the football match they played, drawing 0–0 and losing Beckham to injury.

Eriksson's squad then spent one week training in La Manga before facing Serbia & Montenegro in a friendly at Leicester's Walkers Stadium. Owen led England out for the fifth time as captain and goals from Gerrard and Joe Cole gave the Three Lions a morale-boosting victory a week before their qualifier.

On 11 June 2003, Owen again led out England wearing the captain's armband, but this time the opponents were Slovakia, and the twenty-three-year-old Liverpool striker was winning his fiftieth cap. His appearance made history on two counts, since he became his country's youngest ever captain in a competitive match, and beat the previous record of the youngest Englishman to a half-century of caps by two years. Owen wore the honour well, and claimed two goals to turn around the game, winning 2–1 after going behind.

Owen's brace, a penalty and a header, helped to transform an embarrassing first-half performance into a victory, as the Liverpool striker showed once again that he scored when it mattered. 'Ending the season with a win was exactly what we were looking for,' the skipper said the next day. 'I can't remember as good an England performance as the one we gave in the second half last night.'

The three points maintained a gap of two points between England and group leaders Turkey, but with England's game in hand they knew that two victories and then a draw in Istanbul would take them to the European Championship. It was a healthy position to be in, going into what would be a very short summer break for Owen, who had just ten days off before pre-season started.

11

IT'S MORE IMPORTANT
THAN THAT...

'The horse, Isabelle, reared up on her hind legs so violently that she ended up vertical,' he told the *Daily Post*. 'Louise stayed on at first, but Isabelle lost her balance and fell backwards, dumping her full weight on Louise. She let out a terrible scream when the horse crashed on top of her. I felt my insides collapse.'

Michael Owen described the horror he felt the day that the mother of his child fell in a riding accident, which left her in hospital for a month with a fractured pelvis. Louise made a full recovery, but, with their baby only eight months old, it was a tough time for the young family and made a mockery of Bill Shankly's oft-quoted reference about football being more important than life and death.

The Liverpool season had once again started in hope and expectation, and Gérard Houllier had made further additions to his already impressive squad. Steve Finnan and Harry Kewell joined from Fulham and Leeds respectively but by far the most significant transfer of the summer as far as Owen was concerned was the one that took David Beckham from Manchester United to Real Madrid. As Beckham's vice-captain at international level, Owen was interested to see how 'Golden Balls' fared in *La Liga*, having previously spoken of a desire to expand his horizons.

Liverpool's German international Dietmar 'Didi' Hamann had spoken to Owen about the merits of playing abroad, and the England hero had taken it all on board. 'You would definitely broaden your experience by going abroad,' Owen told the Press Association. 'There are plenty of options there for me. I don't think there are many players these days who would stay at a club from the age of eleven– like I was when I joined Liverpool – to the age of thirty-five.

'Dietmar points to the French side gaining the experience to win the World Cup and I think hardly any of them were actually playing in France. It is probably because the Spanish, Italian and English leagues are the best, where you can learn a lot from different players. Didi has done it himself and by moving abroad he's been very successful and it has furthered his career. There is no doubt it helps your game.'

With Owen's competitive edge, it would be only a matter of time before he tested himself in a foreign environment, unless the Reds matched his trophy aspirations. 'If Liverpool are winning the League every year, there won't be any decision to be made,' the ambitious striker told the *Daily Mail*. 'I am moving into a new house soon and all my family are close by. I have lived there all my life. You don't just jump up and go. I am happy at the moment. If we are a successful team, I will always be happy.'

Having scored twelve goals in the last fifteen games of the previous season, Owen carried his success into the new season, but Liverpool's form was more varied. The Reds lost to Roman Abramovich's new Chelsea on the opening day of the season, despite Owen's scoring his first of the season with a twice-taken penalty, and they drew their next two games 0–0.

In England's first game of the new campaign, Owen added to his international tally in the friendly win over Croatia. But before Eriksson's side played again the Liverpool striker helped his club to their first win of the season, scoring twice at Goodison Park as they beat Everton 3–0. 'I didn't have a good record in the derby until the last couple of years,' Owen said afterwards. 'So it's nice to score today, especially here.'

Following Liverpool's recent success as a counterattacking team, Houllier had begun to play slightly more adventurous football and the subsequent early-season results had led to a certain amount of criticism for the Frenchman. With Owen's goals bringing three points from the neighbours, things were looking up, but the poacher insisted they hadn't been as down as the critics had said. 'Everyone watches TV, sticks the radio on and picks up papers, so you get a general feeling of what the fans are thinking,' added Owen. 'I'm not trying to fool anyone that we've been brilliant before Saturday, but I don't think it's been as bad as has been made out.'

With the Reds' poor start to the season, and their continued reliance on Owen's goals, newspaper talk also turned to his impending contract negotiations. With only two seasons left on his existing deal, Liverpool were keen to sign their talented striker to a longer contract rather than see him walk away as a free agent as Steve McManaman had done four years earlier, in 1999. Owen seemed in no rush to sort it out, saying, 'The club's indicated they're ready to talk. We haven't set a date yet, but I'm sure we will discuss things soon.'

Having risen to the top of the tree at Anfield, Owen was undisputedly England's best striker with fifteen goals in the thirty games since Eriksson took over, but the debate raged on as to who should play alongside him in the European Championship qualifying campaign. Owen's partnership with Heskey had taken Eriksson's side to the quarterfinals of the World Cup, but Wayne Rooney had continued his development at Everton and was looking every inch an international player, despite his youthful impetuosity. 'I don't think anyone would have any fears about picking Wayne,' Owen said. 'He played against Turkey and if anyone's going to wind you up, I think they probably would. He's not played too many games, but I think his temperament is very good. He's a winner.'

After drawing 2–2 at home to Macedonia eleven months previously, Owen and his teammates were desperate for revenge in Skopje. 'It wasn't a case of us not trying,' Owen said of their first match, in the *Daily Express*. 'But rather a combination of things. When you score twice at home you expect to win, but we didn't defend well. We didn't create enough chances and, to be fair to Macedonia, they played well also. It was a kick up the backside for us in a lot of ways.'

That kick gave England the impetus to win their next three qualifiers against Liechtenstein, Turkey and Slovakia and they extended that run to four with a 2–1 victory in Macedonia. Owen failed to score against the Macedonians but he did get the opener four days later, when Liechtenstein came to Old Trafford.

England won the game 2–0, and Owen's strike was his twenty-fourth for his country, taking him level with Geoff Hurst in eleventh place on England's all-time goalscoring records. 'I'm not even thinking about that,' Owen claimed in the *Liverpool Echo*. 'If you look at the figures I'm not even halfway to Bobby Charlton's record yet so there is a long way to go. Obviously every time I score one goal for England it gets mentioned again, but I don't think it's something I would be considering until I got nearer forty.

'To match the record of someone like Sir Geoff Hurst obviously makes me very proud though. He was a great player. There are some great names on the goal-scoring list and I've noticed the next one up on twenty-six is Bryan Robson. So hopefully I can get closer to that one first.'

Once again, in one of his prolific spells in front of goal, Owen was soon breaking another record at club level as he overtook Ian Rush's European goalscoring record for Liverpool, taking his total to twenty-one with the equaliser against Olimpija Ljubljana in the UEFA Cup. Owen had followed his goalscoring exploits with England by grabbing two for the Reds in an away win over Blackburn, and then scored a penalty as Leicester were dispatched the next Saturday.

Those goals had set him up nicely for the trip to Slovenia where he finally pulled away from Rush. Owen had scored his twentieth European goal seven months before, so his seventy-eighth-minute header made the record all his. Ever the team player, Owen dismissed the significance of the goal, and concentrated on the 1–1 draw secured on a difficult away trip. 'Of course I'm proud of the record,' he told the press. 'But more important was that I contributed to a good result for the club. When I first came into the Liverpool team people talked about how quick I was and that I could score goals, but they also said I was not very good at holding the ball up, or that I had no left foot and didn't score with my head.

'Now, with a lot of work, I feel I've proved that there's a lot more to my game. I believe that I've improved my game. I hope this is evident now. I'm proud of the goals I've scored with my head for England, and it was another header on Wednesday. I've worked to improve so many parts of my game. I'm happy now that people are noticing.'

Having beaten Rush's Deeside total at schoolboy level, Owen

had taken a far more important record off the legendary Welshman, and knew that he would have to see Rush the next day, since he was now one of the coaches at Melwood. 'I work with Rushie at the training ground and he is a tremendous influence on me,' Owen told the *Daily Post*. 'He is always urging me to go out and break his record and if there is one person who will be happy for me, it's him.'

Owen continued his pursuit of goals and records with a further strike against Charlton, but Liverpool went down 3–2 at the Valley and followed that with a 2–1 loss to Arsenal at Anfield. His latest goalscoring run had come to an end, but, worse than that, the prolific striker had picked up a shin injury with only a week to go until England's trip to Istanbul for their Euro 2004 qualifier. Ironically, Owen hurt himself tackling his international teammate Ashley Cole, and he had to watch on television as Eriksson's team qualified for the big tournament without him.

Topping the group heading into the last game, England needed only a point against Turkey, and they secured it by drawing 0–0. Beckham put a penalty over the bar, but Sol Campbell and John Terry were superb at the heart of the defence and the clean sheet saw them through. Terry played only after Rio Ferdinand missed a drugs test, and the punishment of the Manchester United defender served only to strengthen the resolve of the England squad, which would help them when they travelled to Portugal for the European Championship the following summer.

England had survived Owen's absence but things were different at club level, as Liverpool stuttered their way through the next three months with few appearances from the former European Footballer of the Year. After missing the Reds' win over Olimpija Ljubljana and the loss to Portsmouth, Owen was rushed back to face Leeds where he scored what would be his last goal until February.

His strike helped Liverpool to beat the Yorkshire side, but Owen clearly wasn't 100 per cent fit and his injury flared up in his next run-out, away to Fulham. Houllier's side won 2–1 at Loftus Road but Owen had to miss another two games to let his ankle heal.

He returned for a 0–0 draw against Middlesbrough, but the striker was rusty after his spell on the sidelines. 'Owen played well but he needs a couple more games to be at his best,' Houllier told reporters after the game at the Riverside Stadium. 'It was a very strange game. There were not many chances – Middlesbrough are difficult to beat.'

Enduring a tough time in the league, Liverpool were enjoying more success in the UEFA Cup, and Owen played against Steaua Bucharest at Anfield as the Reds beat the Romanians 2–1 on aggregate, after drawing 1–1 away. But the victory once again came at a cost as Owen tore a thigh muscle late on. Having finally put his hamstring nightmares behind him, he was enjoying a particularly unlucky spell, and was forced out of Liverpool's next eight games.

Without their leading scorer, any team will struggle, and so it was as the Reds dropped ten points from their seven next league matches, and saw off Yeovil in the FA Cup. The dodgy Premiership form increased the fears that Liverpool would miss out on Champions League football again, and talk once again turned to Owen's potential departure.

Interest from Spain followed with Real Madrid and Barcelona both making their intentions clear. The Nou Camp boss Frank Rijkaard broadcast his opinion on Spanish radio, saying, 'Owen fits the philosophy of Barcelona. He's a player who has done a great job at Liverpool – but maybe his work there is coming to an end. He is a super-dangerous player in the box. He is exactly the kind of player I like but that doesn't necessarily mean we will be able to afford him.'

The feeling was that Owen would stay with the Reds if they qualified for another crack at the Champions League, but another season in the UEFA Cup would see the diminutive striker moving to pastures new. Such talk was very poorly received by the Liverpool fans, who felt Owen was holding the club to ransom and said as much at every opportunity, whether on radio phone-ins, websites or just down the pub.

Owen insisted it was just a matter of time before his new deal was sorted out, and moved quickly to calm the fears of the Kop. 'I want every supporter to know that I'm as committed to Liverpool as any player at the club. I have been the same ever since I first came to Anfield as an eleven-year-old,' he told the *Liverpool Echo*. 'I believe my ambitions can be fulfilled at Liverpool. I find it a little insulting that, after twelve years' service, my loyalty is being questioned. I have signed five contracts with Liverpool, and on each occasion they have been sorted out very quickly and satisfactorily.'

As the New Year started, the thoughts of the outspoken fans were the last of Owen's concerns, because football became entirely inconsequential when his long-term girlfriend, and the mother of his daughter fractured her pelvis falling from her horse, Isabelle. On 4 January 2004 the mare reared up and, although Louise managed to stay in the saddle, Isabelle lost her balance and fell backwards, landing on her rider. Worse was to come, however, as the fall left the pair jammed up against the fence and as the horse struggled to get up she again collapsed onto Louise. The horse tried to get up for a second time, and did so successfully but only after kicking and trampling all over Louise.

Owen and team-mate David Beckham were perceived to have had relatively unsuccessful careers at *los Merengues*, but in fact, Owen's goals-to-minutes-played ratio was the highest in La Liga in 2004/05.

Back in England, Owen debuts at Newcastle United in September 2005, up front with ex-England partner Alan Shearer, Toon legend and the man whose formidable goal record Owen hoped to build on at St James's Park.

Given a warm welcome to the north east, Owen got off to a decent start to the 2005/06 season but just four months in, and only a fortnight after a perfect hat trick against West Ham, his Magpie career shuddered to a halt when he suffered a broken metatarsal playing against Tottenham Hotspur.

Back in familiar action for England after recovering from his foot injury, Owen played a full 90 minutes and grabbed a goal against the Reggae Boyz of Jamaica in a pre-World Cup 6-0 thrashing.

Disaster! After a 1-0 win in the second group game, against Paraguay, fate struck a cruel blow again as Owen's cruciate knee ligament gave way against Sweden in the third World Cup game, spelling the end of his tournament and another long period out from the game he loves.

Away from football, Owen finds plenty to occupy him, with his young family, on the golf course and with his successful stable of racehorses.

Above left: Owen in Manchester United's famous number 7 shirt.

Above right: Lining up for his new team in Champions League action in 2009.

Below: Owen scores against Wolfsburg – the goal was part of his first hat trick for United, on 8 December 2009.

Manchester United fans have taken Owen to their hearts and he has returned the favour, giving his all and contributing vital goals.

IT'S MORE IMPORTANT THAN THAT...

The footballer comforted his wife until the ambulance arrived and then travelled with her to the Countess of Chester Hospital, which had been the scene of much happier times months before. X-rays revealed seven breaks of the pelvis, one of which ran down into the hip, meaning Louise would be unable to put any weight on it for a number of weeks. She also fractured a vertebra in two places and broke a finger, but the good news was that, although there were many breaks in the pelvis, the displacement was minimal and Louise spent only a month in hospital – better than her last bad fall: when she was sixteen Louise broke her femur and had to spend thirteen weeks in traction.

Liverpool were very understanding with Owen during her rehabilitation, and, because he was part of such a large, tight-knit family, there were plenty of other people on hand to help Owen look after Louise and baby Gemma. It was an especially difficult time for the young family and it was the first time mother and child had been separated for any significant period of time. On average, Owen visited the hospital more than once a day, but playing away matches meant that he was absent for a couple of days at a time, and he would make up for it when he wasn't on the road, popping in on his way to and from training.

After initial treatment, Louise was moved to a private hospital, which gave them more privacy from the intrusive press. And, back in the saddle at the earliest opportunity like all keen riders, Louise was on Isabelle by May.

Less than a week after Louise's fall, Owen made his long-awaited return from injury, starting the home win over Aston Villa. After such an extended absence he was expectedly short of his best, but everyone was disappointed when he failed to find the net in six consecutive starts. Owen merely put it down to bad luck.

'Normally, when I come back from a layoff, I need a lot of matches and training sessions because I feel really rusty,' the usually prolific hit man told the *Daily Star*. 'This time I feel as though my touch has been quite good immediately. I don't feel I have lost a lot of sharpness despite being out. To be honest, since I have been back, it has been the same pattern as every other time I have returned from injury. It always takes a couple of games to get my touch and get the goals flowing. I know I just need that first goal to go in to get me going again because I feel fine in every other respect.'

With Owen firing blanks, the Reds were wallowing in fifth place in the Premiership, and a defeat at Tottenham and draws with Wolves, Everton and Bolton did little to improve their position behind Charlton. But, after three minutes of the game against Manchester City, Owen claimed his first goal for three and a half months, setting Liverpool on their way to a 2–1 win, and his good news didn't stop there.

On Valentine's Day the millionaire footballer proposed to his school sweetheart, and she said yes. Owen confirmed the story in the *Daily Post*: 'Yes, we did get engaged on February 14, which was also Louise's birthday. We are very happy together.'

Things weren't so happy on the pitch for Owen, though, and, although he scored another goal the next day in Liverpool's game against Portsmouth in the FA Cup, Pompey fought back for a draw, and won the replay 1–0 at Fratton Park, where Owen missed a penalty.

The cup defeat left Liverpool with just the UEFA Cup and the Champions League place to concentrate on, and some portions of the Anfield faithful felt let down by a squad that had promised so much, and they vented their anger at the manager in the form of death threats.

It was an outrageous and astonishing indication of how twisted a take on reality some people have concerning football, and Owen was shocked and appalled. 'I'm as surprised by it as anyone else,' the striker said to the press. 'There's no place for this kind of thing in the game or in life. But, knowing the manager as I do, he's handling it in the right way. He knows it's just one person and he'll see it for what it is. You can't let it get to you.

'Sadly these days, it seems it can happen to anyone in a high-profile position. I can't tell you how many times it's happened to me now. It's the kind of thing I don't think would have happened years ago but is happening to people in the game regularly now. There are things in football and in life which change, and this is one of the aspects which have come into football more and more.

'If you speak to David Beckham I'm sure he'll tell you this kind of thing's happened to him about a dozen times. It's happened to me lots of times as well. It's not just letters, either: some things have happened that could be considered even worse. To be honest, although it's unfair and awful, nothing surprises me any more. It should not happen and it's not acceptable – but it's almost become part and parcel of the game nowadays.'

Owen's older sister Karen had recently been the victim of an attempted carjacking near her home, and, while the press reported it as a kidnapping attempt because of who her brother is, it later transpired that the criminal duo involved were interested only in her BMW X5.

A traumatic season off the pitch continued for Owen a month later as the builder who had been in charge of redeveloping the his North Wales mansion committed suicide. Mike Flynn was accused of taking money out of the Owen account to use for his own purposes. His company, called Décor by Design, did work at Lower Soughton Hall in Northop after Owen purchased the property late in 2001, for £1.6 million. He had employed Flynn to begin the work of transforming the Victorian building into the house of his dreams.

Owen and his young family had moved into this new home in September 2003, finally able to enjoy the small stable yard and surrounding golf course. But the outrageous cost of building work soon came to light, and Flynn, a family friend of fifteen years, was accused of overcharging by approximately £1.2 million. On the morning of a court hearing when the wealthy builder faced the possibility of jail, he is believed to have taken a fatal overdose of pills.

Owen was shocked and saddened by the untimely death of a man who had been a friend before they fell out over the alleged embezzlement. He refused to be distracted by the traumatic off-field events, however, and, although not enjoying his most abundant spell in front of goal, he continued to score the goals that propelled Liverpool to fourth place in the final Premiership standings. A Champions League spot was the most the Reds could hope for after their dismal winter, but they couldn't find any solace in Europe, where they lost to Marseille in the last sixteen of the UEFA Cup.

Liverpool overcame Levski Sofia 6–2 on aggregate in the third round, with Owen scoring one in Bulgaria, and, although he wasn't hitting the back of the net as often as he would like, his overall contribution to the team had come on immeasurably in recent years – and he was still contributing. 'I scored in consecutive games a couple of weeks ago, so it's not been too bad,' he said to the *Liverpool Echo*. 'Sometimes it's not all about goals. I was happy to have put in a decent all-round performance on Wednesday as much as scoring. When you play away in Europe, you know you've got to put in a lot of hard work defensively too and I thought I did that quite well in Sofia.'

After their good work against the Bulgarians, Liverpool were drawn against Marseille in the next round, where they lost 2–1 in France after drawing 1–1 at Anfield, and there would be no repeat of the European glory of 2001 in 2004. Houllier's side were still dropping far too many points in the league, and they drew with Leeds before losing 2–0 at Southampton, where Owen missed yet another penalty. Having also missed a spot kick against their south coast rivals Portsmouth in the FA Cup the previous month, Owen was determined to make up for the disappointment when Pompey travelled to Anfield for their next match.

He revealed to the press how upset he had been after the cup defeat. 'That Portsmouth game was one of my lowest points ever,' he said. 'The manager was under intense pressure, and I missed a penalty. That day was as bad as I've ever felt. I was so low – I wanted to wrap up the entire season there and then. I remember thinking, "I wish someone would give us that fourth place and we could finish it all now."'

Starting with the Pompey encounter, Liverpool had eleven games left to claim fourth and Owen kept them on track with a brace at Anfield in a 3–0 win. They followed that with two wins and a draw as they kept four clean sheets in a row, and Owen took his total for the season to sixteen, with two more goals against Blackburn. Liverpool were hitting form at just the right time to gain the Champions League place that a club of their standing demands, but on Good Friday they faced Thierry Henry in unstoppable form.

Owen added to Sami Hyypia's goal to put the Reds 2–1 up at half-time at Highbury, but the mercurial Frenchman hit a second-half hat-trick to keep Arsenal's incredible unbeaten league season on track. After losing 4–2 in London, Liverpool dropped five more points at Anfield in their next two games, and their season appeared to be coming apart at the seams.

In such a poor run of form, the last thing Owen would have wanted was a trip to Old Trafford, but the game against Manchester United proved to be an elixir for their season, because Liverpool won 1–0 and followed that with two wins and a draw to finish fourth.

Owen scored against Birmingham and Newcastle to take his total for the season to nineteen from his thirty-eight appearances, not a bad return considering his injuries, the lack of sleep that can be associated with a new baby, the off-pitch trauma of his fiancée's fall, Mike Flynn's suicide and his sister's attempted carjacking.

But Liverpool had fallen well short of their expectations as they finished fourth in the league, thirty points behind Arsenal. 'We know it hasn't been a very good season,' Owen told reporters. 'The players know it and the manager knows it. Getting into the Champions League is always crucial at the start of every season for Liverpool, but fourth place is not good enough for a club like this, especially as the top three have finished so far ahead of us. We can't settle for fourth. There's got to be an improvement next season.'

After such a poor campaign, finishing well off the title pace, and knocked out of all three cup competitions early, Liverpool would struggle to keep hold of their former European Footballer of the Year. And talk of Owen's future once again filled the back pages.

'We'll sort something out this summer one way or another,' Owen said at a press conference for his boot sponsors. 'We've still got to talk about things, but as I stand there are no problems. I'm still here this year and another, so I'm still under contract. But I won't just up and leave on a Bosman [ruling - free transfer]. We've entered discussions and the first set is about where the club is going. It's never been about money but I want to win things. I've never wanted to be anything but successful and I know the manager shares that view.'

But, on 24 May, Gérard Houllier was sacked after six years at Liverpool, and the news filtered through to Owen on his pre-Euro 2004 training camp in Sardinia. The board had decided that Houllier had taken the club as far as he could and it was time for a new man at the top. The Reds had been building and building under their French manager with the Treble-winning 2000/1 season and the second-placed finish the following year the pinnacle of their achievements. But they had been unable to take the next step to Champions and had fallen away with fifth- and then fourth-placed finishes in the Premiership. The League Cup is all well and good, but what the Liverpool fans wanted more than anything was a first Premiership trophy, a first title since 1990, and it seemed that was beyond Houllier.

His success had been built on a solid defensive game, which had excelled in cup competition, but, as he tried to make his team more attractive to watch, he had taken away some of their efficiency, and the results had suffered. Despite all that he had done for the club, it was time for Anfield's favourite Frenchman to move on. And he wasn't the only one.

12

EUROFLOPS

'We built up our expectations so high because we thought we had a real chance of winning it,' he told the *News of the World*. 'And, despite what the cynics are saying about us, we did perform well and went out in very unfortunate circumstances. No one can tell me that any of the teams left in the tournament are better than us. I am sure that there is disappointment in France, Italy and Spain just as there is in England. But, unlike the others, the defining moments did not go in our favour and there was little we could do about that.'

Michael Owen was talking after England were knocked out of Euro 2004 on penalties, and he was right to be disappointed – it was a tournament that seemed to be dominated by the underdogs and was eminently winnable for an incredibly talented England squad.

Preparations for the tournament had been undermined by Chelsea's courting of Sven-Göran Eriksson, in March. The FA had scared off the Russian superpower by signing the Swede to an extended contract with a pay rise – it had done little to help team morale, but the players were still bullish ahead of their trip to Portugal. 'I believe we will win it,' Owen said of the forthcoming tournament. 'We've played together a lot of times and have a lot of experience. We have some of the best players in the world, especially in the really important positions.

'We've got two of the best centre-halves in Europe and plenty of cover despite all the injuries and suspensions. We've got so much quality in midfield: Frank Lampard's grown out of all proportion this year; Steven Gerrard – I've never played with anyone like him; and then you've got the Beckhams and Scholeses of this world, who would walk into any team.'

But the one player who had everyone in England excited was Everton's Wayne Rooney. 'Wayne could be a real surprise package,' Owen went on. 'He has a lot of everything. He holds the ball up really well, he has a great touch and scores goals.'

Rooney had scored only nine goals in his second season on the other side of Stanley Park, but there was plenty more to his game than finishing, and Owen was looking forward to improving their burgeoning partnership. 'Unfortunately for Liverpool, I've had a bit of a break halfway through the season so hopefully it's fortunate for England and myself,' Owen said. 'I'm really looking forward to the tournament – I think all the lads are.'

England's start to the European Championship was highly anticipated by everyone in the footballing world, as they had been drawn in Group B with France, Switzerland and Croatia, and their opening game was against their cross-Channel rivals.

But, before heading to the Iberian Peninsula, Owen had one week of training with the squad in Sardinia. As on the trip to Dubai with England two years earlier, the players were encouraged to bring their families, and so Gemma and Louise joined Owen in the Mediterranean. They stayed with him when the squad returned to England for 'The FA Summer Tournament' in Manchester.

Owen had played only one match for England since September, because injuries had forced him out of the vital qualifier with Turkey and friendly defeats at the hands of Denmark and Sweden. His only appearance for his country in 2004 had been against Portugal in February, and, having not scored in the 1–1 draw with the Euro 2004 hosts, he was without an international goal for nine months.

He soon amended that poor record as he claimed the opening goal against Japan after twenty-five minutes at the City of Manchester Stadium. Gerrard unleashed a low shot from outside the area and his Liverpool teammate was on hand to tuck it home from six yards. England couldn't hold onto their lead, however, and Shinji Ono hit an equaliser early in the second half. The result left Eriksson's side without a victory in five matches since they had beaten Liechtenstein in September, not ideal form for a team supposedly capable of winning the European Championship.

England still had one more dress rehearsal before their heavyweight bout with France, and, unluckily for Iceland, the Three Lions chose the perfect time to roar. Playing again at Manchester City's stadium, Eriksson's side beat the visitors 6–1 to win their mini-tournament. Owen played only the first forty-five minutes and was unfortunate to have a goal disallowed for offside, possibly wrongly. But it was clear who the star of the show was.

Rooney scored two goals, and was a real threat throughout the first half. If he hadn't been replaced at the interval it would have been a question of how many he would or could score. It was scary to think that he was still just eighteen years old.

A certain player had made a massive impact in France '98 at

the same age, and he was asked whether Rooney could do the same at Euro 2004. 'Let's hope so,' Owen said. 'We all hope he's that sort of player who does things like that. Some players are just lucky and do rise to the occasion. It's a bit of an unknown with Wayne because we've never seen him play outside the Premiership, apart from a few qualifiers for England. But the early indications from the games he's played in so far are that he does like to score spectacular goals. Let's hope he can do it as well in the big games. He can be anything he wants. It's up to him how he wants his career to pan out and how much he's willing to sacrifice everything else.'

Owen's achievements were put into perspective when Rooney was asked how much he remembered of that night in St Etienne, when he was just twelve years old. 'I saw the game at my nan's,' the new Boy Wonder told reporters. 'Afterwards, I went outside to recreate it with my mates. People have tried to compare me with Michael Owen at France '98, as I'm the same age as he was then. But I don't think, "This is my chance to do what he did." I'm just a young lad and I want to do my best. But we believe we can do it.'

Rooney's performance against Iceland had given the whole of England a boost ahead of the summer's big tournament, and the game had also helped to settle down Eriksson's starting XI. The team had become quite settled in personnel, as David James had taken over from David Seaman between the sticks and Gary Neville, Sol Campbell, John Terry and Ashley Cole had grown as a back four in the absence of Rio Ferdinand. Owen and Rooney had marked themselves out as the best two attackers and were developing as a partnership. But it was in midfield that there was a problem as the manager tried to balance in the considerable talents of David Beckham, Paul Scholes, Lampard and Gerrard. 'I'm excited about those four players, however they play,' Owen said. 'They've got unlimited ability and they're all world-class players who score goals and create goals.'

All four were undoubtedly top-class players, and England were lucky enough to have them all at the top of their game, but they were too similar and without a left-sided player among them. In the draw against Japan they had lined up in a diamond with Beckham right, Gerrard left, Scholes at the top and Lampard holding. This system gave Beckham and Gerrard the freedom to display their indefatigable energy up and down the flanks. But pushing Scholes forward had meant that Rooney's space behind Owen was cramped. And playing Lampard – a man who made his name by rushing forward to smack the ball goalwards from outside the area – as a defensive midfielder was just absurd.

Eriksson improved things against Iceland by selecting a flat midfield with Scholes moving to the left and Gerrard joining Lampard in the middle, with the central pair being trusted to know when to hold and when to push forward. Although the first team played only the first forty-five minutes in the final warm-up game, it was clear that this system worked better than the diamond, so they stuck with it for the entirety of the Championship.

The England squad took up residence in a hotel in Lisbon, and, although family weren't allowed to stay in the room, Louise and Gemma were staying nearby and the rest of the Owen clan popped over at one time or another to watch their most famous relation.

Interest in England's match with France had been growing almost exponentially since the draw was made, and, as kick-off approached, the fans' excitement reached fever pitch. Despite their failure in the Far East, *Les Bleus* were still rightfully considered one of the best teams in the world. And, with so many of their players earning a living in the United Kingdom, Owen and his teammates knew first-hand just how good their opponents were.

'I believe France are the best team in the world at the moment,' the Liverpool striker said in the *Evening Standard*. 'I don't want to add to the hype but for me they are better than Brazil. We are respectful of them but not fearful of any of their players. We go into this game on their level and not playing for a draw or anything like that. I feel in perfect shape to go and play well. Everything is in place. This group are the best I've ever been involved with and we might not have as good a chance of winning a tournament as we have in the next two years. But it's on the day that matters and a big part of football is the preparation and we've prepared well.'

England's preparation was disrupted by a hamstring injury to Terry, but Ledley King replaced the Chelsea captain in the back four, and he didn't let anyone down as Eriksson's men exceeded expectations in their big game. They led for most of the match after Lampard headed home a Beckham free kick in the first half, but it was not to be their day and France won thanks to two late strikes from Zinédine Zidane.

Beckham even had a second-half penalty saved with the score at 1–0, and it was his Real Madrid teammate Zidane who had the last laugh with a fantastic free kick in the ninetieth minute and a cool, calm and collected penalty deep into injury time. The spot kick came after a Gerrard back-pass sold David James very short and the Manchester City keeper brought Thierry Henry down in the area.

It was a harsh finish to an otherwise excellent England display. Owen was determined to take the optimistic view from the game rather than dwell on the cruel ending. 'The positive side is that, over ninety minutes, we've played the favourites and defending champions and been better than them,' he said after the game. 'The frustration is that we've lost but that's football. If we'd played badly and lost, then we would have had problems. We can't feel sorry for ourselves or blame luck. You need luck to win a tournament and we didn't have it on Sunday night, but let's hope it evens itself out later in the tournament.'

Owen was replaced by Darius Vassell after sixty-nine minutes in Lisbon, and, although he hadn't had so much as a look at goal, the Liverpool man had held a very high line stretching the distance between the French defence and midfield, allowing Rooney more space to create problems, such as when the eighteen-year-old was brought down for Beckham's penalty. With only two goals in his previous six internationals, Owen's lack of opportunity against the French was viewed in some quarters as a display of poor form, and there were calls for him to be left out of the team for the next match.

But Eriksson remained loyal to the striker, whose goals had done so much for him. 'I will not drop him,' the Swede said at a press conference 'I'm not worried about Michael Owen. He is a great player. You can be sure he will be scoring goals for England for many years. He looks sharp and I'm sure he will play even better than against France.'

Neither Owen nor the other Merseyside marauder had made it on to the scoresheet in the opening game, but the young duo made an impact in the next game, against Switzerland.

England welcomed back Terry at the expense of King, but it was Rooney who stole the show against the Swiss. He announced his arrival as an international force, on the biggest stage, with two goals in a 3–0 win in Coimbra. The first, after twenty-three minutes, made him the youngest player to score in European Championship finals, when he headed home Owen's cross; the second made the game safe with a quarter of an hour left to play.

Gerrard added a late third but all the talk after the game was about Rooney's arrival and Owen's supposed demise.

Eriksson again replaced Owen with Vassell in the second half of the match but he dismissed allegations that the two Liverpudlians didn't work as a partnership. 'Wayne and Michael can play very good football together. I've no doubts about that,' the manager said in the *Daily Mirror*. 'It's not a classic partnership with one tall and one small and quick, but they play well together.

'Michael played better in the Switzerland game than he did against France. He was more involved in the game, dropping and taking the ball and making more runs right and left. I think he's coming on and I'm quite sure he will do well. You always have players starting slowly and others who start right at the top. But Michael will score, I'm not worried about that.'

The much-sought-after goal failed to arrive for Owen in their final group match, but England won 4–2 to secure progress in to the quarterfinals. The Three Lions went behind after six minutes, but Rooney again guided his team to victory. Scholes equalised after forty minutes and the young Evertonian scored his third goal of the tournament on the stroke of half-time. In the second half Rooney made it 3–1, and Lampard added a fourth after Igor Tudor had halved England's lead. The 4–2 win gave Eriksson's team second place in Group B, and they were through to the knockout stages, where they would play Portugal.

Owen stayed on the pitch for the whole ninety minutes and had again increased his contribution to the team with one assist, and a hand in two others against Croatia, but the talk was all about England's new Boy Wonder. 'Roomania' was gripping the footballing world and his strike partner still hadn't found the back of the net. 'It bothers me when I don't score,' the suddenly less-than-prolific striker told the press. 'There's always something missing when you win a game and you haven't scored but, if you don't feel that way, then you'll never reach the top.

'Half of me is overjoyed that we're through to the quarterfinals but five per cent of me is disappointed I haven't scored. I like to have the responsibility of scoring goals and I haven't done that yet. It's not like I've been missing chances or anything like that. I had one decent chance against Croatia and chipped it over the bar, but apart from that my all-round game is improving and the bigger the game the more I relish it.'

Facing the hosts in the Portuguese capital for a place in the semifinals of the European Championship was Owen's biggest game since the World Cup, and he was adamant that he could end his goal drought. 'Obviously the next step is to score a goal. I'd love that,' he said to the press. 'It's great to see Wayne scoring all these goals. It takes the pressure off me to a certain extent but, to be honest, I *want* the pressure. I want to be scoring goals. And if we can both click at the same time it will be very good. Wayne is carrying us forward so far, but I still have a big part to play in the tournament. I'm not doubting myself, but the sooner I score the better. Hopefully, there are three massive games coming up for us and I want to be on the scoresheet in each one.'

Owen got part of his wish, since he indeed scored in all of England's remaining games – trouble was, that was only one game, as the Three Lions lost to Portugal on penalties. Enjoying rare luck with injuries, Eriksson picked the same eleven for the third successive game, and England got off to the perfect start when Owen latched onto a defensive error to open the scoring after three minutes.

James hit a long clearance and Costinha was running backwards trying to get a good head on it; but, ever the optimist, Owen immediately ran in behind him in case he didn't get enough on the ball, which he didn't. As the ball dropped, England's now almost veteran striker hit it with the outside of his right boot and into the back of the net.

A nice early goal to settle the nerves should have enabled England to play to their potential, but the players seemed shackled by fear and few of them managed to play to their potential. The team also had to contend with bad luck when the inspirational Rooney was forced off injured with less than half an hour on the clock. The talismanic forward broke a metatarsal in a collision with Jorge Andrade and his tournament was over.

Sadly for England, the team looked clueless without the teenager and they would soon be following their best player out of the Championship. Without Rooney as the focal point of every move, the team had no shape and no structure and they seemed unable to retain the ball. After taking an early lead, England should have gained control of the game but instead the players dropped increasingly deeper, eager to defend their lead, and eventually it cost them.

Portugal found a way through with seven minutes left, and it was no less than they deserved. Hélder Postiga headed Simão's cross past James and the crowd went wild. There was still time for England to attack, though, and, when Owen headed Beckham's ninetieth-minute free kick against the bar, Campbell followed up to bundle the ball over the line. As the players began celebrating, the referee, Urs Meier, saw an alleged push by Terry on Ricardo and the game went into silver-goal extra time.

It was eerily similar to the game against Argentina at France '98, when Campbell had also had a last-minute 'goal' disallowed for a foul on the keeper. And, sadly for England, the end result would be the same.

The first half of the added thirty minutes was very nervy, as neither side was willing to commit too many men to any attack;

but after 110 minutes of the match Rui Costa hit an unstoppable drive from outside the box into the top corner of James's net. With only ten minutes left, England had to attack, and five minutes from time they hit an equaliser, thanks to the Chelsea connection.

Terry nodded down a Beckham corner and Lampard was on hand to swivel on the edge of the six-yard box and smash the ball home, and penalties would once again be responsible for England's exit from a major tournament. Despite missing crucial spot kicks against Turkey and France, Beckham was still England captain and he therefore put himself at the top of the list for the shootout.

As the skipper approached the ball his standing foot dislodged the ball, and when Beckham then struck it he got a horrible contact and sent his effort high over the bar. Owen took England's second penalty and scuffed it down the middle of the goal, because his leg cramped up as he shot, but he got away with it as the keeper dived out of the way anticipating an effort into the corner.

Successful spot kicks from Lampard, Terry and Hargreaves combined with one over the bar from Rui Costa, meaning that at 4–4 sudden-death penalties would be needed to settle the result. Ashley Cole put his away, but Vassell had his kick saved at 5–5. The Aston Villa striker's penalty was well struck and well placed, but Ricardo pulled off a brilliant save and then got up to score the deciding kick. England were knocked out of a fourth major tournament on penalties – and it hurt. Portugal went through to the semifinals, and eventually lost the final to Greece to emphasise just how winnable the competition was for England.

England had many talented players, but, without an obvious left-sided midfielder, playing with three very similar attack-minded men in the middle of the park and overly reliant on Rooney, they had been knocked out of a tournament that they had the quality to win.

Owen defended his captain after the game, joining his manager in criticising the turf. 'The pitch is sand-based and we trained there yesterday,' the goalscorer told the BBC. 'We took penalties and the way a lot of people take penalties puts a lot of pressure on the standing foot. It gave way at the other end yesterday in the practice. It's a big disappointment and it always seems to happen to us. Going out on penalties again is a bitter blow.

'At every tournament there are always five or six teams that are very good and have a very good chance. We definitely believed we were one of them and it's just annoying. It's disappointing. There's no point looking back. We have the World Cup in Germany in two years. Hopefully, we'll be going there with a good, young, fit squad. I'm looking forward to it because of the players we have. Now I'll go on holiday, lounge about and rest the blisters.'

Owen would need his rest ahead of a new season full of challenges at a new club, in a new country.

13

GALÁCTICO

'If I do move, it will be a massive challenge,' he told the *News of the World*. 'But I cannot see myself turning out for another club in this country. Fatherhood hasn't changed my outlook on playing abroad. If it means my daughter Gemma having to grow up living abroad and learning a new language, then fine. I don't see it as negative. But until my contract with Liverpool is sorted out one way or another, nothing is going to happen as far as moving is concerned. I have no reason to move – other than to be successful. If I do go, it will be to win things – nothing else.'

On 13 August 2004 Michael Owen left the club he had joined as an eleven-year-old and joined Real Madrid. The biggest club in the world, the club with more European Cups than any other, *Los Merengues*, or as they have become better known in recent years *Los Galácticos*.

Throughout the European Championship, Owen had been linked with a move away from Anfield. As he entered the final year of his contract, there was no way that Liverpool would allow the former European Footballer of the Year to leave on a free transfer in twelve months' time, so the options were to sign up or go, and in the end Owen went to Spain.

Steven Gerrard had been approached by Chelsea and, although he eventually decided to stay on Merseyside, his long-time teammate decided it was time to seek a new challenge overseas, and went to test himself at the highest level. Liverpool had brought in Rafa Benítez to replace Gérard Houllier, but the Spaniard couldn't persuade Owen to stay, and the England striker couldn't turn down the opportunity to join Real Madrid.

While touring America and Canada with Liverpool, Owen was repeatedly quoted in the press saying how much he loved the club. 'I've been at Liverpool since I was about eleven,' he said. 'Liverpool is in my blood and always will be; no matter what I'm doing I certainly don't want to let the club down. I said I'd never walk out and leave them in the lurch and that still stands. I have a commitment to this club.'

He may have been committed to Liverpool, but he couldn't resist an offer from Real Madrid, so he didn't sign the new contract, and when he arrived back in England word quickly spread that Owen was on his way. The striker was left on the bench when Liverpool faced Austrian club AK Graz in a Champions League qualifier, ensuring he would be able to play for his new club later in the competition. And the move was soon confirmed by both clubs.

Benítez wasn't happy to lose such a talented player so quickly into his Anfield reign, but there wasn't a lot he could do about it. 'When I came here Owen had one year left on his contract,' the new manager told a press conference. 'Real Madrid knew that, and when a big club like them come knocking you cannot control it.'

The fee was believed to be approximately £8 million, with midfielder Antonio Núñez moving to Anfield as a makeweight in the deal, and Owen was soon being unveiled to the press in Madrid. The Real Madrid president, Florentino Pérez, displayed his latest signing, saying, 'I hope Michael Owen will write a new page in the history of this club. We are signing an excellent player.'

Madrid certainly needed to start a new page, after finishing the previous season in fourth place in *La Liga* and without any silverware – an incredible failure for a club the size of Madrid, especially with a wage bill the size of theirs. Owen would contribute on the pitch, but his signing was also hoped to produce more revenue for Real in Asia, where Owen and his new teammate David Beckham had always been popular.

Owen wasn't interested in any of the marketing: he was just excited to get involved at his new club. 'It's a fantastic challenge for me,' he said. 'I'm impatient; I can't wait to put on the famous Real Madrid shirt. I've been to the Bernabéu in the past and now I realise it's the best stadium in the world and home to the best team in the world. I've spoken to Sven-Göran Eriksson and he is pleased with the fact I've signed for this great club. David Beckham often tells me about life in Spain. When I play with England this week I'll probably ask him a lot more questions.'

He was keen to get his young family settled in quickly, and was already lamenting the move away from Anfield. 'I'll come out here with my partner Louise and my little daughter Gemma,' he went on. 'They want to be living with me in Madrid as soon as possible. Liverpool will always be part of my life and I wish them the best of luck in the future. I would like to thank everybody, especially the Liverpool fans, for the marvellous years I spent there. I've been part of that club since I was eleven and it will always be part of my life. That's inevitable.'

Part of the presentation involved Owen's acceptance of his new No. 11 shirt from legendary Madrid striker and honorary president Alfredo Di Stéfano, and his father Terry had been giving him a history lesson. 'My dad has been telling me about the great Real teams of the sixties, about Alfredo Di Stéfano and Ferenc Puskás, two strikers who were just unbelievable,' the new signing said. 'Gento [Francisco Gento López] was apparently the quickest No. 11 my father had seen. Today, I'm so proud to be wearing his shirt.'

It was a good sign that Owen had received a nice low squad number, but there were no guarantees that he was going to be in the starting XI. 'I'm really looking forward to the challenge in front of me,' he went on. 'Raúl, Ronaldo and Fernando Morientes are three of the best strikers in the world – I'm aware of how hard I'm going to have to work to get an opportunity here. Real Madrid are the club of champions. Just being able to train with this group will make me a better player and person.

'Since I was ten I didn't just want to be a footballer: I wanted to be the best footballer in the world. There are still lots of people ahead of me but, if you want to get into that bracket, you have to break out of comfort zones. That, in a nutshell, is why I made the life-changing decision to leave Liverpool for Madrid.'

There were plenty of rumours flying about that Owen's signing had been completed entirely by the president and that the Real Madrid coach José Antonio Camacho didn't want the former Liverpool man. 'Nobody should make mistakes about my wishes: Owen will make Madrid more complete and any players of that quality are welcome here,' Camacho said. 'Owen will mean there is more competition to win a place and keep the other strikers on their toes. Maybe some days they will not be called into the squad.'

Owen's Real Madrid career started with a game in the white shirt of his country, and he got his season off to a goalscoring start with England's second in a 3–0 win over the Ukraine at St James' Park, which continued to prove a happy hunting ground for Owen despite his move. Madrid's first game with Owen on the books was against Wisła Kraków in the Champions League qualifying round, but having signed after the registration date for that round he had to wait another four days to make his club debut.

Raúl and Ronaldo started the game against Real Mallorca, but Owen replaced the Spaniard after twenty-four minutes and created the only goal of the game for his Brazilian strike partner in the Estadi Son Moix. 'Setting up Ronaldo's goal was definitely the next best thing to scoring,' Owen said in the *Daily Telegraph*. 'I had a couple of other half-chances and I would normally expect to bury one of them. You can't have everything on your debut. I'm just pleased to have played for so long and we've got the result.'

Real Madrid's newest striker returned to international duty to help England to two results as they got their World Cup qualifying campaign under way with trips to Austria and Poland. Eriksson came under criticism as England threw away a 2–0 lead to draw 2–2 in Vienna, but Owen stood by the Swede. 'Everyone rates the manager very highly. You want an international manager who creates a great atmosphere and we all get on well. He plays good formations, picks good teams and it's enjoyable coming away with England. He knows an awful lot and his tactics are good. He wasn't happy when he went through a video of the Austria game and it was a mood of disbelief about how we were in such control and let the lead slip. It's just staggering we didn't get three points.'

The Three Lions picked up three points in their next game, winning 2–1 in Chorzów. Owen then returned to substitute duty with Madrid, and replaced Raúl for the final stages of a 1–0 win over Numancia at the Estadio Santiago Bernabéu. 'You don't come into a team like this, with all these players, and expect to walk straight into the team,' Owen said. 'I knew it would be a fight right from the start, and that's obviously what I've got. I'd like to think playing with these players will make me better.'

There was no game time for Owen as *Los Merengues* got their Champions League campaign under way with a 3–0 defeat away to Bayer Leverkusen. 'Everybody's disappointed because 3–0 is not good but we've games to put it right,' he told the press after watching the embarrassment unfold from the bench. 'I always want to play but it wasn't to be. I'm always confident I can do things if I get a chance, but the game wasn't there for me tonight, so I'll wait for the next game. I'll just wait for my chance.'

It was an appalling result and, when it was followed by a 1–0 reverse away to Espanyol, Camacho decided he'd had enough and he quit. Having lost control of the massive egos in the dressing room the former Madrid defender felt powerless and left his assistant Mariano García Remón in charge of the team. 'I can see I'm not going to get this team to perform. I'm not capable of changing things,' the strict Camacho said as he resigned.

Owen summed up the feeling of a lot of the players when he spoke of the latest departure. '*Surprised* is the word,' Owen said. 'I've not been involved in too many managerial changes. This would certainly be the first that happened after three League games.' The England striker had made his first start in the game against Espanyol, but, as Camacho left, a new coach came in with new ideas and Madrid's No. 11 found himself back on the bench. When a second start finally came around Owen was forced to limp off after fifty-two minutes against

Deportivo la Coruña with a thigh strain. The injury kept him out for only a couple of games, however, and he was fit again in time for England's next batch of World Cup qualifiers.

The first of these was one to relish for Owen, since it gave him an opportunity to shine against the country he had lived in for almost all his life. Ahead of the match against Wales, the media began to debate whether the Madrid striker deserved a place in the England team, considering his lack of game time in Spain. But Owen was confident in his ability. 'I know I haven't set the world alight but I'm not concerned,' said the off-form striker. 'I'd prefer people to write nice things, but I'm more than 100 per cent sure that the headlines about me will be reversed.

'I know better than anybody that you can be as low as anything and then be on top of the world. I'm not worried about it. I knew it would be difficult going out to Madrid, but I'm still up for the challenge and I'm still hungry. I know that I'll do well because I'm not a quitter, and I'll fight to the death.'

Owen received a boost when he claimed a goal at Old Trafford, but there was some debate about the goal, as Frank Lampard's shot deflected in off the striker's heel with three minutes on the clock. 'After you've gone a while without a goal you often get one that comes off your backside,' Owen said when interviewed on the BBC. 'Frank is standing by me, so I don't want an argument. But, initially, I thought it just hit me and went more or less in the same path. Having seen it again, it has taken quite a big deflection.'

England went on to win the game 2–0, and, although that goal was eventually given to Lampard, Owen had one of his own four days later. Eriksson showed his continued faith in him away to Azerbaijan, handing Owen the captain's armband in the absence of Beckham, and the Madrid striker repaid his coach's confidence with the only goal of the game in the Tofik Bakhramov stadium.

Named in honour of 'the Russian Linesman' – the man who allowed Geoff Hurst's oft-debated goal in the 1966 World Cup final – the stadium in the Azerbaijan capital was a fitting place for an England striker to return to form. Owen headed home Ashley Cole's cross midway through the first half, and that strike was enough to secure the three points and keep England on top of Group 6 with ten points from four matches. 'It was a great ball from Ashley but it was difficult because the ball was swirling about all over the place,' said Owen. 'It was important for us to win the game – that's the main thing. The fact I scored was secondary. A game's not just about scoring. I can play well and not score. It was also a great honour and responsibility to be captain.'

His two performances for his country had given Owen a much-needed fillip after his difficult start to the season, as he later revealed to the *News of the World*. 'That was the turning point for me,' Owen said. 'That was a "thank you, England" and "thank you, Sven". It was perfect timing and the perfect thank you for sticking by me when I hadn't played every game out here for Madrid. That international week couldn't have come at a better time for me. It made me look forward to playing ninety minutes again because I wasn't playing out here as much as I'd have liked at the time. So, after two good wins, it gave me a lot of confidence to come back to Spain.'

It was good to see that his Real Madrid coach had been taking note of his player's international contributions. 'I think his scoring for England was very good for him,' García Remón said of the former Liverpool striker. 'He needed to play well. I have confidence in two players ahead of him and Owen needs to understand that. But what he has done with the international side is great for him. We consider him to be extremely important to the future of Real Madrid, and sometimes the future comes little by little.'

Little things off the pitch can make a big difference as well, and his house hunting certainly didn't help Owen's early-season form. 'The difficult bit so far has been living in the hotel for eight weeks,' he said. 'It's hard to live in one room with a child who wants to run around the garden. I need to find a house, to learn the language and meet a few people. When things aren't perfect off the pitch they aren't on it, either.'

Things on the pitch started improving for Owen after his return from international duty as he forced his way into the first XI and started five consecutive games for Madrid, and scored in the first four of them. He had been left on the bench for the game away to Real Betis but he replaced Walter Samuel at half-time and did enough to warrant a place upfront with Ronaldo for the big Champions League clash with Dynamo Kiev, as Raúl dropped into midfield.

The Ukrainian side were top of Group B with two wins from their first two games, and Madrid, third on three points, needed a win at the Estadio Santiago Bernabéu to kick-start their European campaign. Making his Champions League debut Owen scored the only goal of the game after thirty-five minutes, knocking in Ronaldo's cross from close range to register his first for *Los Merengues*. 'To score settled me right down and I've been waiting for that moment since I came here,' Owen told the *Daily Telegraph*. 'The one thing I've been lacking is a goal and it was a relief to get off the mark.

'It's a great feeling to score here. To score the winner in a Champions League game in front of your home fans is special. Since I've been here things have slowly got better and better. It's not easy to come to a new country and be stuck in a hotel room, but things are starting to come together on and off the pitch.'

Owen was replaced to a standing ovation after sixty-six minutes, and it was clear that the *Madridistas*' hearts were warming to the little Englishman, as was the coach. 'I was really happy with Michael Owen's performance because we needed a lot of mobility in attack and he provided this,' said García Remón. 'He's improving.'

With the coach happy, Owen started once more when Valencia were the visitors four days later, and the twenty-four-year-old striker repeated his trick grabbing the only goal of the game to give his club three more points. 'It's been an important week for both me and for the team,' Owen said in the *Independent* after his second goal of the week. 'I'm feeling more comfortable all the time and it's always good news to get on the scoresheet. The two wins have given us an important boost and even though we aren't scoring that many goals we are improving.'

As is often the case with Owen, one goal had opened the floodgates and he got another in his Copa del Rey debut against Leganés, which Madrid won 2–1. It was the first time Owen had played ninety minutes for *Los Galácticos*, as the manager took the cup as an opportunity to rest Ronaldo and Raúl, but the England forward was just happy to complete a full match for his new employers two and a half months into his Spanish adventure.

'I have scored my third goal for Real Madrid and I am very happy about it, although the most important thing is that we have qualified for the next round,' he told the *Daily Post*. 'It's not a question of awarding me a medal because the goals are the result of everyone's work. I have always worn a smile, I was simply needing a bit of time, but bit by bit I am getting better.'

Things improved off the pitch as well for Owen as he finally moved into a house. He had found a £5,000-a-week rented mansion in the suburb of La Moraleja, and he felt that knowing he was going to be moving out of the hotel had helped him to turn things around for Real. 'I'm feeling much more confident on the pitch at the moment because I'm much happier *off* the pitch,' the Madrid man said in the *Daily Mirror*. 'I can't wait to unpack my things properly. Living in a hotel for three months is hard work. It was one of the things that contributed to my slow start here. Room service is nice, but just one room between three of us is not ideal. Coming to a new team, learning a new language, living in a hotel all the time, people don't realise how difficult it can be to adapt to these things.'

The newly settled striker made it four from four on the way to a 2–0 win against Getafe, and Owen was certainly enjoying his hot run of form. 'The goal streak will come to an end one day but hopefully that's quite a while off,' he said. 'I'm used to scoring goals and that's my job and it's nice to be able to do it.'

Unfortunately, Owen's streak came to an end, away in Kiev in the next game, but after scoring four goals in his five consecutive starts he was quickly restored to the role of bit-part player after failing to find the net in the 2–2 Champions League draw. He didn't even get consecutive starts for another month and a half, despite grabbing goals as a substitute against Malaga, Albacete and Levante. 'It's always disappointing when you don't start,' Owen said. 'But what can you do when you're playing with a great group of players? You know you're not going to start every game. I suppose next time I'll have to score five in five games.'

Owen did have the honour of playing for his country at his club ground, as Spain entertained England in a friendly at the Bernabéu. In the press frenzy building up to the game, he was asked how things were going in his new homeland. 'At the start I felt the pressure,' he told reporters. 'You're the new lad in the class, and you think all eyes are on you. If you put a foot wrong then it's, "Oh my God! Everyone's seen that mistake and they think I'm a bad player." If you've been here for a while, you even laugh about your mistakes or you get the mickey taken out of you. I'm beginning to lose that feeling, though, and obviously the more you play, score goals and integrate with the team, then it makes it more relaxed.'

Owen lost bragging rights to his neighbours, because England lost 1–0 in the Spanish capital, but he was soon back to impressing the locals in the white shirt of Real Madrid. Any defeat to Barcelona is a bad result for Real Madrid; losing 3–0 to their fiercest rivals and being left seven points behind at the top of the table made Owen's first Madrid game in the Nou Camp one to forget. But the atmosphere would make that very difficult. 'The noise was deafening,' said Owen. 'My ears were ringing at the end. It was louder even than when I went to Celtic Park with Liverpool. It's a kick in the teeth but you can't say all is lost in November.'

Real Madrid still had plenty to play for and there was no one at the Bernabéu even willing to talk about surrender let alone run up a white flag. *Los Merengues* qualified for the last sixteen of the Champions League by beating Roma 3–0 away, but they were still a little inconsistent in the league and would soon hire a third manager of the season.

Owen scored Madrid's first against Racing Santander away, but the Cantabrian side were a resilient outfit and took the lead twice, and it took a last-minute winner from Zinédine Zidane to claim the last points under García Remón. Owen started against Santander and also in the 1–0 defeat Sevilla three days before Christmas, which proved to be García Remón's last game.

But, while the new coach was being lined up, Owen was looking forward to his first winter holiday since turning pro. 'I'm desperate for Christmas but sometimes you don't want a break when you're playing well,' he said as he told the press of his plans to spend it in Liverpool. 'We all get a week off and I'm looking forward to spending Christmas in my house. But I think I'm going to the Southampton game on the 28th and I might go to training at Melwood as well to say hello to the lads.'

While Owen was catching up with his old teammates, Real Madrid got rid of his old manager, replacing García Remón with Vanderlei Luxemburgo. The former Brazil manager took control of Real Madrid over the Christmas break, and Owen didn't start two games in a row under his third manager of the season until the end of February. But Luxemburgo got off to a successful start with seven consecutive wins in *La Liga*, to close a thirteen-point gap on Barcelona to just four points, and he was forgiven his sparing use of Owen.

Despite his limited appearances, the England striker continued to score, and got goals from the bench against Real Zaragoza and Osasuna to help maintain the run. Owen also scored in the Copa del Rey, as Madrid were knocked out by second-division side Valladolid on away goals, and added to his England caps in the dour 0–0 friendly draw with Holland at Villa Park.

The lack of opportunity in Luxemburgo's team was clearly an irritation to Owen, who was shown by statistics in the Spanish newspapers to be the most lethal goalscorer in *La Liga* on account of his impressive goals-to-minutes-played ratio. 'I want to be in the starting XI,' he said to the press. 'I won't sit around and ever be happy on the bench. I don't ever want to be that type of person who's happy with not succeeding. My name's been linked in England with a couple of teams but that's only because I haven't been in the starting XI for a month or two now. It's only natural, I think.

'As soon as the first manager came in I was a sub and gradually played more and more. Then the second manager, it was exactly the same. It starts from scratch again with the new manager. Everything you've done earlier counts for a lot because there are points on the board and the fans have watched. As regards the new manager, the slate has been wiped clean again. You have to start again and impress him because if I don't play well now I don't think he'll be watching the tapes. I won't have much of a chance of playing if I don't do well.'

After scoring the winner against Osasuna, Owen was rewarded with his second league start under Luxemburgo, but Madrid's fine run came to an end with a 2–0 defeat at the hands of Athletic Bilbao. The players may have had one eye on their forthcoming Champions League clash with Juventus, and, although they beat the 'Old Lady of Turin' three days later 1–0 in the Bernabéu, Luxemburgo's team lost the second leg 2–0 in extra time in Italy to end their European campaign.

Owen was reduced to substitute appearances in both games, meaning his first season in Spain would end with only two Champions League starts for the most successful of all European teams. But he was working his way back into the side, and, in between the two games against Juventus, Owen had been chosen for his first consecutive starts of 2005, thanks to Raúl's bout of flu.

A 2–0 defeat away to Deportivo la Coruña further dented Madrid's title aspirations, but Owen got the first goal to set *Los Galácticos* on their way to a 3–1 win over Real Betis before Raúl returned to the first team and the Englishman returned to the bench. Just as Owen's season again seemed to be going through the doldrums, an international week came to the rescue to revive his spirits, and his fortunes in front of goal.

The former European Footballer of the Year had started talking more about a possible return to the Premiership, as he grew increasingly frustrated in *La Liga*. 'If I came home tomorrow, I would know that I have proved my abilities,' Owen said in *The Times*. 'I think about it a lot because I've got a lot of time to think over here and especially when I come back to meet up with England. Every time I join up, I feel I am coming back as a better, stronger player. People wonder whether English players can make it abroad, particularly strikers, and I believe I've passed that test. I'm into double figures and I'm scoring goals as often as anyone in Spain considering my time on the pitch, or lack of it.'

Facing Northern Ireland in a World Cup qualifying game at Old Trafford, Owen scored his twenty-ninth goal for England, as they won 4–0, and, after a victory by such a margin, there was talk of running up a cricket score against Azerbaijan in their next game. One of the minnows of world football, the former Soviet country had lost 8–0 to Poland, and the press were eager to see England get more goals than the Poles.

'There is going to be pressure on us,' Owen told reporters. 'But obviously 8–0 is a score you don't often see in international football. We'll be happy to get the three points and if we can score a couple of goals that's a bonus. Comparisons are bound to be made with what Poland have done and I know the staff and coaches have seen the match. There were a lot of mistakes made in the Azerbaijan team and I don't think they'll make as many mistakes again. Every shot Poland had seemed to go in.'

The quotes must have been twisted on their way through to the Azerbaijan coach, Brazilian Carlos Alberto, as he launched an incredible attack on the England striker, after the Three Lions won 2–0 at St James' Park. 'Who is he, anyway? What has he won? He should wash his tongue and clean David Beckham's boots,' said the 1970 World Cup-winning captain. 'This man, the small one who doesn't play in the Real Madrid first team, said if Poland beat Azerbaijan 8–0, England should score eight goals and he'd score five of them. Where are those goals tonight? This man, this midget, I refuse to talk about him any more. I will talk about Beckham, Rooney, Ferdinand or Lampard but not this midget.'

Owen was adamant about what he had actually said. 'If he checks my pre-match quotes he will realise that I never said anything about scoring five goals,' the England striker retorted to the Brazilian through the media. 'I would never be so disrespectful. He would, though, be perfectly within his rights to criticise my performance – I've certainly had better games in an England shirt. I'll learn from the experience and continue to improve as a player and person because of it.'

The striker's miserable night was compounded by a booking that ruled him out of the autumn clash with Wales. 'I'm not used to the sort of personal criticism that came my way from Carlos Alberto this week, but I had bigger concerns when I flew back to Madrid,' Owen said to the Press Association. 'I was far more upset about the booking that means that I will miss England's next World Cup qualifier against Wales in September.

'I can understand Gazza's tears in the 1990 World Cup semifinal. To miss a qualifying game in Cardiff might not seem as important but, for me, it was shaping up as one of the biggest matches of the year. I will not be playing any cup finals with Real Madrid and it's not looking too pretty for us in the Spanish league, so a trip to a packed Millennium Stadium was something to relish. It has been a happy hunting ground in the past, but now I will have to sit in the stands.'

Things improved on the pitch at Madrid, however, as Owen started the last nine games of the season. He scored the winning goal at Albacete, filling in for a sick Raúl, and got another, far more important goal a week later as Madrid beat Barcelona 4–2 at the Bernabéu. Playing upfront again with Ronaldo, with Raúl returning in the midfield, Owen got the fourth goal as *Los Merengues* closed the gap at the top of the table to six points with seven games left.

'It was one of the best matches I've been involved in,' Owen said after the superb victory. 'I'm pleased with my performance, I'm pleased with everyone's performance – I don't think there was a bad player on the pitch. When a big game comes along you always have that extra edge.'

It was the kind of night that had motivated Owen's move to the world's most famous club, and he received a well-deserved standing ovation when Luis Figo replaced him with ten minutes remaining. 'The fans have really taken to me. I have scored goals consistently and I'm really happy about that,' Owen told the *Daily Mail*. 'We knew that we had to win tonight and six points is still a lot. But there are seven games to go and we will be trying our best. It would be great to win the title in my first season. There are not too many Englishmen who can say they have scored in this match.'

Luxemburgo didn't dare to drop Owen after a win over the Catalan side, and nor should he have done so. Indeed, the Englishman's stock had risen to such an extent that he wasn't even dropped when he didn't score in the wins over Levante, Villareal and Real Sociedad. But the team were working, and they made it six wins in a row with Owen among their number, as they beat Racing Santander 5–0, with the Englishman grabbing one. But *Barca* were also winning and the gap was still six points with only three games left, and Madrid's fading hopes of the title evaporated completely when they drew their next game away to Sevilla.

The home side took the lead, but Madrid struck back when defender Javi Navarro put the ball into his own net under pressure from Owen, and, although a Zidane goal seemed to have secured three more points, a last-minute goal from Júlio Baptista made it 2–2. The result meant that Barcelona needed only one point from their remaining three games to claim a first title in six years, as they had a better head-to-head record, and they got that with a 1–1 draw later the same evening.

'It was really frustrating because we made a huge effort to try to win the game,' Owen told the *Independent* after the title was lost. 'But we have been trailing Barca for much of the season and even though we have put together two good runs of results Barcelona haven't slipped up and it has been very difficult for us to get close to them.'

Having seen the title slip away, Real failed to lift themselves for the Madrid derby against Atletico, and drew 0–0, before closing the curtain on the campaign with a 3–1 win over Real Zaragoza. Owen scored the opening goal, before being replaced at the interval by Luis Figo, as the manager gave the Portuguese midfielder a last forty-five minutes in a Real Madrid shirt.

The Iberian legend had already agreed to leave the Bernabéu in the summer, while Owen's future was far less clear. In his first year in Spain the Englishman had endured some tough times, but had ridden them out. And, by starting the last nine games and scoring four goals in the process, Owen had moved to thirteen league goals for the season.

Including his cup goals, the striker claimed sixteen in total for Madrid, which is a poor return from forty-five appearances, but far more respectable when you realise that only twenty-six of those were starts. Apart from his end-of-season run of games, and another similar sequence at the end of García Remón's reign, Owen had barely started two games in a row. His season had been decimated by inconsistent team selection, but he kept on scoring.

His goals had helped Madrid finish the season on eighty points, second to Barcelona by four points, and he had fired England to within touching distance of the 2006 World Cup. Owen added three more goals to his tally before going on holiday, however, as he grabbed a hat-trick to beat Colombia 3–2 in New Jersey.

Joining the England tour late due to the longer Spanish season, the former Liverpool striker underlined his importance to Eriksson's side with all their goals in the Giants Stadium. It was only a friendly win for England, but the first two strikes were notable for Owen, because they took him level with and then beyond Alan Shearer, Tom Finney and Nat Lofthouse, who had scored thirty international goals each.

With thirty-two goals, Owen moved to fourth on the all-time list of England goalscorers with just Bobby Charlton, Gary Lineker and Jimmy Greaves ahead of him. 'Everyone thought I'd beat Shearer's record in the last game,' the twenty-five-year-old said. 'So did I because I had so many chances. But I've finally done it. It's been a great end to the season for me, I got one at the weekend for Real Madrid and three here.'

Speculation continued about Owen's future, and his past was there for all to see as his old club won the Champions League. Having left Liverpool to play at the highest level and win silverware, Owen was asked about watching his former teammates come back from 3–0 down at half-time, eventually to beat AC Milan on penalties in Istanbul. Despite finishing the season trophy-less in Spain, he had no regrets and was happy for the Reds. 'It was fantastic. It was really unbelievable. Amazing, all those goals. It was incredible,' Owen said to the news agency Agence France-Presse. 'It happens once in a lifetime. How often does a team let a three-goal lead slip by? Italian defences have a history of not giving away much. But, as I said, it's a once-in-a-lifetime thing. It's like in boxing when a guy is knocked down three times and he gets up to win.'

It was the trophy that Real Madrid want above all others, and they were sure to reinforce their squad in their pursuit of the cup they had won nine times. Many strikers were linked with the club, and Owen was realistic enough to know that the decision to stay at the Bernabéu could be out of his hands. 'I spent many years in England, all of my career,' Owen told the press. 'I did well over there and, perhaps, that's why I'm still talked about. If someone comes and tells me there's a club interested in me and that I have to go, then I'll have to do that.'

But, before playing any more football, in Spain or England Owen took advantage of a rare summer without a tournament and finally married his long-term girlfriend Louise Bonsall. The pair married at the Carden Park Hotel near Chester in a very private ceremony in front of a dozen relatives and close friends in June 2005. But they also celebrated their vows with a huge party at their house, and sold the picture rights to *Hello!* magazine. It seemed a bizarre move for someone who had always been so private with his private life, but, when the wedding plans began to add up, they decided it would be easier to have one group of paparazzi policing the event rather than have hundreds of photographers trying to sneak their lenses into the celebration. After their splendid wedding, the happy couple enjoyed a fabulous honeymoon before Owen returned to football – and a third club.

14

MORE METATARSAL MADNESS

'The only consolation is it has happened at the end of the year and not towards the end of the season,' he told the press. 'It means I have plenty of time to be fit for Newcastle and England. I've spoken to the doctors and it's going to be at least two and a half to three months. Plenty of people I know have had this injury – Wayne Rooney, David Beckham, Gary Neville and Steven Gerrard – so I'll talk to them to see how to deal with it.'

Michael Owen had a right to be upset after breaking a bone in his foot, which effectively ended his season in December, but he took the injury in his limping stride and focused on getting fit for the World Cup. He had taken to life at Newcastle like a duck to water, and had immediately got back among the goals on his return to Premiership, but what should have been a promising season building up to the big tournament in Germany ended with Owen in a race to prove his fitness.

With Owen's lack of game time during the previous season,

there had been constant transfer rumours emanating from both England and Spain, and the footballer's quoted words revealed much of his mindset during those times. 'I've never wanted to be a *Galáctico*, with all that it means,' he told the *Daily Mirror*. 'I only want to be on the back pages and playing good football. Then you can call me what you like. It doesn't matter.

'I've never really wanted the off-field attention. I just want to play football and be remembered for being a decent player when I retire and for what I did so that I can enjoy the rest of my life. Maybe I'm not considered the main man but if I had that much of an ego I wouldn't have come here to play. There are plenty of main men at Real Madrid and I've never been one of those who want to jump out and say, "I've got to be the one." I'm happy in the background.'

The summer had been spent in limbo with various voices from the Madrid hierarchy stating unequivocally that Owen was staying, while the press continued to speculate on his likely destinations. And the old saying 'there's no smoke without fire' was certainly true in this case.

Real Madrid signed two extra strikers to bolster their forward line in the summer of 2005, and, after the Brazilian duo Robinho and Júlio Baptista signed, it became apparent that Owen was no longer wanted at the Bernabéu. 'During my four days off, there've been two big signings confirmed by the club and I can understand why this has resulted in speculation about my future,' Owen said in a statement. 'Real Madrid contacted my advisers over the weekend and explained that they wanted me to stay but that they would not stand in my way if the right opportunity arose for me to return to the Premiership. With the knowledge of Real Madrid, there's been brief dialogue with three or four Premiership clubs, although no formal negotiations of any kind have taken place. I look back on the past year with a lot of good memories. If I had to make the decision again, I would still have chosen Real.'

With the World Cup only ten months away, there was no chance of Owen's staying at a club where he would be fourth- or fifth-choice striker, and it was time for him to head home to England. He was linked with Chelsea, Arsenal, Manchester United and Liverpool before Newcastle United emerged as the leading contenders. The previous season's Premiership top three all had specific systems and strikers that worked within those systems. Chelsea had Didier Drogba, Arsenal had Thierry Henry and Manchester United had Ruud van Nistelrooy, while Liverpool were reluctant to spend £17 million on a player they had sold twelve months before for around £8 million, and had already recruited Peter Crouch to strengthen their attacking options.

Owen's preferred destination was Anfield, having spent so many years there, while the lack of European football at St James' Park certainly didn't count in the Magpies' favour, after they were knocked out of the Intertoto cup by Deportivo la Coruña. 'I said that my ideal situation was to start the season in the Real Madrid team and if not I would prefer to return to Liverpool,' Owen told reporters. 'The Real Madrid president understood and said he would try to help me achieve this. If the transfer can't be finalised in time, I've agreed to go to Newcastle United but only on a one-year loan. I need to be playing regularly in World Cup year.'

Newcastle manager Graeme Souness revealed that his club's bid had been accepted by Madrid, and they were waiting on Owen's decision. 'It's now up to the player and his advisers to say yes or no to the move,' the Toon boss told the *Daily Telegraph*. 'I'm a confident sort of person; I'm an optimist and a pessimist at the same time and I'm hopeful that Michael Owen will join us and he obviously knows players at our club and he will be speaking to them about what we can offer.

'Real Madrid have spent a lot of money on new strikers and I would imagine that like any other club they would like to recoup some of the money on a player that might not be involved too much this year. It's common sense, as far as I see it.'

As the transfer window drew to a close there was talk of a bid from Everton, but the offer from the Red half of Merseyside was 'too little, too late' and, rather than face another season on the bench, Owen plumped for Newcastle.

Having completed the deal, the former European Footballer of the Year revealed he was looking forward to linking up again with his old England colleague Alan Shearer. 'Alan was a great help throughout and instrumental in my decision,' said Owen in the *Liverpool Echo*. 'I had spoken to him many times over the past few weeks and he should work for the Newcastle tourist board when he finishes playing football. He even offered to give up his No. 9 shirt but I have declined. No. 10 will do for me. I will regard playing alongside him in his last season as an honour. He has been, and still is, a great striker and there is no way that Newcastle should be where they are in the table with that calibre of player.'

Souness compared his new signing to that which brought Shearer home nine years previously. 'He's someone who can become a legend with Newcastle United fans,' the Newcastle manager said of Owen. 'In football, the hardest thing to get in your team is someone who puts the ball in the back of the net, and Michael is the best at doing that. I can understand people who liken it to the signing of Alan Shearer. I'd say it's the biggest transfer I've been involved in as a manager of any football club.'

Owen signed a four-year deal worth an estimated £80,000 per week, and there were 20,000 Geordie fans at St James' Park to see him presented with his new black and white No. 10 shirt. And he told them of his mission statement. 'My job is to score goals and I can guarantee I will bring that to this club,' Owen said. 'I can absolutely promise the fans the only thing they will get from me is 100 per cent and my aim, like everybody at the club, is to win things. That's what I'm in football for and if my goals lead to Newcastle winning trophies then that's my job done.

'It'll be amazing because this club hasn't won anything for so long. When they do, and not if, it will be like winning the World Cup. Newcastle is a massive club and the support here is unbelievable. I'm so excited, I really want to play for them straightaway. I had a great season in Spain and scored a lot of goals but I wanted to get back to the Premiership. It's where I belong. I'm pleased because I had three options, Real Madrid, Liverpool and Newcastle. When it came down to it a deal couldn't be made with Liverpool and I desperately wanted the buzz of waking up on a Saturday morning knowing I was playing in the Premiership, so I chose this option.'

Owen was joined at St James' Park by a number of other signings as Newcastle looked to build on their disappointing bottom-half finish in 2004/5, and in came Scott Parker, Albert Luque, Nolberto Solano and Emre Belözoğlu to help the trophy challenge.

While still a Real Madrid player Owen had got his season under way with a substitute appearance in England's crushing friendly defeat, losing 4–1 to Denmark in Copenhagen, and in beautiful and yet depressing symmetry his first game as a Newcastle player was another away defeat for England. Owen had missed the 1–0 win over Wales in Cardiff through suspension but returned to the team days later as Eriksson's side lost 1–0 to Northern Ireland.

Before the game in Belfast, Owen had spoken of his joy to be back in the demanding spotlight of his home country. 'The pressure is intense on us and that's what makes English football great,' Owen told the press. 'I go on to a pitch knowing every eye is on me. When you make one bad pass, you know it's going to be spoken about the next day because there is that intense pressure.

'Moving out to Spain for a year, I missed a bit of that. I picked up a paper and didn't understand what they were saying about me. I wake up every morning and there's a drive in me. I switch on the telly and see the leading goalscorers' chart, the next page flicks over and it's the league table. I'm permanently driving myself to do better and better. There's a buzz in waking up, and having it in my blood every day to grit my teeth and do whatever's needed.

'Spain was fantastic, but it's a lot more relaxed than here. I like waking up knowing that I'm going to a stadium that'll be deafening, that whatever I do will be on the back pages of the paper, either rubbish or good. I can't expect to get praised all my life. I know as much as anyone that criticism is part and parcel of the job and I bounce back.'

A defeat against Northern Ireland brought plenty of critique with it, and Owen dealt with it admirably. 'It was a poor performance and it wasn't good enough,' he told a press conference. 'It was good to get back playing competitive football, but not in that manner. It was a disappointing result but at least I'm playing, fit and looking forward to Saturday's game.'

The Saturday in question brought Fulham to St James' Park, and, with no goals and just one point from their first four league games, the Magpies were hoping the new arrival would be able to kick-start their stalling season. But with so little competitive action under his belt Owen was justifiably below par in a 1–1 draw, and, although he had helped Souness's side get a first goal of the season, he was determined to sort out his own form as quickly as possible. 'It was a great occasion for me, making my debut, as it's the sort of occasion you can only dream about,' he said. 'Obviously, you want to put in a brilliant performance and get a goal, but today it was not to be. However, there will be future days when I'm sure that will happen.'

The first of those days came the following weekend, when Owen scored the second of Newcastle's three goals in a win at Blackburn. It was the first victory of the season for the Magpies and brought three much-needed points to ease the pressure on Souness. 'The first win of the season is always important,' Owen said after the game. 'We've had a lot of injuries, but once you've got the first three points everything looks rosier in the garden and now we've got players coming back. As soon as we've got our injured players back, that's when they should judge us and the manager.'

Souness was delighted with his new signing, who had found his form more quickly than could have been hoped, much to the amusement of his manager. 'You have to smile, don't you?' the Scotsman said. 'It was his second game for us and I suppose that's a long time for him not to score! It just beggars belief.'

Owen made it two from two the following week, to get his first home goal for Newcastle and secure a second win of the season, as Manchester City were beaten 1–0. But the match winner was keen to share the plaudits. 'I scored the goal but there were plenty of great performances,' he told the press. 'The back four kept a clean sheet and Shay [Given] made a fantastic early save. I thought Alan Shearer gave them a tough time – I would have hated to have played against him. I read some quotes from the manager saying I still hadn't scored at home and laughed. After three games here the confidence is growing and we have seven points. We're on a roll and I'm delighted with the win. It was a special feeling to have people calling my name after I scored, especially so loudly.'

Owen's latest hot streak was cut short by a leg injury picked up in training, and he was forced out of the 0–0 draw at Portsmouth, but it wasn't serious enough to keep him out of England's last two World Cup qualifiers, where six points would guarantee their place in Germany the following summer. Newcastle's new striker was desperate to get the goals that would help England on their way, and in a revealing interview with the *Sunday Mirror* he told how much he thinks about goals. 'There is no better feeling than seeing the ball hit the back of the net,' he said. 'It is what I go to sleep thinking about and what I wake up thinking about. Every time I eat something or drink something, it's always on my mind. Thinking about goals gives me that extra little bit on the pitch. It's what my life is all about, scoring goals; I eat, sleep and drink it.'

Owen failed to score against a manager-less Austria side, but a 1–0 win at Old Trafford and other results that went their way meant that Eriksson's team qualified for the World Cup. With twenty-two points from their nine games, England were guaranteed a place in the finals as the best group runner-up, even if they lost to Poland. But there was to be no easing up from the England squad and they got a second win in Manchester 2–1, with goals from Owen, who was captain once again in the absence of David Beckham through suspension, and Frank Lampard, leaving them top of Group 6.

The Newcastle striker's goal had given him the share of another record, as he was now joint level with Gary Lineker having scored twenty-two competitive goals for England. 'Gary Lineker was probably my biggest hero as a kid, so it's nice to equal his record,' said Owen. 'Hopefully I can beat it before long but obviously I'll have to wait until the World Cup Finals themselves to do that. It's always nice picking up these records, but I'm more interested in having a great run at the World Cup.'

Owen's thoughts were already turning to Germany the following summer, and he was confident that he would be in one of England's strongest ever squads. 'We should be optimistic,' he said. 'When you get to a World Cup you need players you can look at and think, "He can win a game on his own." We've got the likes of Frank Lampard and Steven Gerrard. If just one puts in a fantastic performance in a game, that could get us through maybe to the semifinals.

'Then you look around and see a Wayne Rooney and other players and think, "If he can turn it on, that bit of magic might open up another top team." The more top players you've got, the more chance you've got of creating a bit of skill and magic – and Wayne is definitely one of those sorts of people.'

Newcastle's good form was disrupted by the international break and they lost 1–0 at Wigan before putting together a run of five consecutive wins. Owen missed the 3–2 derby win over Sunderland with hamstring trouble but returned with a bang the following week with a brace against West Bromwich Albion at the Hawthorns. Owen had settled in to the northeast quickly, and his off-field happiness was evident in his on-pitch displays. 'My daughter Gemma's not shown any signs of a Geordie accent yet, but it's only a matter of time!' Owen told the press with a smile. 'But our second baby's due in February and we've put roots down here.

'We're in a place in Northumberland. We have another kid due, but we don't know if it's a boy or a girl yet. We found out with the first one but not this one. I've been getting out and about with my daughter after training and know where all the parks, playgroups and farms are to keep her occupied. I've settled in better than I thought. It took a while at Real Madrid with hotel rooms and stuff, and we were dreading the first couple of months but it's been great since I arrived.'

Newcastle had been good for Owen and he had been good for them, helping them to fourteen points from seven games, and they made it seventeen from eight with a 1–0 home win over Birmingham. And, with another Magpies victory in the bag, Owen returned to England duty for a heavyweight clash against Argentina. 'This is an important game,' he said. 'We need to gauge how we're doing against one of the other favourites. The performances are taking more importance coming up to the World Cup.

'Now we've qualified we need to gain confidence individually and collectively. When you win there are so many spin-offs – you gain confidence, the whole country's happy and you get a better send-off going to the World Cup. It all tends to roll into one. And if you lose there are question marks here, there and everywhere.'

England came from 2–1 down in Geneva to beat the South Americans 3–2, and it was Owen's two late headers that transformed a disappointing loss against a team far more blessed technically and tactically into a victory for those English virtues of stamina and tenacity. 'If we'd lost, we would have still believed we had a chance of going to the World Cup next summer and having a good tournament,' Owen said afterwards. 'Just because we've won, it doesn't mean we're going to win in Germany but it does give the confidence a lift.'

The confidence in the squad, and the whole of England, was lifted after a fine result, where Rooney provided a threat throughout and Owen got the goals to win the game. The partnership was coming on in leaps and bounds, but by the time the World Cup came along they would both be struggling for fitness, and subsequently form.

Owen suffered a small injury setback on his return to Newcastle, and a groin strain put him out of action for a month before he came back to face Arsenal at home. The Magpies' form suffered without their record signing and they crashed out of the Carling Cup and dropped eight points from three league games, before Owen's return.

Like a lucky charm, Owen brought Newcastle results just by his mere presence, as Souness's team beat the Gunners 1–0, despite the fact that Owen was well short of match fitness after his spell on the sidelines. The England striker looked far sharper the following week, and West Ham bore the brunt of it as the gifted footballer bagged a hat-trick at Upton Park on the way to a 4–2 win.

His goals only served as a reminder as to how incredibly average Newcastle were without their *Galáctico*. Having joined the club when they had taken only one point from their first four games, Owen had played eight games, scoring seven goals, and helping his new team to nineteen points from a possible twenty-four. In the games the England man had missed since signing, the Magpies had picked up five points from a possible fifteen. And Shearer was quite rightly delighted with his new strike partner. 'He really is the difference between our being an average side and a very good side,' the former England captain told the press. 'Our partnership is going well and, if we can both stay fit, then we will cause people problems. We both have great belief in our own ability and our games suit each other.'

Unfortunately, that partnership wasn't able to develop, because Owen's season was effectively over within a fortnight, but not before the former Liverpool striker made an emotional return to Anfield. 'It's hard for me to know what it's going to be like until the game,' Owen told the *Liverpool Echo* before the game. 'There are lots of things I've thought about. What do I do if I score? What do I do if Carra gives me a kick up the backside? These aren't things I'll know how to react to until it happens. I'm going to be playing against people who are my best friends. I speak to Carra every day, and play golf with Didi Hamann every week.

'I have to be professional and do my best for Newcastle. I can't say I won't enjoy scoring a goal, because that's what I love to do. But I can't say I'll enjoy it, either, because it's against Liverpool.'

That particular puzzle was left unsolved as Newcastle were beaten 2–0, but more disappointing for Owen was the reaction of the Kop, who jeered his every touch and abused him with chants throughout the game. 'You should have signed for a big club' was one of their favourites; 'What a waste of talent!' kept them mildly entertained; while, 'Where were you in Istanbul?' seemed a bit of a low blow.

As low as Owen might have felt after his miserable return to Anfield, he would have felt a lot worse five days later, when he broke the fifth metatarsal in his right foot in a collision with his England teammate, Tottenham goalkeeper Paul Robinson. But, with the World cup still five months away, the estimated two and a half to three months' rehabilitation period didn't present too much of a concern. 'It's disappointing, but everyone gets their fair share [of injuries],' Owen said. 'If there's any consolation I've got plenty of time before the World Cup.'

Another bonus was that the England medical staff were well drilled in aiding recovery from such an injury, because Beckham, Rooney, Gerrard, Neville, Danny Murphy and Scott Parker had all been struck down by similar breaks in recent years.

It seemed that the injury would be little more than an inconvenience for Eriksson's side, since Owen would miss only a handful of warm-up matches, but at club level it was far more serious. The break meant that there would be almost no more

Newcastle action for Owen in 2005/6, and he appeared only once more for his club as he returned as a substitute for the league clash with Birmingham at the end of April.

It was Owen's goals that had transformed the Magpies' results, easing the pressure on their under-fire manager, and with the prolific little striker out of action Souness was in trouble. Newcastle lost the game at White Hart Lane 2–0, after Owen hobbled off and the manager was sacked little more than a month later.

Owen had an operation on his foot, after being assured that it would give him the best chance of a 'strong and quick recovery', and in the days after the injury everybody was confident that the Newcastle striker would be back well before the end of the Premiership season. But complications and a second operation meant that Owen eventually took to the pitch in Germany after featuring in just four games in 2006.

The New Year did bring some good news for Owen, though, as he celebrated the birth of his second child on 6 February 2006. James Michael Owen was born at 12.56 pm at the Countess of Chester Hospital, weighing 7 lb 9 oz (3.4 kilos). Owen said, 'Louise and James are both doing well and we're all thrilled.'

Owen was especially delighted by the birth of his first son, and he was keen for James to extend the footballing Owens to a third generation. 'People have asked me if I'd like him to be a footballer, and of course I would,' the happy father said. 'My dad was perfect with me from that point of view.

'I played golf, cricket, snooker, did athletics, rugby, even a bit of boxing. I loved it all. I'd like to get my children involved in sports but if they don't like it that's fine. The most important thing is for your children to be decent people.'

Owen made his first appearance for Newcastle under caretaker-manager Glenn Roeder in the Magpies' penultimate league match, and he played the final thirty minutes as a substitute, but walked very gingerly away from the ground. Fortunately, there was no further damage to the foot, but a first game back had taken its toll and Owen didn't appear for the final game of the season at home to Chelsea.

In Owen's first season for Newcastle he had shown he still had his knack for scoring goals, as his seven from ten starts showed, but after his injury the Magpies had cruised through the rest of the campaign to finish seventh in the league, and he was looking forward to getting them further up the table when he returned to fitness – but no one could have predicted how long he would have to wait for that opportunity.

15

GET WELL SOON

'It was a nightmare injuring the major structure in my knee,' he said. 'But I'm positive I'll come back as brand-new as ever. I just want to get the main operation done and get on with the rehabilitation. To start with, I'll just be trying to move the knee and get everything feeling fine. Obviously, the time's going to be spent healing. But I'll be trying to keep as fit as I can and as strong as I can, so, when I'm ready to return, I have as little time as possible in the reserves and in practice matches, and get straight into what I want to be in, and that's the first team.'

Michael Owen's reputation for being injury-prone certainly wasn't helped in 2006. After entering the World Cup unfit after his broken foot, the Newcastle striker left it with a career-threatening knee injury.

As England were going into the World Cup, there was plenty of speculation: there were all the 'will they/won't they?' recovery issues over the injured players; there was Sven-Göran Eriksson's decision to step down after the tournament and all the talk about his replacement and whether an Englishman or a foreigner was better suited to the job; there were, on top of all this, the usual summer transfer rumours. But, as the competition in Germany grew closer, everything seemed to sort itself out.

Wayne Rooney, Ashley Cole and Michael Owen had been backed in their fitness battles, while Ledley King had not. Eriksson's assistant, the then Middlesbrough boss Steve McClaren, agreed to take over at the top from August 2006, and Owen insisted he would be with Newcastle the following season as he looked to pay back the club for the way they had stuck by him through his injury torment.

As the warm-up matches edged closer, Owen revealed he was back to full health. 'I'm feeling fine – and I have been fine for quite a while now,' he told the press. 'I've been training since the season finished; I've been training with no problems for a while now and I'm excited about the World Cup. We have three games to look forward to before we go to Germany but there are no doubts at all in my mind about being fit for the first game with Paraguay, no doubts at all.

'If there was a World Cup game tomorrow, I'd be in a fit condition to play. I feel fresh and raring to go. Maybe I've played fewer games than ideal going into the World Cup but before the last one everyone was saying we had played too many games.'

But with Rooney having broken a metatarsal as well, and facing a much more desperate race to get fit in time for the World Cup, some people were concerned that the extra responsibility would prove to be too much for the Newcastle striker. 'Is there more pressure on me to score if Wayne's injured?' Owen asked the press corp. 'It's one thing being able to handle it and the other thing is enjoying it, and it doesn't really affect the way I play. I know I can handle pressure.

'If anyone plays for England, plays for them on a regular basis and plays either for or against the top Premiership teams like Chelsea and Manchester United, you've got to be able to handle pressure. It just comes with life, really. It washes over me. I can stay focused no matter what people say or people write, or whatever else. If you stopped to think about it, there are obviously going to be millions of people watching us back home and it's going to be built up into a big frenzy as well, so there's going to be masses of pressure in that sense. But I don't go to sleep thinking about the pressure: I go to sleep thinking about that little rectangle that I've got to smack the ball into, and that's about it.'

Owen started his first game of 2006 in England's first warm-up match, a 'B' international against Belarus at Reading's Madejski Stadium. With Rooney still injured it gave Peter Crouch his fourth opportunity to line up alongside Owen and, although England lost 2–1, it was a much-needed run-out for the rehabilitating Newcastle striker, who came off after sixty minutes. As well as Rooney and Crouch, Eriksson had also selected seventeen-year-old Arsenal forward Theo Walcott, making Owen the oldest striker in the England squad.

The latest Boy Wonder had made an impression on Owen despite having not played in the Premiership for the Gunners. 'I think he handles the weight of expectation fine,' the twenty-six-year-old said in the *Daily Star*. 'He's quite a level-headed lad. I think everyone expected him to handle it fine. It was unfortunate we weren't on top of our game and playing good football and creating that many chances on Thursday because Theo is like me. He wants the ball. He is like any striker. If we are not getting good quality ball in and around the final third, he can look as ineffective as anyone. Theo got kicked a bit – that's football, Premiership, international, particularly being a striker. We get kicked up in the air more than anyone.'

With Rooney injured Owen was more important to the England

cause than ever and it was vital that no one should kick him out of either of the remaining friendlies, because, without their two world-class forwards, the Three Lions would find it difficult to fulfil Owen's prediction. 'I still think the teams we took to other competitions were good enough to win, but this is probably the best one, with even better players,' Owen told *The Times*. 'The good thing is that the team we had in Japan has developed. We have the same nucleus that has been together for so long.

'All the top teams that win things understand each other and have played with each other for a long time. Look at the France team that won the World Cup and European Championship – they were really experienced, then it breaks up and the next generation might not do anything for a few years. We have that great mixture of youth and experience and even the experienced ones are only twenty-five or twenty-six, so it is a useful blend.'

The first team looked sharp in their final two warm-up games, and beat Hungary 3–1 at Old Trafford, before thrashing Jamaica 6–0 on the same ground four days later. Owen grabbed his first goal since December in the win over the Reggae Boyz but Crouch grabbed all the headlines after scoring a hat-trick and launching into a robotic dance celebration after each of his goals. Against the Caribbean side Owen played a full ninety minutes and with that England were ready for Germany.

Owen still looked a little rusty in the match against Paraguay, and was replaced by Stewart Downing after fifty-five minutes of a 1–0 win. The England team weren't at their best either and relied on an own goal to win the game, as Beckham's third-minute free kick was headed home by defender Carlos Gamarra. The former European Footballer of the Year shrugged off press criticism for his poor performance in Frankfurt and insisted he could win the Golden Boot at the World Cup. 'I was asked the other day who's going to be top scorer,' Owen told the *Northern*

Echo. 'What a stupid question! Me. That's the aim anyway – that's what I prepare for. I want to do well, I want the team to do well and, if it can't be me, I would love it to be Wayne Rooney or Peter Crouch. If we won the World Cup and I was their little sidekick, I'd be delighted. But I'm confident I can contribute too, even though I wasn't able to score against Paraguay.'

Owen failed to score against Trinidad and Tobago either, and was replaced after fifty-eight minutes as Rooney made his World Cup debut from the bench in Nuremberg. Goals from Crouch and Gerrard helped England to win 2–0, and there was the suggestion that Owen might start the final Group B match on the bench. 'I'm not worried,' Owen said ahead of the Sweden clash. 'If I'm sat on the bench, I'm sat on the bench. I've been on the bench in my career before. If the manager thinks that's the right thing, then he'll obviously do it. That's football. We've got twenty-three players and if I'm on the bench then so be it. I wouldn't say that I've played the best two games of my career, but I'm quite content. I'm not that type of player like Wayne Rooney, who's always involved, even when we're playing bad. My job is to get on the end of crosses.'

The crosses certainly weren't coming, and, playing alongside the giant Crouch, Owen had to work hard to try to get hold of any of the long balls that were being pumped forward to the big man. The flicks that you might expect from the little-and-large partnership were also hard to come by, and Owen had seen one solitary chance come his way in his two appearances.

The diminutive striker remained confident that, if more chances came his way, he would be back among the goals in no time. But in all of the furore about Owen's lack of form it was easy to forget that England had won both their games and were set for the knockout stages, where they would face Ecuador or the hosts Germany. 'I would probably prefer to play Ecuador,

I think of the chairman, Freddy Shepherd, who has invested all that money, and Glenn Roeder, the manager, who has kept in touch through the tournament and been very supportive. And all those great fans who have only seen me for eleven matches.'

The blow was softened for Newcastle by the knowledge that the FA's insurance would be contributing to Owen's salary while he was in recovery, but that wouldn't be putting the ball in the net or points on the board in the Premiership.

Owen did receive some good news, though, in Colorado, where he was being treated at the clinic of knee specialist Dr Richard Steadman. A preliminary scan in America revealed no damage to the medial ligament. 'We've had all the scans done over here and basically we're thinking, from what the scans say, that it's a cruciate,' Owen said to the *Daily Telegraph*. 'It's a rupture. You can't see the cruciate on the scan, so it's obviously floating about somewhere in the knee, but apart from that there is minimal damage. There is nothing else that needs operating on, so that is a big bonus. Not so much of a bonus in terms of time limits, but just in coming back, where you have just one injury to come back from and not plenty of things going on in your knee.'

But the good news didn't last for Owen as he needed two operations, and the second to repair the ligament wouldn't be possible until two months after the first one, to repair the cartilage. 'We went to the US thinking there was only going to be one operation but there was a little more damage than first thought,' Owen told the *Daily Mirror*. 'It went against the rehabilitation needed for a cruciate so we had to do the operation separately. The plan is to go back there in six or seven weeks, but hopefully that will be the last I see of America. I'm just hoping the next op can be successful.'

Owen bought his first horse in the summer of 1999, having been introduced to a trainer by former England captain David Platt. Owen was initially torn between buying a colt and buying a filly, and so in the end he went for both. He named the filly Etienne Lady as a tribute to his wonder goal against Argentina, and it took a little longer to come up with a name for the colt, but in the end he managed to dedicate the horse to his whole family. 'Talk to Mojo' comes from the initials of his siblings and his parents: T-A-L-K – Terry, Andrew, Lesley, Karen; T-O – Terry Owen; M-O-J-O – Michael Owen, Jeanette Owen.

Talk to Mojo brought Owen his first win as an owner, on 16 July 2000 at Newbury with odds of 10–1, but the footballer hadn't expected to win and hadn't backed his horse, and he hadn't even travelled down to Berkshire to watch him run. Despite his missing this early success, Owen's horses have brought him much joy since, and some winnings as well. His best horse was Treble Heights, who won her maiden race at Chester in August 2002. This time the Owen clan were there *en masse* and all had some money on the filly as she came in at 4–1.

Further purchases include Top Man T, named after his dad; Private Soldier, who is his mum's horse, which she named after her dad; and Speciali, which Owen named after a pair of his boots. Etienne Lady is now breeding, and Owen thinks it more likely that he will be involved in horses than football when the time comes to hang up his boots, possibly working as a breeder.

The big family house in Northop has stables. Louise has always been a keen rider, and Owen seems to have become increasingly fond of his horses, treating his favourites to a very pampered retirement. Owen now lives in another mansion near Belsay, Northumberland, which keeps him close to Newcastle, and has developed something of a property portfolio overseas with investments in Dubai and Portugal, among others. But the house in North Wales is the property nearer to both sets of grandparents, and was transformed into Owen's dream house after much work, so he will keep it no matter where he is playing his football.

But the big question for Owen was whether, after his recuperation, he would be able to reclaim the form that made him one of world football's most feared forwards. Would he be able to score the quantity and quality of goals that took him to the Ballon d'Or in 2001, and led to his being sought after by the giants of European football and finally signed by the world's biggest football club, Real Madrid?

16

THREE YEARS OF FRUSTRATION – 2006-9 WITH NEWCASTLE AND ENGLAND

When Michael Owen returned injured from the World Cup to face a serious operation on his knee, it heralded the start of probably the most frustrating years of his career. In typical Owen style he remained bullish, insisting he had no doubts he would be back fit and scoring goals in record time.

But in many ways the injury proved to be the least of Owen's concerns as Newcastle lurched from one disaster to another and England's fortunes followed a similar pattern.

The first hint of what was in store arrived almost as soon as Owen's flight touched down and he found himself at the centre of a club versus country row. Newcastle were furious at the prospect of being without their star player for such a long period, particularly as he had been injured not while wearing the black and white of his paymasters but while playing for his country.

The club demanded serious compensation from the FA, with some reports suggesting they wanted as much as £20m to cover his wages, lost revenue and the cost of buying in a replacement – £10m striker Obafemi Martins. There were even suggestions Newcastle could take out an injunction preventing the FA from selecting Owen in future England squads, although such claims had a ring of tabloid sensationalism about them. But there is no doubt the row was a fierce one, with FIFA eventually introducing a compensation fund for injuries sustained at World Cups in a bid to prevent it happening again.

By the time Owen began training again for the first time, in February 2007, the row was in full flow and it took until the summer to sort it, with The FA eventually agreeing a revised payment of between £7m and £10m.

On the pitch, Owen made his comeback on April 10 in a behind-closed-doors friendly against Gretna and, of course, scored in the process. But although he played his first full game for Newcastle in over a year later that month, against Reading in a 1–0 defeat, the trauma was not yet over.

His injury nightmare struck again at the end of the season when he was carried off on a stretcher after colliding with team-mate Matty Pattison in a match against Watford. It was only concussion but with reports rife that Owen could be set to leave Newcastle at the end of the campaign, it was not the image the striker wanted fans to remember.

Newcastle chairman Freddy Shepherd, too, was not a happy man at the prospect of losing his star player just as he was regaining fitness and urged Owen 'to show some loyalty' rather than engineer a move away from Tyneside.

Owen responded in the way you would expect and eventually, in July, he signalled his willingness to stay by saying: 'I believe that these can be good times to be at Newcastle, which is why I am more than happy to be here.'

Mind you, life at Newcastle was far from rosy. Manager

Glenn Roeder resigned in May 2007 after being summoned to a board meeting following the team's dismal run of just one win in 10 games, leaving Nigel Pearson to take control for the final weeks of the campaign as fans protested against the board.

The arrival of Sam Allardyce as Newcastle's new manager didn't help either, especially as the club undertook a change of ownership shortly after which sparked a dramatic fall from grace that nobody could have predicted.

Mike Ashley, owner of the Sports Direct retail chain, completed a £134m take over of the Toon in the summer of 2007 and appointed Chris Mort as his chairman, meaning old hands such as former chairman Freddy Shepherd and owner Sir John Hall were no longer the men in charge.

Ashley, 25th on the *Sunday Times* Rich List with a fortune of £1.9 billion, quickly proved to be something different. He chose to watch matches from the terrace, for instance, and even when he sat in the directors' box insisted on sporting his Newcastle replica kit – no doubt to the dismay of the suits who sat alongside him.

From his position alongside the Toon Army faithful he seemed to be influenced by the reaction of the crowd, and appeared to turn against Allardyce's management style. The former Bolton man hadn't been his appointment – he was tempted to the club by previous chairman Shepherd – and he hardly had a reputation for the kind of football that Ashley and so many of his fellow supporters craved.

By the time Allardyce had been in the job for eight months and taken charge of just 24 games the clamour for his head was already reaching fever pitch.

United weren't winning games, but more importantly they weren't playing the kind of football the fans demanded. By the time the New Year arrived things were desperate, with a home defeat against Manchester City and an away reverse at Wigan heightening the pressure.

When Newcastle, sitting 11th in the Premiership, produced a miserable display to draw 0–0 at Championship side Stoke in the FA Cup – a match they were fortunate not to lose – the axe finally fell. On Wednesday January 9 2008, Allardyce left the club 'by mutual consent'.

His departure set off a frenzy of speculation as to who would replace him, with Mark Hughes, Jose Mourinho, Didier Deschamps, Alan Shearer, Graeme Souness and Steve McClaren all mentioned in dispatches. And when Newcastle were thrashed 6–0 at Manchester United, collapsing embarrassingly in the second half, it became clear something had to be done quickly.

Harry Redknapp was promptly installed as favourite to get the job but there was a shock in store for Mike Ashley when he offered the post to the Portsmouth boss – only for him to turn it down.

Was this how low Newcastle had sunk? One of the greatest clubs in the world, yet unable to persuade the manager of Portsmouth that his ambitions could be more easily achieved at St James' Park?

To Ashley there seemed to be only one way out – and he produced what at the time seemed a masterstroke by persuading the Messiah, Kevin Keegan, to return to the club.

'I think Keegan is an extraordinary appointment,' BBC commentator Gary Lineker said at the time, echoing the views of a nation. 'And quite an exciting one as well. They tend to appoint from the heart in the North East and it seems they've done it again.

'One thing you know about Keegan is he's very good at getting what he wants, making boards listen and react in terms of the investment and the people he wants to bring in.

'He's hugely popular of course, almost won the league title and I think the fans would all love it if they pulled it off this time.'

Fans flocked to St James' Park to welcome the Messiah back and there was talk of a new era on Tyneside and a return to the glory days of exciting football and European nights under the lights.

Just for a second it seemed possible, too, with Owen scoring in a 4–1 FA Cup replay demolition of Stoke City in January 2008 as Keegan watched from the stands.

The striker was also handed the captain's armband by Keegan and although it took until March for Newcastle to win their first league match under Special K, Owen scoring in a 2–0 victory over Fulham, the atmosphere had certainly been lifted.

A good run of four wins and two draws, including six more Owen goals, took Newcastle into mid-table and with talk of big-money signings to come over the summer a new era appeared to be on the horizon.

It looked good for Owen, too, because despite all the injury problems he ended the season with 11 goals and, at last, seemed at home in the black and white shirt.

In typical Newcastle fashion, however, they managed to stuff it all up.

The following season began promisingly enough with a 1–1 draw at Manchester United, a 1–0 victory over Bolton courtesy of an Owen header and a 3–2 extra-time Carling Cup victory at Coventry in which Owen also found the net.

But something wasn't quite right between Keegan and his employers and the tensions at board level would eventually hit melting point as the big-money signings everyone expected failed to materialise.

Keegan left on 2 September, just hours after the closure of the transfer window, and even intensive talks with Ashley could not resolve the issue. Keegan later sued the club, successfully, for unfair dismissal.

Owen must have despaired at the situation, which also saw Mike Ashley offer the club for sale and then take it off the market in the space of the next few months. A crowd of just 20,577 turned up for a League Cup match against Tottenham in late September, the lowest for a competitive match since 1993, and although the shock appointment of former Wimbledon boss Joe Kinnear sparked a small revival it quickly became clear the Toon were in for a relegation battle.

It's little wonder, then, that in December 2008 Owen rejected the offer of a new contract and insisted he would look for a new club at the end of the season. With Newcastle in dangerous water in the Premiership he promised he would not bail out in January and would stay to fight relegation, eventually contributing 10 goals for the campaign. But it proved to be a thankless task.

Kinnear underwent heart surgery in February 2009, leaving assistant Chris Hughton in temporary charge of the team. And then, in a desperate bid to save the season, Ashley appointed fans' favourite Alan Shearer as manager for the final eight games of the campaign.

Even that wasn't enough to save the Toon from the drop, though – their fate was sealed by a 1–0 defeat at Aston Villa on the final day of the season.

The unthinkable had happened; Newcastle had been relegated. And, of course, inevitably it meant Owen's Newcastle career was over.

Maybe that was for the best, because those three tough years on Tyneside since the 2006 World Cup had virtually destroyed his England career, too. Injury ruled him out of England's opening six qualifiers for Euro 2008 but he returned to score against Estonia and break Gary Lineker's record for the most goals in competitive England internationals – 26.

He also scored twice in the 3–0 victory over Russia in September 2007, which seemed to pave the way for England to reach the finals in Austria and Switzerland. But the qualifying tournament ended in disaster as England lost 4–2 at home to Croatia and miss out on a place in the finals, with manager Steve McClaren sacked the very next day. And Owen has barely had a look-in since.

The arrival of Fabio Capello as manager has seen the striker largely ignored, currently stuck on 40 goals and 89 caps, just nine goals short of all-time record holder Bobby Charlton. It's inevitable that some people will conclude that Owen's time at Newcastle had a serious effect on his reputation.

'I know my reputation as a footballer and as a professional suffered at Newcastle,' Owen later admitted in an interview in the *Guardian* newspaper.

'I'd never try to shirk my share of the blame for the club being relegated. I played 33 games last season and I know I could have done a lot better.

'But some of the criticism that was levelled at me was bordering on the ridiculous.

'I tried to understand it, but if you step back and analyse some of the things being said about me then you would realise how crazy it all was.

'The bottom line is that if you don't play well, if you don't score, if you don't win, you become a target.'

Perhaps the biggest problem for Owen after leaving Newcastle is that it is still difficult to shake off the image of being 'injury prone'. 'It does irritate me that so many people have doubts, but if there is one thing I am angered by, the injury thing would be it,' Owen said after leaving the club.

'There is no doubt I have had injuries in my career. But there is a long list of players that have had a broken metatarsal. I was foolish trying to rush back for the 2006 World Cup and my leg had just come out of plaster.

'It's true I didn't set the world alight in the last year at Newcastle. That is no one's fault but mine. We were not playing well as a team and I wasn't doing my bit either.

'But I played 33 and 32 games in the last two years in a Newcastle team that was not in Europe and did not go on a decent cup run. Still I was continually labelled injury-prone, which gets up my nose. I am 29 and have played over 500 games for club and country. That says it all.'

Fortunately for Owen, he wasn't the only person thinking that way. And just as one door was closing, another very attractive one was about to open...

17

SEVENTH HEAVEN AT OLD TRAFFORD

Manchester United's number seven shirt has always been one of the most glamorous and prestigious in the history of European football. Think George Best, think Bryan Robson, think Cristiano Ronaldo.

So when Ronaldo, the man who inspired United to Champions League glory in 2008 and to three Premier League titles in a row, finally left Old Trafford to chase the money at Real Madrid in the summer of 2009, manager Sir Alex Ferguson had a dilemma.

Where on earth do you turn to fill the boots and shirt of a legend?

The answer, provided at a packed press conference on July 3, 2009, shocked everyone. The answer was Michael Owen!

When you analyse it, the decision was certainly a brave one. After all, Owen doesn't share the same sublime skills as Ronaldo and Best on the pitch and certainly not their love of the high life off it – unless you put training racehorses in the same bracket as dating Miss Worlds and wearing skimpy shorts in calendar shoots!

But, as the glossy 32-page brochure put together by Owen's agents in a bid to find him a new club highlighted, he is a superstar in his own right and a man with huge experience at the very highest level in the game. The fact that he was available on a free transfer from Newcastle appealed to frugal Fergie, too, of course. But what he was really signing was guaranteed goals and true world class stature.

And that's why Ferguson is adamant his number seven will help fans forget about the old one.

'Michael gives us experience in the penalty box, which is vital,' the Scotsman said after Owen agreed terms. 'He has always had that little knack of losing defenders in the last third. I know he will score a lot of goals for us. He has been great at that for years.

'Michael is a world class forward with a proven goalscoring record at the highest level and that has never been in question. Coming to Manchester United with expectations that we have is something that Michael will relish.'

Owen signed a two-year contract at Old Trafford and it quickly became clear that Ferguson, who also tried to sign him as a teenager but was beaten to his signature by Liverpool, had immense faith in his new arrival – especially after handing him that number seven shirt.

'He's fantastic in the last third of the field, he knows when to run and when to hold his runs and the experience he gives us in that position is going to be vital for us,' he said ahead of the new season as United toured the Far East to prepare for the 2009/10 campaign.

'We gave him the number seven and it's a jersey that's been worn by some high profile players. I think he is that. His profile for the last decade has been outstanding.

'To choose someone to wear that shirt you have to be confident he can carry that. He has a confidence in himself to do that. The important thing was to give it to someone who has the confidence to use it and I think Owen was the natural one to get it.'

The only question now is: can Owen live up to that billing and guide United to further glory and take his own career to a new level? In short, can he live up to the shirt?

Not surprisingly, the answer from the England star so far has been a resounding 'yes' and he has a inner self-confidence that the move will turn out to be the best of his career.

'When United came in for me I thought about the players I'd be alongside, playing at Old Trafford in a team that you know will create chances. Then I went to bed and when I woke up the next morning it really hit me,' he said at his Old Trafford unveiling.

'I thought, "Hell I can win a league title here and play in the Champions League". Let's just say that I am very excited!

'This is a fantastic opportunity for me and I intend to grab it with both hands. I am now looking forward to being a Manchester United player and I am fortunate that I already know so many of the players here. I missed pre-season last year and I am pleased that I will be starting at Carrington from day one.

'I want to thank Sir Alex for the faith he has shown in me and I give him my assurance that I will repay him with my goals and performances.'

The move came out of the blue, so it was no wonder Owen was thrilled. He had also been strongly linked with Hull City but, with all respect to the Humberside club, that would have been a million miles away from the glamour of Old Trafford.

Yes, a move to Hull would have provided less pressure and possibly more opportunities to start games. But, as you'll know by now, Owen is a man who likes a challenge.

'This is a big chance to show that I can do it again, to show that I can handle the pressure and the expectation,' he explained. 'I've handled the pressure and scrutiny before and all the managers I've played under will all say I can handle it.

'The number seven shirt has pressures of its own and some great players have worn it in the past, but I will do it justice. The manager asked me to wear the shirt. He said a player needs broad shoulders for it and he asked me if I felt I could handle it.

'I said "yes" without hesitation. I know it represents so much. Two big players have left Manchester United, in Cristiano Ronaldo and Carlos Tevez. There were a lot of goals in Ronaldo and I'm here to hopefully fill that gap.'

It's probably true to say that Owen wasn't necessarily Ferguson's first choice, having also been linked with a series of other strikers over the course of a long summer. But, as the striker told the *Guardian*, that news made little difference to him after finally achieving the transfer he so craved.

'In previous years it has been the little things that have gone against me, like clubs not being able to agree a fee, but this time it has gone in my favour,' he said.

'You have bad and good luck in your career which people don't get to find out about. I don't care whether I was first or 100th choice. I just want to do well for Manchester United.

'If this challenge does not put a spring in your step and a smile on your face, nothing will. I still believe I can do well.'

That self-confidence was quickly justified when Owen scored his first goal for United on his debut – scoring in the 84th minute after coming on as a substitute against a Malaysian XI in a pre-season friendly in Kuala Lumpur.

Wearing the famous Number Seven shirt for the first time he came off the bench in the 60th minute in a packed Bukit Jalil National Stadium and sealed a 3-2 victory with a neat finish from inside the area.

'You train for weeks in preparation for that all-important first game and to score on your debut feels great,' Owen told United's official website after the match.

'It's always nice to get off the mark, not just when you join a new club but any time. I was sat chatting to Wayne Rooney in the dressing room afterwards and he feels the same way after getting off the mark for the season.

'It's obviously doubly good for me with it being my first goal for the club, and even though it won't really count in the grand scheme of things, it does make you feel better. Hopefully I can score a lot more.'

In fact, Owen scored three more in United's pre-season games before making his competitive debut for the Red Devils when he came off the bench against Birmingham City in August 2009.

Inevitably his first goal followed soon after – against Wigan a week later in a 5–0 victory for Fergusons's champions. But it was his first home goal that really made the headlines.

That's because it came against deadly rivals Manchester City in the very last minute of injury time – and earned United a stunning 4-3 derby day victory.

The goal means Owen has now scored in four different derby fixtures – for Liverpool against Everton, in the *El Clasico* for Real Madrid against Barcelona, in the Tyne-Wear derby for Newcastle against Sunderland and now for United against City.

And, more importantly of course, it finally ended any suggestion that United fans were reluctant to take him to their hearts because of his Anfield past.

'The reception for me has been great,' he later told Sky in a television interview. 'Although I must admit when I first signed it was one of the things I thought, "What type of reaction will I get?" But they've been absolutely fine, there's been no problem whatsoever.

'And then scoring in the derby, if there were any people on the outside who were still wondering what reception I'd get, that allayed everything.

'For it to finish as it did, and with me managing to grab the winning goal, it certainly made me feel even more at home at my new club.

'To score such a dramatic goal against our arch rivals did a lot for me. I had contributed to winning a game. I felt part of the club. I felt great among the lads and the fans.'

Owen has since played for United against Liverpool at Anfield and even if that match ended in a disappointing 2–0 defeat the question of his commitment to Manchester is unlikely to be raised again.

In the build-up to that Anfield clash Owen described United as 'probably the biggest club in the world' during an interview for Umbro in Ireland, and his comments caused quite a stir at his former club.

Typically, ever the diplomat, Owen quickly clarified his comments by saying: 'I didn't set out to offend anyone. What I said was, in terms of support, revenue and stadium, Man United are probably the biggest in the world but Madrid, Barcelona and Liverpool are up there with them in other areas.'

But whatever he meant to say or intended to say, the debate was lapped up by United fans who were already singing Owen's name and taking him to their hearts. True, he hasn't quite forced his way into the side as a permanent partner for Wayne Rooney yet, starting some games and being left on the bench for others. But importantly, he has also remained largely fit since arriving at Old Trafford and all the signs are he is easing into his new life at the other end of the M62 pretty well.

He has already notched up his first Champions League goal

for United, in a home match against CSKA Moscow, and ranks the goal against City as one of the most important and enjoyable of his career.

With United challenging on all fronts as usual, the only question mark that remained concerned his ability to force his way into the England squad and end the season not only as a trophy winner with his club but as a World Cup star for his country.

Logic said that if Owen was playing for United at the highest level and scoring goals then he would be almost impossible to ignore once the squad for South Africa was decided in May 2010. But unfortunately, as has been the case so many times over Michael Owen's career, there was a lot more to it than that.

England manager Fabio Capello hadn't selected Owen for an England squad since his second match in charge, an away friendly against France in Paris in January 2008 and seemed, at best, reluctant to rock the boat by changing his policy.

Owen's rivals for the shirt – players such as Jermain Defoe, Peter Crouch and Carlton Cole, had all been scoring and playing regularly in the Premiership and had consistently been selected ahead of him. More than that, Capello seemed irritated and uncomfortable when asked about Owen's future chances and stuck rigidly to an insistence that the striker had not played enough games and is not fit enough to risk.

Owen steadfastly refused to criticise Capello's decision to leave him out and instead insisted he would be ready if and when he got the call.

'I have just got to continue doing well and see where that will take me,' he said. 'I have been in the provisional squad quite a few times, though the final squad is the one you want to be in.'

Somewhat prophetically, he continued: 'It's good to see England doing so well but unfortunately every time the squad comes around I seem to have picked up a small injury even though I'm back to fitness now. Or maybe at Newcastle at times I was a bit out of form.

'There are no excuses for me. Obviously now I need to play really well for my club and score a few goals and hopefully get back in it. I have always been optimistic about that.

'I haven't changed as a player – I'll always score goals. I've got a record to show that. I think everyone knows what they will get from me and I've proved it in World Cups before.

'But the last thing I want to do is start a Michael Owen for England campaign and say all the reasons why I could or should be selected. I'm at ease with myself and the situation and I know what I've got to do and that's to play well for Manchester United.

'I've not spoken to Fabio Capello about it and I don't need to – I know the situation, I need to play well and score goals and do well for United and then I could get picked. But as I say I'm at ease with it. I don't lie awake at night thinking this or that. It's simple enough equation – play well and you'll be in and don't and you won't.

'As I say, I have had a letter every time to be in the preliminary squad. I know from being in those squads that the manager, Fabio Capello, is keeping an eye on me. I am confident I will play for England.

'To get into that squad and go to the World Cup is the ultimate aim for every English footballer, but that's not until the summer. I still have time to do as well as possible.'

Sadly, Owen didn't get that seat on the plane to South Africa. Yet another injury was to blame – a seemingly innocuous hamstring problem sustained during United's Carling Cup final victory over Aston Villa on 28 February turned out to be more serious than first thought, ruling him out for the rest of the season and putting paid to his dreams of England glory. But it's easy to forget amid all the fuss about his injuries that he is still only 29 years old and in his prime. So let's hope he bounces back, as he has done so many times in the past. His career is certainly not over, and he could yet have his fairytale ending.